GLOBAL E-COMMERCE AND ONLINE MARKETING

Watching the Evolution

Edited by Nikhilesh Dholakia, Wolfgang Fritz, Ruby Roy Dholakia, and Norbert Mundorf

QUORUM BOOKS
Westport, Connecticut • London

Library of Congress Cataloging-in-Publication Data

Global e-commerce and online marketing : watching the evolution / edited by Nikhilesh
Dholakia . . . [et al.].
    p. cm.
    Includes bibliographical references and index.
    ISBN 1–56720–407–4 (alk. paper)
    1. Electronic commerce. 2. Internet marketing. 3. Globalization. I. Dholakia,
Nikhilesh, 1947–
    HF5548.32.G557   2002
    658.8′4—dc21   00–068787

British Library Cataloguing in Publication Data is available.

Library of Congress Catalog Card Number: 00–068787
ISBN: 1–56720–407–4

First published in 2002

Quorum Books, 88 Post Road West, Westport, CT 06881
An imprint of Greenwood Publishing Group, Inc.
www.quorumbooks.com

Printed in the United States of America

The paper used in this book complies with the
Permanent Paper Standard issued by the National
Information Standards Organization (Z39.48–1984).

10 9 8 7 6 5 4 3 2 1

Contents

Illustrations

TABLES

Preface

This book is the result of collaborative work between a number of researchers in the United States, Germany, Sweden, Denmark, South Korea, and New Zealand. In particular, the collaboration between the Research Institute for Telecommunications and Marketing (RITIM) at the University of Rhode Island in the United States and the Institute for Marketing at the Technical University of Braunschweig in Germany has been pivotal in developing this book. Industry experts from firms such as Andersen Consulting, Continental AG, McKinsey & Co., Telia, Volkswagen, and ZUMA have joined the academic group of authors as coresearchers and contributors to this book.

The result is a unique book that provides in-depth and international insights into the way that e-commerce and online marketing are evolving. In this book, you will find not only strong managerial insights but also plenty of empirical research evidence as well as fresh conceptualizations to comprehend the intricacies of the fast-changing world of e-commerce. The diversity of global perspectives presented in this book helps to illuminate the nature of e-commerce in ways that cannot be found in books that reflect only the North American perspective. We hope that the content of the chapters will be useful to managers, students, and policymakers alike.

A number of individuals have helped greatly in conducting the background research for this book and in putting together the diverse content from different parts of the world. We would especially like to acknowledge the help that we have received from Kuan-Pin Chiang, Zhenhong Hu, Martin Kerner, Nir Kshetri, Tobias Lührig, Jerry Paquin, Miao Zhao, and Detlev Zwick. Office assistance provided by Amy Van Amersfoort has been invaluable.

We would like to acknowledge the encouragement provided by Edward P. Mazze, Hasbro/Verrechia Chair and Dean of the College of Business Administration at the University of Rhode Island, and Eric Valentine, publisher of Quorum Books, at various stages of this project.

July 2000   Nikhilesh Dholakia,
                                                                Wolfgang Fritz,
                                                         Ruby Roy Dholakia, and
                                                               Norbert Mundorf

1

Online Marketing: An Introduction to the E-Commerce Revolution

Nikhilesh Dholakia, Wolfgang Fritz, Ruby Roy Dholakia, and Norbert Mundorf

INTERNET AND THE NEW ECONOMY

If the Internet and its associated technologies were suddenly removed from the face of the Earth, the impact on advanced economies–particularly the United States, Canada, the European Union, and Japan–would be disastrous. The economies of these regions would go into a tailspin. Tens of millions of people would feel totally frustrated because they would be unable to obtain essential information or conduct necessary transactions. Telecommunications traffic would be seriously disrupted, with sweeping impacts on sectors such as financial services and transportation. Millions of information workers–ranging from technicians to high-tech chief executive officers (CEOs)–would lose their jobs.

The Global Perspective

Although the commercially oriented Internet took off only after the invention of the World Wide Web protocol in the early 1990s, the Internet has woven itself into the very economic fabric of the advanced economies of North America, Europe, and Asia. The emerging markets of Latin America, Asia, East Europe, and Africa are taking rapid strides to join the global revolutions in the Internet, mobile communications, and e-commerce. As Microsoft's publicists like to put it, the Internet has become the "digital nervous system" of the new economy. On a global scale, not just the Internet, but also the mobile communications networks are creating a framework for electronic commerce. The world today and in the foreseeable future looks very different than in the closing years of the twentieth century. The following facts and projections provide a flavor of the global dynamism of the emerging electronic economies in various parts of the world[1]:

- At the end of the first quarter of 2000, the number of Internet users in the world was pegged at about 305 million. Of these, 137 million were in the United States and Canada, about 85 million in Europe, and about 70 million in the Asia-Pacific region.
- By early 2000, nearly 40 percent of the world's Internet users had made a purchase

online.

- Nearly two in three Americans over the age of 12 had access to the Internet in 2000, and half of them went online every day.
- Internet usage in Germany grew by 53 percent in 1999, and there were nearly 16 million German Internet users by mid-2000.
- By 2003, the number of Internet users worldwide is easily expected to pass 500 million.
- The number of Internet users in China is expected to surpass that in the United States by 2010.
- Despite the continuing economic crisis, the number of Internet users in Russia reached nearly 8 million in 2000 and was expected to triple in the next few years.
- The number of wireless subscribers in the world already exceeds the number of Internet users. By 2004, the number of wireless services users is expected to outnumber fixed-line Internet users by 2:1.
- On every continent except North America, the number of people using wireless devices exceeded those surfing the Net. Wireless e-commerce, also called m-commerce, is now the focus of many up-and-coming businesses in Europe and Asia.
- By mid-2000, 7 million of Japan's 57 million mobile phone users were subscribing to NTT DoCoMo's i-mode mobile Internet service, which allows access to over 7,000 Web sites.
- By late 2000, more people in China had mobile phones than in Japan. The number of Internet users in China exceeded 12 million and was doubling every six months.
- Europe leads the world in the penetration of wireless devices. Rather than rely on the Internet, however, a vast number of European wireless users employ SMS and WAP protocols-which are somewhat different than the Internet–for communications and commerce.
- In India, where per capital income is under U.S.$400, WAP-enabled, wireless e-banking services became available in 2000.

All over the world, Internet and related technologies are creating the conditions for conducting business by electronic methods. While the United States holds a position of leadership in e-commerce, there is a clear trend of rapid growth of Internet infrastructure in other parts of the world. In terms of electronic commerce based on mobile communications networks–also called m-commerce–Europe and Asia have established a lead over the United States.

Electronic Commerce and Online Marketing

While the majority of commercial Web sites in the world merely publicize a company and its products, an increasing proportion of Web sites are becoming transactions oriented. The convenience of Web browsers and mobile access methods has resulted in a massive spurt in electronic commerce.

Electronic commerce and its broader paradigm–e-business–are transforming all business functions (Kalakota and Robinson 1999). Marketing is no exception. How will electronic commerce transform marketing? In what ways do online marketing methods differ from conventional marketing techniques? What factors lead to the success or failure of online marketing strategies? These are the questions that we begin addressing in this chapter and continue addressing in the rest of the book.

We begin with an assessment of the size of the e-commerce sector. Then we provide some useful ways of classifying e-commerce activities. Next, we discuss some of the factors that lead to the success or failure of online marketing strategies. The elaboration of these factors constitutes the bulk of this book. We provide an overview of the chapters to follow and offer some concluding comments for this introductory chapter.

SIZE OF THE E-COMMERCE SECTOR

Estimates of global e-commerce projected the total value of such commerce at about U.S.$7 trillion by 2004. North America was expected to account for about half of this followed by the Asia-Pacific region and Europe, each region accounting for under a quarter of the e-commerce revenue. Only 12 countries are expected to account for nearly 90 percent of all e-commerce.

These broad estimates could change substantially because of new technologies or rapid social and cultural change. Also, within the broad sweep of these estimates, we are likely to see a wide variety of e-commerce patterns across the world. The overall size and growth of the global e-commerce sector in various countries would depend on a number of factors: the data communications infrastructure, the availability of e-commerce options, and the willingness and ability of people to transact online.

Global Data Communications Infrastructure

There is little doubt that data communications infrastructure, either in the form of the fixed Internet or in the form of wireless devices with data communications capabilities, will keep growing rapidly for years to come. This is even more evident from a global perspective than from a perspective that focuses primarily on North America. For example:

- Global Crossing, a new U.S. based telecom company, created a globe-spanning fiber-optic network that linked major business centers of Europe, Asia, and North America, setting the stage for seamless global provision of Internet and e-commerce services.
- Flat-rate phone and Internet services, which helped boost Internet use in the United States, were also available in Canada, Australia, New Zealand, and Mexico and were being introduced in Germany, Hungary, Italy, Japan, and the United Kingdom.
- Nearly 200 free Internet service provider (ISP) firms were operating in the United Kingdom Even Internet and media giants such as AOL and Bertelsmann had opened subsidiaries offering free Internet services in the United Kingdom.
- The introduction of free ISP service in Italy gave a substantial boost to Internet usage in that country. Telecom Italia signed up nearly 2 million users in four months for its free Internet service.
- By 2010, demand for broadband services in Europe and Asia will surpass the

Table 1.1
Classifying E-Commerce by Business and Consumer Sectors

		Target of e-commerce initiative	
		BUSINESS	CONSUMER
Source of e-commerce initiative	BUSINESS	**b2b** Business-to-business e-commerce Examples: eSteel, Chemdex	**b2c** Business-to-consumer e-commerce (e-Retailing or eTailing) Examples: Amazon.com, eToys
	CONSUMER	**c2b** Consumer-to-business e-commerce Example: Guru.com	**c2c** Consumer-to-consumer e-commerce Example: eBay

demand for such services in the United States.

- Internet portals such as Yahoo! and Lycos are developing "voice portals" that would allow millions of people without access to a personal computer (pc) to use the Internet with the help of a telephone and voice commands.

As the infrastructure advances, location and distance will be less relevant, and e-commerce activities–on both the seller and the buyer side–will become increasingly global (Cairncross 1997). Of course, many countries–especially in Asia, Latin America, Africa, and parts of Eastern Europe–will not be able to afford the type of telecom infrastructure based on fiber optics that the advanced countries have. In these developing nations, wireless as well as television-based infrastructure and e-commerce solutions will hold strong appeal, and substantial e-commerce will be conducted with voice-based technologies.

Availability of E-Commerce Options

While the availability of a communications infrastructure is a precondition for e-commerce, the infrastructure by itself would not lead to the emergence of electronic markets. For e-commerce to flourish in a country, there must be e-commerce options available to the people. The United States has a commanding lead in terms of the number and variety of "dot-com"-style e-commerce companies that sell everything from software to steel. At the end of

2000, the United States had nearly 600,000 e-commerce sites. In Europe, Asia, and elsewhere, e-commerce activities started later than in the United States but are now gaining strong momentum:

- Between 1999 and 2003, the combined share of Western Europe and Japan in global e-commerce will rise from 29 percent to 47 percent.
- E-commerce sales in the Asia-Pacific region grew by almost 200 percent in 1999 and were expected to pass U.S.$7 billion in 2000.
- Online retail sales in Europe were expected to soar from under U.S.$3 billion in 1999 to nearly U.S.$170 billion in 2005.
- Sweden was emerging as the world's leading electronic retailing country. Nearly 10 percent of retail sales in Sweden was expected by electronic methods by 2005.
- From under 2 million in 1999, the number of online stock market investors in Europe is expected to jump to nearly 17 million in 2003.
- To overcome Japanese reluctance to pay for online purchases by credit cards, electronic retailers allow Japanese consumers to order online but pick up their purchases at a neighboring 7-Eleven or similar convenience stores and to pay by cash.
- Over 90 percent of Internet shoppers around the world report that they are "somewhat satisfied" or "extremely satisfied" with their online shopping experience.

While lack of infrastructure will limit e-commerce options in large developing nations such as China and India, the emergence of cable television (TV)-based and wireless methods of Internet access will begin leveling the playing field for e-commerce firms in such nations. In anticipation of such alternative access methods, dot-com-style e-commerce companies are sprouting in all parts of the world.

Willingness and Ability to Transact Online

The willingness to buy and sell online varies across the world. There are cultural differences, as well as differences associated with types of transactions (e.g., business-to-consumer versus business-to-business), experience levels of users, and design and convenience of the commercial Web sites, and other factors. Several real or perceived barriers stand in the way of online marketing:

- One-quarter of companies polled in Australia in 2000 did not provide a secure, encrypted method of payment over the Internet. This acted as a damper on Australians' desire to buy on the Net.
- Between 1998 and 1999, complaints about online fraud in the United States jumped by 38 percent, with auction sites responsible for the majority of the complaints.
- A British study in 2000 found that people were quite aware of the Internet and its pervasive impact, but "mistrust, fear, and cynicism" characterized their views of the Internet.
- A study of Fortune 500 corporate Web sites characterized 28 percent of these sites as "unimaginative" with "poor site maps."

Table 1.2
Classifying E-Commerce by Physical and Digital Characteristics

		Digital Product	Physical Product
Digital Communication	Digital Delivery	Exclusively Digital Commerce Examples: Software from Beyond.com sold via Net ads, eMatter available from Fatbrain.com, MP3 music	E-Commerce with E-production Examples: Digitally delivered, printable greetings, photos, etc. sold via the Web
	Physical Delivery	Digital-ready E-Commerce Examples: Music CDs sold by CDNow, Amazon.com	Standard E-Commerce Examples: Dell Computers, eBay auctions, Amazon.com books
Conventional Communication	Digital Delivery	Media-supported Digital Commerce Examples: Digitally delivered software, movies, music sold via TV	Media-supported E-production Examples: Digitally delivered, printable greetings, photos, etc. sold via TV, magazines
	Physical Delivery	Digital-ready Conventional Commerce Exampls: Music sold through record stores	Conventional Physical Commerce Examples: Gasoline Pumping Station, Selling Detergent at Wal-Mart

- In Japan, keyboard-oriented technologies do not appeal to people, and they are reluctant to order online because they do not trust at-home delivery services.
- Japanese Internet users are deeply concerned with the security of credit cards and other personal information and want a variety of online payment systems to experiment with.

- 84 percent of Japanese Internet users, 75 percent of Latin American users, and 52 percent of Western European users prefer operating in a language other than English.

For online marketing to succeed, it is essential to overcome the real or perceived problems of security, privacy, and trust. In the business-to-business (b2b) sector, transacting companies often have long-term relationships, and the legal framework to protect the transactions is well established. It is not surprising, therefore, that b2b e-commerce constitutes the dominant proportion of e-commerce, and this segment of e-commerce is growing the fastest.

The ability to do online business depends, first and foremost, on the availability of some form of data communications infrastructure, be it fixed Internet or a wireless method. In many of the emerging markets and even in some of the advanced economies, even if consumers have access to a data communications method, they lack other means of conducting online transactions. In countries like China, Brazil, and India, the availability of credit cards is low, making it difficult to set up payment systems for those willing to buy online. Only half of Internet users outside North America pay for e-commerce purchases by credit card compared to 75 percent payments by credit cards in the United States and Canada. Creative ways of overcoming such barriers, however, are evolving around the world:

- In Brazil, banks sponsor free Internet services that not only allow online banking but also allow users to pay for goods purchased at the bank-sponsored "electronic malls" by using funds on deposit at the bank.
- Malaysia has introduced e-Purse, a stored-value smart card available in "reloadable" as well as disposable versions. The card can be used in physical stores, and transit systems, as well as for Internet purchases.
- In Europe, a relatively high penetration of smart cards, digital wallets, and other secure payment methods provides alternatives to online credit card usage.
- Banksys in Belgium has introduced a smart card terminal that can be attached to a PC. People with such a terminal and the bank's stored-value smart card can shop at a number of merchants offering everything from food to electronic gadgets.
- In addition to use of credit and debit cards, Rediff.com, a shopping site in India, allows payments by check, and Value Paid Postage (similar to COD in the United States) and via a bank account at ICICI, an Internet-oriented bank.
- Japanese consumers can reserve concert tickets on the Web, finish the seat selection process at special Internet kiosks in convenience stores, and pay the store checkout clerk by cash.

Constant improvements in security, payment systems, and delivery systems are helping to dismantle the barriers to using e-commerce methods to buy goods and services. The challenges are, of course, tougher in those countries where the Internet infrastructure is limited, and credit cards are not widely available, or where there is reluctance to use credit cards on the Internet. Several solutions to these problems are becoming available. Also, as mobile commerce or m-commerce evolves, the telephone bill will become an important method of collecting payments for electronic purchases.

CLASSIFYING E-COMMERCE ACTIVITIES

Because e-commerce, e-business, and online marketing are rapidly evolving fields, any attempt to classify them cannot be exhaustive. New business models that lie outside our classification schemes will keep appearing. Nonetheless, the classification frameworks we provide capture most of the ongoing e-business activities as well as provide a glimpse into e-commerce activities that are yet to appear on the scene.

Classifying by Source and Target

A popular way of classifying e-commerce activities is in terms of the source and the target of e-commerce efforts (see Table 1.1). In the e-commerce arena, b2b and b2c have already become popular terms. The c2c sector was almost single-handedly created by eBay. The c2b e-commerce activities include home-based "free agents" offering their services via the Internet to business customers. In terms of dollar revenue, the b2b sector is the giant among these: it accounts for nearly 80 percent of all e-commerce. In terms of number of users, however, the consumer-to-consumer (c2c) sector comes out on top. For example, eBay has 20 million users—more than any other e-commerce site can claim.

Classifying by Extent of Digitization

In e-commerce, a distinguishing feature is the use of digital communications. Further digitization can occur in terms of digital delivery of products. At present, digital products are limited mainly to software, information, and some music. In the future, more and more products will get digitized and be ready for digital delivery. The great risk in this is the ease of copying and redistributing the digital products without paying the developer of the product. Digital delivery will therefore depend, to some extent, on the evolution of security and authentication methods. Physical products can also be delivered by digital means if (1) their design and manufacturing specifications can be coded, and (2) machines can be located at the customer's end to receive these specifications and to produce the goods. We can already see this happening in the case of products like greeting cards and photographs. In the future, we will undoubtedly see other physical products that can be digitally delivered (see Table 1.2).

The multiple ways of classifying just discussed show that e-commerce and online marketing are living, evolving phenomena. One requisite for success is the ability to navigate through the complexity of e-commerce forms and to focus on a workable business model with potential to create synergies for the marketer and strong appeal for the market.

SUCCESS AND FAILURE FACTORS

A comprehensive understanding of what leads to success or failure of e-commerce and online marketing ventures across the world will evolve over several years. Some early indications about the factors that people to buy online (or to gravitate to traditional ways of buying) are already evident, however. Based on our ongoing research, we find that:

- Those who use the Internet a lot also buy online a lot. This same behavior is beginning to happen with those who use mobile communications a lot: these people are the prime prospects for m-commerce.
- The more time that a person spends at an electronic commerce site, the greater the chance that he or she will make a purchase at that site. Also, such a person is likely to purchase a greater amount than someone who spends very little time at the site. This has unleashed a great race to develop attractive, "sticky" e-commerce sites.
- Long waiting time (in terms of accessing or navigating a site) is a prime enemy of e-commerce. Compared to the physical world, people are tremendously impatient in the electronic environment. Because of this, great efforts are being made to provide high bandwidth connections and to streamline the Web-surfing experience. The challenge is especially tough for m-commerce, where the small screens of the devices are very limiting. Similarly, voice-based e-commerce–a necessity for many global contexts–creates special challenges in terms of efficient surfing.
- When faced with a long waiting time or Web site breakdown, inexperienced Internet users are likely to abandon the Web and move to a physical commerce location. Experienced Internet users, on the other hand, are likely to try a competitive Internet site. Because of this, e-commerce sites that are not the leaders in their category have a chance to prove themselves to experienced users.
- Those who are satisfied with an electronic buying (or supplying) experience are likely to repeat that experience.
- For those satisfied with electronic commerce in a category, the proportion of their business in that category done by electronic means will increase over time.
- Sites that offer their users a high degree of perceived control are likely to enjoy continued patronage and growing frequency and size of transactions. For this reason, a lot of attention is being paid to customization and personalization of the e-commerce experience.

The preceding success factors represent fairly self-evident propositions. Yet, the developing e-commerce businesses sometimes ignore them. Also, the listing merely provides a starting point in terms of developing e-commerce and online marketing strategies. As seen earlier in this chapter and as becomes evident in the other chapters, there are many cross-national and cross-cultural variations in terms of the success and failure factors for e-commerce.

OVERVIEW OF CHAPTERS TO FOLLOW

Following this introductory part, this book consists of five parts followed by glossary of Internet and e-commerce terms, bibliography and references for all chapters, and a list of contributors. Part I explores how Internet marketing challenges conventional business paradigms. It addresses changes in markets as well as infrastructure and discusses their implications for business processes and market structures.   Dholakia and Dholakia identify characteristics of the knowledge society and information economy. On this backdrop they illustrate changes in market and value processes resulting from the transition from the Industrial Age into the Information Age. They point out that an increasing influence of the consumer on the value chain and changing roles of marketing characterize this transition. From an essentially one-way monologue with limited feedback, marketing changes into an active conversation potentially involving numerous "communities of corporations and consumers." The authors also point out that primarily developing countries, or about one-sixth of the population, benefit from these changes. Nevertheless, the Information Age also affects emerging markets of Asia, Latin America, Eastern Europe, and Africa.

Dholakia, Dholakia, and Park use the Internet to analyze the impact of infrastructure innovations on markets and marketing. The theoretical framework consists of agency theory, transaction costs, and network externalities.

Dholakia, Dholakia, and Laub focus on the marketing mix in electronic commerce. In particular, they explore if the four Ps (produce, price, promotion, place) can be applied to electronic market transactions and which modifications are required. They point to the limits of the conventional four Ps in e-commerce settings. While it remains uncertain if there is a need for a completely new paradigm, the chapter offers suggestions for new ways of marketing in the Internet era.

Part II focuses on selected results of empirical studies regarding the influence of the Internet on marketing in international markets. In chapter 5, Fritz and Kerner compare Internet marketing in Germany across three different industries: media, banks, and insurance.   This empirical comparison sees the media sector as an industry leader in e-commerce, while banks and insurance seem to be reluctant followers. This study shows that the media industry has a considerable e-commerce orientation, while the other two are still focused on the communication and public relations function of the Internet. Nevertheless, the banking industry in particular also seems to show a trend toward e-commerce.

In chapter 6, Fritz discusses to what extent traditional retailers are threatened by electronic commerce. While the danger is not yet clear and present, the potential exists, especially for those product categories that lend themselves to Internet business. The strategies pursued by retailers, including their own Internet presence, appear to be largely insufficient.

Wikström and Frostling-Henningsson discuss the outlook for online grocery shopping in Sweden in chapter 7. In many ways, Sweden is a fertile ground for grocery-oriented e-commerce. The study reported in this chapter shows, however, that electronic grocery shopping runs into some limits, even among those families that are strongly committed to this method of shopping.

In chapter 8, Rask presents results from a study of how small and midsized are responding to the challenge of Web-based international marketing in Denmark. He formulates three prototypical strategies of Web presence and shows the complex ways in which firms progress along (and sometimes backtrack along) these Web presence strategies.

Lührig and Dholakia examine the growing phenomena of Internet auctions in chapter 9. Apart from the spectacular emergence of eBay as a c2c firm, the major impact of auctions is in the b2b arena.

Part III focuses on theoretical frameworks for online marketing. Chapter 10 explores the ways in which attributes of online retail stores differ from the attributes of physical stores. It develops a model to understand the process of loyalty formation to online stores and offers managerial insights about enhancing the attributes of electronic retailers.

In chapter 11, Wikström, Carlell and Frostling-Henningsson offer some additional evidence from their study on Internet grocery shopping in Sweden (see chapter 7) and suggest a model of Internet shopping in which the virtual realm "mirrors" some aspects of the real store.

In chapter 12, Dholakia and Fortin examine the growing field of advertising on the Net. They argue that interactivity and vividness (also referred to as the creation of "rich media") are emerging as key concepts for understanding and classifying various types of Internet ads.

Part IV addresses special problems and opportunities of online marketing, such as Web site design, online data acquisition, virtual communities, privacy, and access issues. In chapter 13, Mevenkamp and Kerner develop guidelines for the design of corporate Web pages. Using multiple methodologies, they derive suggestions and guidelines from the analysis of Web offerings of a large computer company.   They conclude that businesses need to analyze wishes, preferences and habits of their target users to shape their Web presence, rather than rely blindly on "common sense" suggestions.

Bandilla and Hauptmanns (chapter 14) illustrate the use of the Internet for marketing research. The Internet has the potential to conduct research with very large numbers of respondents within a short time frame. These benefits are offset by several major drawbacks, in particular problems with sampling and respondent self-selection.   The chapter addresses the suitability of various Internet services for online research.

In chapter 15, Bennemann and Schröder examine the growing use of virtual communities as an instrument of Internet marketing. When successful, such communities can become a tremendous source of support to a firm. But what makes such communities successful? Bennemann and Schröder delve deeply into this issue based on the results of the study of the virtual community affiliated with an American trucking company.

The Internet opens the world to the consumer but at the same time renders the consumer open and sometimes vulnerable to the world. Chapter 16 presents a framework for examining privacy issues in e-commerce settings. In essence, the framework shows that the actions and perceptions of both the marketer and the consumer create a set of interactive spaces. Many of these spaces are problematic from the consumer's perspective. It is therefore likely that privacy concerns will remain and perhaps keep rising on the political agenda.

Speaking of politics, promising and promoting Internet access have become "good politics" in most parts of the world. While Internet access continues to grow at a phenomenal rate, there will continue to remain a global divide between the Web "haves" and "have-nots." Even within the affluent nations, concerns about the "digital divide" are surfacing. In the future, while the advanced nations will strive for universal Internet access, the emerging world will keep experimenting with a variety of technologies and social policies to bring the Internet to people who may not have access to telephones or even electricity.

Part V consists of two chapters dealing with some of the ways that companies and organizations are transforming because of Internet and e-commerce. In chapter 18, Zwick, Dholakia, and Mundorf compare and contrast the overall Web strategies of five comparable pairs of American and German firms. On most dimensions, the American Web sites were more advanced than the German ones at the time they were studied. A major exception was the dimension of globalization. German Web sites were globally oriented, while the American Web sites had at best a very weak global orientation. In chapter 19, Mundorf and his coauthors examine the emerging patterns of Internet-aided distance education. Results from an Internet-based transatlantic learning project are presented to show how connecting students from different countries can enhance their global learning and cultural awareness.

SUMMARY AND CONCLUSIONS

In the year 2000, Internet and e-commerce entered their "globalization phase" in a stunning and decisive way. While the content of the Web was still largely in the English language, the number of Internet users whose native language was not English exceeded the number whose native language was English. Not just the developed nations of Europe and North America but also a number of emerging nations, some with vast populations such as China, India, and Brazil, have made serious and long-term commitments to e-commerce. Japan, an affluent nation that found the keyboard-based approach of the early phase of the Internet unappealing, has plunged into the new mobile methods of Internet access based on phones and palmtop devices.

Along with galloping globalization came the first wave of dot-com failures. In Europe, the fashion merchandiser Boo.com crashed, creating waves of panic in the Internet economy. In the United States, high-profile e-commerce firms such as Peapod, CDNow, Toysmart.com, QuePasa.com, and drkoop.com burned through their cash and faced the prospects of either radical restructuring or closing shop altogether.

The continuing forces of globalization, technological upheavals, and relentless competition require a balanced and reflective approach to e-commerce and online marketing. This book delivers such an approach. The chapters that follow, authored by marketing and e-commerce researchers and industry experts from many countries, delve into the fundamental and long-term drivers of the Internet infrastructure, e-commerce models, marketing approaches, and customer behaviors. While you will find plenty of dot-com examples sprinkled throughout the book, the main strength of the chapters lies in their novel conceptualizations, the well-argued frameworks, and the research-based evidence. These are the enduring tools that will help you in exploring, understanding, and managing e-commerce activities and online marketing in the coming years.

QUESTIONS FOR DISCUSSION

1. Five years from now, how will e-commerce activities be similar and how will they be different across the advanced nations of North America, Europe, and Asia?

2. Ten years from now, how will e-commerce activities be similar and how will they be different when comparing the advanced nations as a group and the emerging markets as a group?

3. What qualities must a firm have to succeed as an online marketer on a global basis, including advanced nations and all the emerging markets? Which ones of today's firms seem to possess or are working to develop such qualities?

Part I

Impact of the Internet on Marketing

2

Markets and Marketing in the Information Age

Nikhilesh Dholakia and Ruby Roy Dholakia

THE INFORMATION AGE

Many forces are propelling the advanced and emerging economies across the globe into the Information Age. Sharp boundaries between information functions and types that existed up to the Industrial Age are getting erased. A vast information space is opening up that is reshaping and will continue to influence the nature of economies and societies for decades to come.

What forces are driving all these changes? Among the primary drivers are:

- *Digitization*: The conversion of all forms of information into a digital form makes it easy to store, transfer, process, and mix information that, in previous times, stayed in separate compartments and domains.
- *Deregulation*: Realizing that technology is making it possible to move information in easier ways and across multiple paths, most governments are dismantling the controls on the movement of information and on the media that had existed during much of the industrial era.
- *Decreasing costs*: Because of rapid technological advances in fields such as semiconductors and fiber optics, unit costs to process, store, and move information are dropping, thereby pushing price-to-performance ratios ever lower.
- *De-tethering*: To keep up with fast and global lifestyles and work styles, information technology devices are abandoning the "tether"–the wire that keeps them tied to one location. E-commerce is transforming into its mobile variant "m-commerce."
- *De-centering*: Various types of information and communication networks across the world are getting interconnected because of the growth of the Internet. There is no center anymore in many aspects of life.

At a fundamental level, these five forces are technological, political, economic, social, and cultural in character, respectively. The specific labels and content of these forces will change with time, but for the foreseeable future, the fundamental shifts at these five levels will continue to occur as the Information Age unfolds (see Figure 2.1).

Figure 2.1
Forces Shaping the Information Age

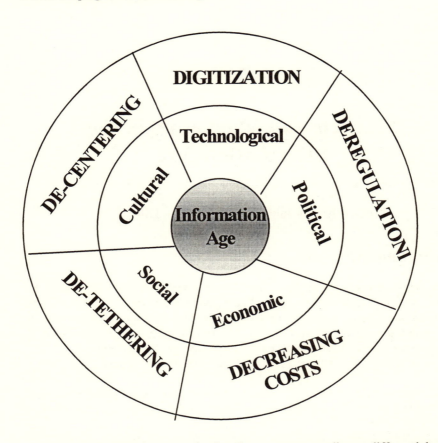

At the present juncture, the five forces are proceeding at differential rates. Furthermore, there are differences in the strength and impact of these forces across the nations of the world, a point that we revisit in the discussion of the global aspects of the Information Age.

Let us do a quick reprise of the five forces. After the invention of the World Wide Web format of the Internet, people started realizing that there is merit in digitizing the content that they own or create. Therefore, digitization is proceeding at a rapid clip. Not only current content but historical and archival content are also getting digitized. This has obvious implications for data storage, which is expected to grow at a high rate for years to come.

Deregulation is happening worldwide, but its progress is uneven, slowed by political pressure from companies and employees who feel that very competitive markets threaten their interests. Among the major countries, the United States leads in deregulation. There are, however, smaller countries such as New Zealand and Chile that have deregulated faster and further than the United States.

Costs are declining very fast for information processing and storage activities and have also begun to decline for the movement of information. Just as cheap computing and storage transformed the world of business, abundant and cheap bandwidth will bring in a second wave of the information revolution.

De-tethering, or "going mobile," has become a major force in some of the advanced economies of Northern and Southern Europe, as well as in affluent parts of Asia. The United States, which (along with Scandinavia) led the world in mobile telephony in the 1990s, is, in fact, slipping in a relative sense. Mobile communication devices have become attractive lifestyle symbols for the elite all over the world.

De-centering induced by the Internet and virtual ways of working and living are happening at the leading edges of the information economy. The impact of de-centering will become pervasive with time. In terms of Internet readiness, some countries such as the United States, Canada, Finland, Sweden, the United Kingdom, and Australia are leading the rest of the world. Because of its sheer economic weight, however, the United States that is developing the world's first Internet-based mega-economy. Let us turn our attention to the nature of the information economy that is emerging as a result of the combined impact of these forces.

INFORMATION ECONOMY

An information economy is emerging, gradually eclipsing the industrial economy. This has already been evident in the United States since the mid-1990s and is likely to be the case in many other regions of the world in the first decade of the twenty-first century. There are three main parts of the information economy:

- *Information firms*: At the core are the companies that represent the technological essence of the information business. These companies span industries such as computers, telecommunications, software, automation, electronics, and media (including the Internet).
- *Information-intensive firms*: These are companies and industries that have information at the center of their business operations. The vast and global financial services industry fits into this category, as do industries related to education and research.
- *Information-aggressive firms*: In most industries, some firms take aggressive leadership in transforming their business operations using information technology (IT). Even though they may be in businesses as diverse as bookselling or aircraft manufacturing, such firms are best characterized as Information Age firms. Such firms, if successful with their IT-driven strategies, gain market share and thereby challenge others in their industries to follow suit.

As the Information Age widens and deepens, we will see growth in all three parts of the information economy, but most dramatic changes will occur in the third category. There are still relatively few firms (and industries) where fundamental redefinition of business using IT has taken root. In fact, we can say that when the major firms in an industry completely redefine their business using IT, that industry moves into the second (information-intensive) category. Similarly, a few information-intensive firms–such as Andersen Consulting or E-Trade–become such intense users of IT that they become information firms. The three parts of the information economy are highly symbiotic, and the 1990s witnessed the tremendous and favorable economic impact of these symbiotic relations on the U.S. economy, even in a global setting that was characterized by crises.

Taken together, the three parts of the information economy already account for nearly 50 percent of the employment and gross domestic product (gdp) of the advanced economies of the world. These percentages will continue to grow well into the twenty-first century. As the Information Age unfolds, activities from other "ages" will diminish, but they will not disappear. We will continue to have residual activities from the Stone Age (hunting and gathering), Agrarian Age (agriculture), and Industrial Age (manufacturing). The surviving parts of the earlier ages will be considerably more informationalized than they are today. The percentage contributions of the ages that are more distant in origin, however, will shrink drastically, as is evidenced by the already small role of agriculture and even smaller role of hunting (e.g., fishing) in the advanced economies of today. These residual activities of earlier ages together constitute a limit on the information economy. The information economy will expand until the activities of the earlier ages can be compressed no further. Of course, in due course, the information economy itself will be compressed by the rise of a new type of economy–one that merges biotechnology with IT–whose outlines we can only barely imagine at this stage (Kurzweil 1999; Tapscott 1995).

To understand the changes occurring in the markets and marketing activities in the Information Age, we have to pay close attention to all three elements of the information economy. The information firms are, and will be continue to be, in the driver's seat for a couple of decades. These firms are developing and applying the basic information technology tools and are investing in the core infrastructures of the Information Age. Some of these firms are also models of information-aggressive firms. For example, Dell Computers is not only a leading computer maker but also one of the best exemplars of applying information technology for the purposes of customized e-marketing and agile manufacturing.

Over time, the information-intensive and the information-aggressive firms will come to play the defining role in shaping the Information Age. This is similar to the situation in the Industrial Age, when steam engine makers provided the initial core technology and defined the early character of industrialization, but eventually the Industrial Age was profiled by industries such as textiles, railways, automobiles, steel, machine tools, shipbuilding, and electrical machinery. In the Information Age, the financial services sector has taken an early lead in applying the newly emerging technologies, akin to the textile sector in the Industrial Age, but it remains to be seen which other sectors will also emerge as key economic sectors of the Information Age. Even though we are at an early stage of the Information Age in this sense, some information-aggressive firms have already started to change the character of markets and marketing. Amazon.com in book retailing, Priceline.com in travel services, and eBay in auctioning and trading are well known examples in this regard.

INFORMATION AGE MARKETS

Markets are systems of transactions governed by distinct rules that have existed since ancient times but were refined greatly by the rise of capitalism (Pandya and Dholakia 1992; Polanyi 1944; Sahlins 1972). In hyperindustrial economies, market transactions occur across fairly elaborate value chains or, more appropriately, value networks. In the pre-Internet stage, information technology often helped major firms to strengthen the transactional links across value chains by proprietary approaches such as the use of Electronic Data Interchange (EDI). With the growth of the Internet, information links opened up, and proprietary architectures became less appealing. In coming years, we will see a movement toward solutions that maintain the advantages available from the openness and ubiquity of the Internet (and its successors) as well as offer some proprietary advantages in terms of Intranets and Extranets.[2]

Transactions that occur in private spaces such as offices are less visible than transactions that occur in public spaces such as retail stores. In the Information Age, market transactions are occurring increasingly in electronic or virtual spaces, which are often labeled as cyberspace (Gibson 1984) or marketspace (Rayport and Sviokla 1994). As transactions shift to electronic and virtual spaces, they become less public and less visible. Often, only transacting computers are aware of what is occurring, and human agents have to ask for special reports to find out about such transactions. For those willing to probe deeply, however, electronic transactions offer a gold mine of consumer information, and this has given rise to many concerns about the privacy and sharing of consumer data.

The most visible market transactions in a value chain are those occurring at the level of the end user or the consumer. The majority of such transactions occur in public and physical retail environments. Although things such as credit and debit cards and cash registers with scanners have introduced a lot of information technology into the consumer-stage transactions, compared to other stages of the value chain, the consumer stage is relatively less "informationalized" (Davis and Davidson 1991).[3]

This will change in the next phase of the Information Age. The last link in the value chain, the one leading to the consumer, is moving the virtual cyberspace. As this transition accelerates, vast changes will occur in the information economy. It is as if there was a free-flowing pipe, but a clog constricted one part of it; and that clog (at the consumer level) is being dissolved by information technology. There will be a step increase in circulation and flow of goods and services. Markets will be energized by the removal of bottlenecks. This can be observed most clearly in stock and commodity markets where informationalization, even now reaching the consumer level, has dramatically pushed up the volume and variety of transactions in stock exchanges such as Nasdaq in the United States and the Neuer Market in Germany.

Figure 2.2
A Simplified Representation of the Industrial-Age Value Chain for Delivering Goods and Services

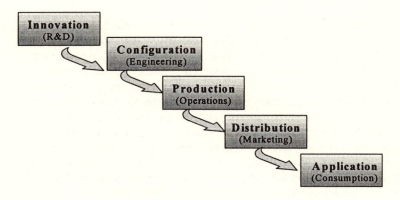

Since we cannot expect people to buy and consume beyond certain physical limits, most of the changes that we can expect will be qualitative rather than quantitative. New forms of competition will arise, and a new economy, already emerging, will begin to rival the "old economy" (created in the industrial era) in terms of size and power.

MARKETING, VALUE CHAIN, AND INFORMATIONALIZATION

Let us consider a simple representation of the value chain by which goods and services are created and delivered to end consumers (see Figure 2.2). The activities that we call "marketing" were confined to the last link of this chain for many decades. With competition and increasing market orientation in most industries, marketing activities began to stretch deeper into the value chain—toward production, configuration, and innovation. The influence of marketing consumer. Technology moved too fast for the conventional marketing process to work in a full-blown manner.

As the last link of this chain gets informationalized, it not only steps up the flow of goods and services to the consumer, but also opens up the possibility for the consumer to reach deep into the value chain. When this happens, consumers begin to shape production, configuration, and innovation activities inside firms or networks of firms (see Figure 2.3). Interactive networks permit easy communication among firms and customers. Furthermore, information technology speeds up cycle times throughout the value chain, including now the final consumer stage of the chain (Dholakia 1999). Competition shifts from cost-cutting and product differentiation strategies to opening up clear and interactive channels linking the consumer and the corporation. Marketing changes from a monologue (by the corporation) with a weak feedback (from the consumer side)

Figure 2.3
The Emerging Information-Age Value Chain

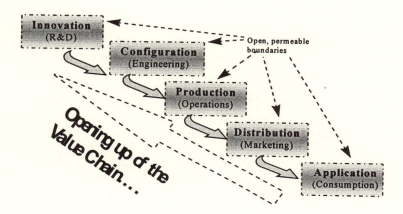

to an active conversation, even a multilogue involving communities of corporations and consumers (Firat and Dholakia 1998).[4]

IMPACTS OF INFORMATION TECHNOLOGY

The impacts of information technology on markets and marketing will unfold over many decades. Some of the contours of things to come, however, are already becoming visible. Let us examine some of the main dimensions of markets and marketing that will change.

Consumer-Level Impacts

Learning, Knowledge, and Skills

Marketing interactions in the Information Age trigger interesting changes in the knowledge and skills of consumers as well as providers. In general, cybertransactions require fairly knowledgeable consumers and service providers. Buying a book or conducting a stock trade on an Internet Web site is a relatively complex operation, at least for first-time users. Once the learning has taken place, however, cybertransactions can lead to significant reductions in transaction costs, in economic as well as psychic terms.

Consider the case of stock brokerage services. By providing a full range of high-quality services, Merrill Lynch emerged as the biggest brokerage service firm in the United States. In terms of supporting its financial consultants and traders, Merrill Lynch became a world leader in IT support to its employees, delivered right to their desktops. In addition to current market information and databases, Merrill Lynch account service executives even had dedicated radio and video broadcasts available to them. As electronic trading gained momentum, and telecommunications improved, Charles Schwab–a discount brokerage firm– adopted an aggressive marketing strategy to win accounts. Schwab promised lower commissions and offered 24-hour telephone access to brokers and account executives. Using technologies such as interactive voice response, Schwab extended the informationalization stage to the end user. With the growth of the Internet, E-Trade entered the field by offering Web-based trading services directly on the end customer's desktop. E-Trade customers had 80-90 percent of the key support information on their desktops, the type of information that in the early 1990s was available only on the desktops of account executives in major brokerage houses such as Merrill Lynch. By forgoing some of the nice, but nonessential customer, services (such as fancy printed statements, gold Visa cards, and plush offices), E-Trade offered commission rates that were only about 20 percent of those charged by Merrill Lynch and were also about one-third of those charged by the discount broker Schwab. As competition heated up in electronic brokerage, Schwab responded by aggressively shifting a lot of its customers to Web trading, and Merrill Lynch started offering a variety of Web-based trading and information services. At the low end, competitors such as Suretrade and Ameritrade emerged that undercut even E-Trade by 50 percent or more.

The informationalization of the consumer stage is predicated on learning and skill improvement by the end customer–there must be a willingness on the part of the end customer to invest some money and effort in learning and skill enhancement in return for discount prices and greater control over services. In some cases, employee skills also have to be upgraded. In the case of Peapod, a company that offered online grocery shopping services to busy households, the employees who pick and pack the orders (received electronically) had to be well trained. For example, when picking and packing fresh fruits and vegetables, they had to ensure that the freshest and best produce was packed. In some instances, investments in such employee skill development may begin to reverse the long-term trend of de-skilling of retail employees in the United States.

With the Information Age unfolding, technology skills and knowledge of vast segments of the population are improving, through schooling as well as on-the-job training. This would continue to open up new opportunities for existing firms that are willing to take on the creative challenges of Information Age marketing as well as for new entrants that keep inventing novel methods of electronic marketing.

Loyalty, Identity, and Mobility

Established brands with strong consumer loyalties will face the challenge of extending the brand equity into the virtual cyberspace. In the making of a brand identity and building up of brand equity, physical factors–shapes, sizes, packages, designs, logos, retail displays–play a significant role. While it is possible to have cyberspace analogs for most of these, the impact of these elements in cyberspace is usually not as intense as it is in the physical world. Furthermore, in cyberspace, switching costs (in money as well as effort terms) are extremely low–a message or an image can be made to vanish with just one click, and a competing brand can be examined and purchased with just a few more clicks. In effect, information technologies lower the mobility barriers for consumers. They can move with ease from image to image and from brand to brand. Coupled with the fact that entry barriers for new, competitive entrants are lower, this means that it becomes relatively difficult to hold the attention and loyalty of consumers in cyberspace. Some brands, such as Coca-Cola or Nike, are likely to be creative and strategic enough to take on this challenge, but other brands may not be able to hold on to their loyalties and equities in cyberspace.

Brands that are created entirely in the virtual cyberspace, such as Amazon.com (an Internet bookseller) and E-Trade (an Internet stock brokerage service), have the opposite problem: they lack the physical cues that can help shape and sustain their brand identities. Such brands often have to make great efforts to translate their electronic successes into the physical world. Take the case of Gateway 2000, a direct seller of computers that uses the telephone and the Internet as the sales channels. To overcome the disadvantage of being a virtual organization, the company used physical cues and humorous imagery to distinguish itself from both direct and reseller-dependent competitors. Using its remote South Dakota location to advantage, Gateway created an association with rural settings: pastures, barns, and cows. The company shipped its computers in great big boxes painted like the side of a cow, and cow images were used in its print and television advertisements as well as on the Web site. Finally, the company opened Gateway stores in key markets, complete with the cow motifs, and began to advertise that customers could "call, click, or come in."

In the years to come, we are likely to see refinements in the conceptualization as well as nurturing of cyberidentities and cyberloyalties (Abbott et al. 1999). Studies of how identities are formed, sustained, and transformed in cyberspace are already under way and will influence marketing efforts of firms (Turkle 1995).

Experience Frames

By experience frames we mean frames of space and time in which buying, selling, and consuming experiences occur. Shopping is not merely an instrumental act but also an experiential process. Today's retail environments provide some of the most fantastic settings for direct experiences in a safe, community-like milieu. Even the most richly designed cyberbrowsing and cybershopping environments do not even come close to a great retail setting. It is true that virtual reality technologies will gradually shrink this gap, but physical retail settings will retain their superiority as an experience frame for decades to come. In fact, by using information technology in physical settings, retail environments can become even more fantastic than before, as evidenced in theme parks and high-tech concept stores and malls.

One of the biggest challenges facing firms operating in cyberspace in the coming years will be to create electronic experience frames that can compete effectively with physical experience frames. Ways have to be found to make the electronic marketplace experience comparable to the physical marketplace experience. This is not easy, especially since physical spaces in major retail centers and theme parks are being updated and rendered fantastic and spectacular in a variety of ways (Dholakia, Firat, and Venkatesh 1997). Moreover, such physical spaces have the advantage of offering a safe, community-like experience because of masses of people visiting them. While some forms of virtual communities are emerging, the experience in such virtual communities–in terms of shopping experience–is likely to be limiting.

In the next several years, in terms of experiential aspects of the marketplace, advantages will lie with firms that can create or influence attractive and alluring physical as well as virtual spaces for consumers and also provide effortless ways of moving from one to the other. Firms such as Disney, Coca-Cola, Lego, Nike, Hilton, DreamWorks, and MGM Grand are well positioned for this. With the emergence and refinement of virtual reality (VR) technologies, however, things are likely to change at some point. Just as firms like Amazon.com and E-Trade emerged to take advantage of the Internet as a transactional tool, we will surely witness the rise of a new breed of firms that are able to use VR advantageously to create alluring and captivating virtual marketplaces. Such firms will usher in virtual settings that equal or surpass their physical counterparts or at least offer an experience-per-dollar ratio that is unbeatable.

Supply-Side Impacts

Market Structure

In many industries, when the last steps of the value chain leading up to the consumer get informationalized, there is a lowering of competitive entry barriers. Relatively small-scale firms as well as savvy start-up enterprises are able to tap into markets that were hitherto accessible only to firms with large and established distribution networks. Examples of this are found in a variety of industries: Gateway 2000 in computers, Amazon.com in bookselling, and Virtual Vineyards in wine distribution. As and when these new entrants succeed, they begin to alter the market structure. Industries that were characterized by relatively stable, oligopoly-style patterns of competition suddenly become arenas of high and dynamic competition or "hypercompetition" (D'Aveni 1994). So far, this process is visible in relatively few cases and mostly in the North American market. In the next few years, we can expect the market structure changes to occur more rapidly, pervasively, and globally.

Institutional Arrangements

In some cases, Information Age marketing methods give rise to institutional arrangements that are reminiscent of the preindustrial era. In preindustrial settings, a customer could send a list to the local grocer, and the grocer would deliver all the listed items. Peapod's shopping service does exactly this, except now the shopping list is sent electronically, the delivery time is scheduled online, and a physical process is visible to the consumer only in the last step: the actual delivery of the ordered groceries.

The Information Age thus not only creates new institutional arrangements–cybershops and electronic retailers–but also often harks back to a preindustrial era of customized products and services. A firm like eBay, for example, re-creates the electronic version of old-time trading methods such as swap meets and flea markets.

Global Impacts and Implications

Access Inequities

The discussion so far has assumed the conditions prevailing in advanced economies with fairly well developed information infrastructures. Reality is different at the global level. Half the world's population is yet to make its first telephone call. Of the 6 billion people in the world, only about 1 billion have access to a good, universal information infrastructure.

Even in the advanced countries with well-developed telecommunications systems, there are substantial differences in terms of digitization, bandwidth availability, and computing power (Dholakia 1997). The all-fiber "intelligent island" of Singapore is quite different from remote rural areas of the United States, where even digital telephone exchanges may not have made an appearance yet. Furthermore, with computerization and the Internet, another distinction is surfacing between the United States and the rest of the advanced world. In terms of computing power measured in terms of available MIPS (millions of instruction per second) per capita, the United States has rapidly climbed to a level that is more than twice that found in most advanced economies of Europe and Asia (Roche and Blaine 1997). In terms of Internet connectivity, the United States and Canada also exhibit profiles that are dramatically more advanced than those in other major developed countries (Kalin 1999).

Global Opportunities in the New Economy

There is no doubt that the early opportunities for the firms constituting the information economy–the information firms, the information-intensive firms, and the information-aggressive firms–lie in the United States and a handful of other countries that have advanced information infrastructures and a substantial, installed base of computing power. These markets will continue to define the products and services of the Information Age for years to come. For the visionary firms of the information economy, however, it would be a mistake to focus attention solely on these leading markets. Although highly promising, these markets account for only 0.5 to 1 billion of the world's 6 billion consumers.

In the coming decades, another 3 to 4 billion consumers would aspire to be a part of the information economy and to taste at least some of the fruits of the Information Age. Because of sheer demographics, the majority of these aspiring consumers will be in Asia (Tanzer 1997).[5] Latin America, Eastern Europe, and Africa will also offer substantial opportunities.

The leading segments of these emerging markets will resemble the advanced countries in terms of the information infrastructure. These leading segments are likely to respond to Information Age products and services in much the same way as the consumers in advanced countries do. This was already evident in the late 1990s, for example, in the rapid adoption of the Internet by the upper-middle-class segments in India, where the per capita annual income was not even U.S.$400.

Substantial opportunities, however, will also lie in the emerging markets beyond these leading segments. These "secondary segments" in the emerging markets will not have access to, or be able to afford, a basic (wired or wireless) telecommunications service or a desktop or tabletop information appliance (the hybrid PC-TV combination, in whatever forms it evolves) in the foreseeable future. They would, however, have access to some form of television and public telecommunications terminals such as pay phones or kiosks. They may even have access to rudimentary, pagerlike wireless telecommunications devices.[6] They will have some disposable income available for consumption and investment purposes. For Information Age firms aspiring to be global players, one of the biggest challenges will be how to reach out to these secondary, but very substantial, segments in the emerging markets. Firms such as Nokia, investing in the development of phone-based Internet delivery methods, are likely to be rewarded in such settings.

On a global scale, the foreseeable shape of the new information economy can be characterized as a three-legged stool. The first leg will be the advanced economies of the world. The second leg will be the advanced, relatively rich consumer segments in the emerging economies of the world. The third leg will be the secondary segments in the emerging economies—people with some discretionary buying power who would like to participate in the information economy, but on cheaper and more economical terms than those applicable to the first two legs. In order to be stable, long-term global marketing strategies in the Information Age will have to pay attention to each of the three legs of the stool.

SUMMARY AND CONCLUSIONS

The Information Age is being shaped by technological, cultural, and economic factors that have great momentum. Such forces are symbiotic and mutually reinforcing, and this is accelerating the pace of change. A new information economy is emerging, led by the firms that create and deploy various information technologies. In the foreseeable future, the leadership of the information economy is likely to pass to information-intensive and information-aggressive firms. These are firms that use information as a raw material and use IT to transform and redefine their business.

The new information economy will reshape markets and transform the nature of marketing. Business processes, including transactions at the end customer level, are getting informationalized. Market transactions are moving into the virtual cyberspace. In informationalized value chains, end customers may have opportunities to reach deep into the organizations serving them and to influence the distribution, production, configuration, and even creation of products and services.

As these trends accelerate, they will create challenges for existing major brands. Such brands will have to come up with new ways of projecting brand equity and maintaining consumer loyalty in cyberspace. These new forms of marketing may open up many opportunities for new players who, unburdened by the legacies of the Industrial Age, can create innovative business models tailored specifically to the Information Age.

Finally, on a global scale, the changes in markets and business models brought about by the Information Age will propagate rapidly from the advanced countries of the world to the leading segments of the emerging economies. There will, however, be substantial opportunities in the secondary segments of emerging markets. Such segments will not, or cannot, respond to the business models that work in affluent market settings endowed with strong information infrastructures. Substantial opportunities will be available to firms that figure out business models for extending the key benefits of the Information Age to these secondary segments.

QUESTIONS FOR DISCUSSION

1. Five years from now, which industries are likely to represent the leading edge of the "information-intensive firms" and "information-aggressive firms"? Why?

2. If the value chain is increasingly opened to customer manipulation, what will be the ultimate result? Will it be possible for customers to use IT not just to design but even to "invent" the products that they want? In which types of industries are we likely to see such extreme changes?

3. Ten years from now, what will the information infrastructure look like in parts of the world that are not advanced? How can proactive firms take advantage of the rudimentary, but yet connected, infrastructure that may become available in developing countries?

3

Internet and Electronic Markets: An Economic Framework for Understanding Market-Shaping Infrastructures

Nikhilesh Dholakia, Ruby Roy Dholakia, and Myung-Ho Park

Infrastructure innovations have had far-reaching impacts on markets and marketing in the past. The latest such infrastructure revolution-the Internet-is presently under way. Marketers need to focus their attention on how Internet-based and other forms of electronic commerce will shape markets and marketing in the future. In this chapter, an economic framework based on agency costs, transaction costs, and network externality is presented to examine how the Internet might transform electronic markets and marketing institutions and practices in general.

INTRODUCTION

While new methods of marketing communications and product distribution emerge from time to time in competitive settings, new market-shaping infrastructures appear but rarely. In the past 150 years, we witnessed the occasional, but far-reaching, transformation of markets and of marketing through the emergence of revolutionary infrastructures such as the railways, the electric grid, the telephone system, and the highway system (see, e.g., Klein 1994). Each of these infrastructure innovations created new markets, transformed existing markets, spawned new marketing institutions, and altered marketing practices and concepts in significant ways.

The latest such infrastructure revolution is presently under way. The advancement and convergence of telecommunications and information technologies have ushered in a new infrastructure for information exchange (for reviews of Information-Age convergence, see National Academy of Sciences 1994). Variously dubbed as the "information superhighway" or "I-way," "cyberspace," "information infrastructure," and a virtual "marketspace" (for definitions or early use of such terms, see Anderson 1995; Gibson 1984; Kirkpatrick 1994; Rayport and Sviokla 1995), a definitive label for this new and evolving infrastructure is likely to emerge only in a retrospective sense. After key parameters are settled over time through public and private policies that are attempting to bring some order to the wild growth of this new electronic frontier (for public policy perspectives, see Hart, Reed, and Bar 1992; Miller 1996), we may at some future date arrive at a definitive label for today's dynamic era. In this chapter, we will focus on that part of the new information infrastructure that has already achieved a high degree of global standardization: the Internet.

The key question addressed in this chapter is this: How has the Internet shaped (and will continue to shape) markets and marketing? We answer the question by analyzing the market-shaping characteristics of the Internet from an economic perspective. Using this perspective, we will examine how the Internet is shaping, and will continue to shape, markets, marketing institutions, and marketing practices.

The discussion in this chapter is organized into three major sections. The first section provides a brief review of electronic markets, the growth of the Internet, and its emerging implications for electronic markets. The second section discusses the economic impact of the Internet on markets, marketing institutions, and marketing practices from three perspectives: agency costs, transaction costs, and network externality. The third and final section offers concluding comments and discusses the emerging research needs from a marketing perspective.

INTERNET AND ELECTRONIC MARKETS

Electronic Markets

Electronic markets and electronic commerce are not new concepts. Electronic markets have existed since the 1970s, sometimes even earlier. Ranging from credit-card transaction systems (Orme et al. 1995) to airline reservation systems and store-specific electronic shopping systems (Malone, Yates, and Benjamin 1989), electronic methods of buying and selling have been around for a while. By the late 1980s, Malone, Yates, and Benjamin (1989) concluded that the development of electronic marketplaces was inevitable and that ultimately, many (if not most) transactions would be conducted electronically. Bakos (1991; 296) introduced the terms "electronic marketplace" and "electronic market system," which he defined as "an interorganizational information system that allows the participating buyers and sellers to exchange information about prices and product offerings." Other terms appeared with the growth of Internet and its transformation into a commercial medium.

Internet as a New Infrastructure

The Internet grew out of the defense (ARPAnet), scientific (NSFnet), and academic (Bitnet) computer-based communications networks that were sponsored and supported by the U.S. government (Hart, Reed, and Bar 1992). Selected members of the academic community and some government agencies were its primary users for nearly two decades. Within these user categories, however, the user base and scope of usage of networked text-based communications expanded rapidly in the 1980s and the 1990s. Net usage expanded from university scientists working on defense projects to nearly all professors in the United States and from major research universities to all types of educational institutions, including community colleges.

Parallel to these government-sponsored networks, companies had been building Local Area Networks and Wide Area Networks for their internal communication needs. From the late 1980s, after the formation of the Internet Corporation as a coordinating agency, it became clear that there was more to be gained by the merging and internetworking of these disparate public and private networks than by keeping them separate (National Academy of Sciences 1994).

Facilitating Conditions

The popularity of text-based communications such as e-mail, newsgroups, discussion groups, bulletin boards, and chat lines had laid the groundwork for the rapid growth of the Internet. People realized that they could communicate with thousands of others with similar interests and access electronic information at thousands of locations through protocols such as Gopher, FTP, and Telnet. Real excitement and explosive rates of growth, however, were triggered by the invention of the multimedia World Wide Web (WWW) protocol. Invented at the CERN laboratory in Switzerland and refined at the NCSA laboratory in Illinois, WWW and the Mosaic browser opened up new vistas of Internet usage and electronic commerce (Hoffman and Novak 1995).

WWW and easy-to-use Web browsers such as Mosaic, Netscape, and Internet Explorer facilitated access to, and use of, the Net in a variety of ways. First, these graphic interfaces were inviting and involving and became more enticing as sound, animation, and video capabilities were added. Second, graphic displays set the user free, to some extent, from the tyranny of the keyboard; finding and manipulating information became a point-and-click experience. Third, new Web sites and competition among Web portals provided fresh and exciting content every day. In the world of television, this would be like having new channels, shows, and movies added to the schedule every day.

Internet and Electronic Markets: Emerging Implications

The Internet has been shaping up as an ideal marketing communication medium. When it is used as both a communication and a distribution medium, it confers a dual advantage. This is why publishers, software companies, music houses, movie companies, graphic designers, photographic services, banks, insurance companies, reservation systems, and education and training providers became very interested, and some leading players started deriving early benefits of the Internet.

The business potential of the Internet beckoned many firms. By the end of 1995, there were 40,000 commercial Web sites (Gupta and Chatterjee 1997). By December 1996, about 627,000 domain names had been registered. This number exceeded 1.5 million by the end of 1997 (Friel 1997) and reached 5.3

Table 3.1
An Evolutionary Perspective on Market Transactions

Historical Phase	Premodern Preindustrial Age	Modern Industrial Age	Postmodern Information Age
Overall characterization of market transactions	One-to-One	One-to-Many	Many-to-Many
Nature of relationship	Personal relationship	Mediated relationship	Electronically mediated, simulated "one-to-one" relationship
Market Response	Immediate and Direct	Delayed and Indirect	Immediate and Direct
Volume of Transactions	Limited	Large	Large
Market Reach	Local	National	Global
Information Sources for Buyers	Personal sources of information	Media-dependent, plus some Word of mouth	Net-based impersonal and "personal" sources
Connection among Buyers	Limited, personal	Nonexistent, or Very Limited	Extensive, Impersonal

million by early 1999 (DomainStats.com 1999). Sites began to get talked up in the media or get listed as "cool sites" or "hot sites" by various services such as Yahoo!. Such superior sites were as likely to belong to small and midsized firms as to large firms.

Not only marketing firms rushed to be connected to the Internet; millions of users also made a dash to the new medium. Estimates in the mid-1990s ranged around 2 million new connections every 30 days. Many of these individuals had their computers connected by high-speed links, while others attempted to navigate cyberspace with slower, modem-based links. People using the Net could surf (go from one Internet site to another), browse (explore the contents of a site), lurk (drop in on an ongoing discussion without contributing to it), or ask for specific information.

A strong advantage offered by the Net is its transparent global reach. Firms from any part of the world can create a strong Web presence and reach out to potential customers globally. Similarly, users from any part of the world can be connected to the Net and access information, goods, and services from any supplier small or large, local or global. According to one study, in the mid-1990s Australia was the second largest Internet user in relation to its population, with over 50 percent of its Internet use by corporations (Tse et al. Sutton, Tsang and Stuart 1995). By the late 1990s, the largest Internet markets outside the United States were in Europe, with the United Kingdom, the Netherlands, Germany, and the Scandinavian countries exhibiting prolific growth (Tomic 1998). By 2000, Internet growth in Asia became explosive.

These connections between marketers and customers and among customers themselves have transformed almost every dimension of market transactions.   Suddenly, it has become possible to have many-to-many connections (see Table 3.1) and yet simulate a "one-to-one" relationship (Peppers and Rogers 1993). Despite the large volume of transactions generated over widely dispersed (time and geography) markets, the Internet provides immediate and direct responses to a supplier's offerings. Users are becoming informed and knowledgeable by connecting with communities of like-minded users. Realizing the benefits of such electronic communities, marketers and cybermediaries have started promoting and supporting such electronic user-to-user interactions.

ECONOMIC IMPACTS

In economic terms, electronic infrastructures such as the Internet affect the market system by influencing the economic benefits and costs experienced by institutions. We treat the overall marketing system as consisting of sectors of institutions such as households, firms, and government agencies (Pandya and Dholakia 1992). Thus, the overall marketing system in the United States comprises all households, firms, and government agencies in the country and the relationships among these. When a new infrastructure, such as the Internet, becomes significant in terms of size (i.e., number of institutions and nodes connected), it starts affecting the economic benefits and costs within an institution as well as across institutions. Three important types of impacts have been identified in the literature dealing with the economics of electronic infrastructure: agency costs, transaction costs, and network externalities. We review these three types of impacts briefly, followed by an integrative view of economic impacts of the Internet.

Agency Costs

In any institution where the owner, manager, or leader (in other words, the overseer of the institution) has to delegate activities and operations to others (the operatives or agents), a divergence between the interests of the owner/manager/leader and those who carry out the delegated tasks is likely to arise. This gives rise to a category of costs called "agency costs" by economists (Fama 1980; Jensen and Meckling 1973; Ross 1973). These include costs of coordination and monitoring of operations, as well as opportunity costs when operatives make decisions that are not in the interests of the overseer. While the agency cost literature has focused mostly on the behavior of managers and workers in a firm, in principle a broadened concept of agency costs and benefits can be extended to all types of institutions (including households and government agencies) that populate a marketing system.

Information technology (IT) has two distinct impacts on agency costs (Gurbaxani and Whang 1991). On the one hand, information technology makes it possible to effectively coordinate and monitor the activities of the agents running the day-to-day operations of an institution, including far-flung global operations. By doing so, IT lowers agency costs. The massive delayering, downsizing, and reengineering in the American economy offers evidence of the paring of agency costs by firms, albeit with the accompaniment of significant human misery (Brynjolfsson, et al. 1994; Miller 1996). A different impact on agency costs may occur because IT enables the delegation of operating authority to an ever-wider range of operatives. This is the essence of another contemporary business trend: the employee "empowerment" movement, which has gone particularly far in IT-intensive firms such as FedEx. Empowered employees (or agents) can make quick decisions in situations that may, for example, require an on-the-spot redressing of a customer complaint. Such empowered agency is likely to bring economic benefits to the owners and overseers, especially in service-oriented businesses (Berry and Parasuraman 1991). It could also potentially give rise to opportunity costs due to agent/operators acting contrary to the interests of overseers. Firms that have taken the empowerment philosophy to heart believe that the economic benefits far outweigh the potential costs.

As far as marketing activities are concerned, the growth of the Internet opens up possibilities of extending the "agency" for a variety of marketing-related functions to operatives located at the farthest reaches within a firm's organization and even into other firms and the household sector. The agents located outside a firm may be intermediaries or customers. The following typify some of the early patterns of such interinstitutional and intersectoral transfers of agencies:

- Through its Web site, FedEx allows customers to track the progress of their packages using the airbill number.
- For a period, Compaq's Digital Equipment unit allowed interested parties to "log on" to, and "test-drive," one of its new computer models through its Web site.
- On the Dell and Gateway computer company Web sites, customers can configure and build the computer systems of their own choosing.

Because the Internet cuts across all institutional sectors–firms, government agencies, nonprofits, and households–it enables the maximization of economic benefits possible through an extremely wide extension of agency for selected tasks. Not just tasks such as selling, promoting, ordering, and shipping can be delegated, but also (eventually) tasks such as inventory management, product design, product testing, and even production scheduling are likely to be delegated. Along with garnering the anticipated competitive benefits, firms undertaking such extensions may also expose themselves to potential opportunity costs and risks stemming from such "universal and open agencies."

From a marketing systems perspective, we are likely to see the emergence and growth of institutions and methods to control and manage the potential risks and opportunity costs of wide-ranging agencies. To deal with such risks and costs, new forms of insurance, regulations, payment systems, and security arrangements are already being experimented with, and more are surely on the way.

Transactions Costs

It is now well accepted that transactions across institutions are not costless and that contractual or hierarchical structures emerge to control and minimize transaction costs (Williamson 1975). Researchers on marketing channels have utilized transaction-cost analysis extensively to understand channel structures and behaviors.

Information technology offers possibilities of reducing transaction costs or shifting these to buyers (Bakos 1991; Benjamin and Wigand 1995; Gurbaxani and Whang 1991; Malone, Yates, and Benjamin 1989). If consumers order tickets through an online system, for example, airlines save the costs associated with travel agent commissions and ticketing agents. Even before Internet-based stock trading became popular, Charles Schwab passed on some of these savings to its customers: it offered 10 percent discount commissions on stock trades placed through its automated, phone-based Telebroker system. In the past, systems to facilitate smooth, low-cost transactions (such as the Sabre airline reservation system and Schwab's Telebroker) required investments in proprietary and specific information technology assets. In a market system where Internet access is ubiquitous, the possibilities of minimizing transaction costs open up to anyone who has a few thousand dollars available to set up an Internet server (Hoffman and Novak 1995). American Airlines, Schwab, and countless other service providers have quickly moved the capabilities of their formerly proprietary and dedicated transaction systems to the universal platform of the Internet. Such transaction cost savings, as well as the potential to reach untapped markets, are some of the factors fueling the phenomenal growth in Internet-based commerce.

Many administered and vertically integrated marketing systems evolved, at least in part, to minimize transaction costs (Arndt 1983; Gummesson 1987). As the Internet and similar technologies drive down transaction costs, the rationale for such vertical arrangements will partly disappear. We have seen some movement toward "hollow" and "virtual" corporations (Rheingold 1993). The growth of the Internet and electronic commerce will intensify the pressure on some vertical market systems to loosen their interfirm linkage, or to delink altogether (Benjamin and Wigand 1995). Of course, Internet-based commerce also spawns interorganizational arrangements of a different kind. New, looser, and open forms of organizational arrangements emerge to deal with the fluidity of markets in cyberspace (Sarkar, Butler, and Steinfield 1995). Internet portals–both generic and specific to particular categories–have evolved as the first-level cybermediaries. Such new intermediaries have interposed themselves between producers (or service providers) and consumers by taking advantage of new, emerging economies of scale, scope, and knowledge (Lee and Clark 1996). These are places where consumers often stop first, as soon as they enter the Internet, and then thay may proceed elsewhere. To ensure that consumers do not stray too far and revert back to the portal sites, concepts of "stickiness" and "aggregation" have appeared. These are ways of minimizing search costs, increasing the productivity of search, and extending the scope of search (within a category, across multiple categories). Portals also facilitate easy transfer to cognate and related activities (e.g., from seeking information to suggesting related books, music, and investments), encourage user-to-user communications, and provide external benefits (such as entertainment, news, scheduling, weather, and financial services).

Network Externalities

Many infrastructure technologies are network technologies; they create networks of people and institutions by linking them together. The economic benefit of the network derived by each linked node increases as the size of the network expands. Thus, the telephone network was of little value when just a few people had phones, but its value increased enormously when universal service was established. Economists have labeled this effect "network externality" (Katz and Shapiro 1985, 1986) and have recommended the formulation of sales strategy based on the benefits of such externality (Shapiro and Varian 1998). Network externalities of earlier networks, such as the telegraph and telephone networks, have had a substantial impact on the American marketing system (Fischer 1987; Mueller 1993).

In terms of network externality, the impact of the Internet is likely to be far greater than for prior networked technologies such as the telegraph and the telephone. This is because the rate of growth of the Internet is unprecedented in the history of electric and electronic networks, and its reach is global. If the mid-1990s growth rates were to be sustained, for example, the entire population of our planet would be connected to the Internet by 2003 (Negroponte 1995). While this is unlikely to happen, as the rate of growth has dampened somewhat, it does give an indication of the order of magnitude by which Internet growth exceeds the growth rates that characterized other networked electric and electronic technologies.

In most types of networks, the potential value of a network increases in proportion to the size of a network. Thus, in a television network, the larger the reach of a program or channel, the more valuable it is to advertisers. The television network, however, is a one-to-many network, and the increase in potential value of the network is directly proportional to the size of the network. Positive network externality benefits are obtained in many-to-many networks such as telephone, fax, and e-mail networks. In such networks, the relationship between the value and size of the network is curvilinear. In the initial stages, the potential value of the network is low as network size increases. After a critical size is reached, however, the potential value of the network rises exponentially.

Each new user past the critical size adds potential value at a proportion greater than the size of the network. Perceptions of rising value begin to drive the size of the network-those unconnected feel the need to get connected to derive value, and the rates of growth zoom upward. Such a critical size was evidently reached for the Internet in the early 1990s.

The potential value of a many-to-many network translates into realized value for the users-economic as well as noneconomic value-depending on the needs and activity patterns of users. Telephone networks are of value to the household as well as the business sectors because they enable users in these sectors to keep in touch and engage in transactions. Fax networks, on the other hand, are used primarily by businesses because households do not find it easy to convert the potential value of a fax connection into realizable economic or social value.[7] As a network, the Internet offers multiple ways of communication, and therefore its potential value is realizable by all types of users-households, the corporate sector, and government agencies. This is one reason that the Internet growth has been so dramatic.

CONCLUDING OBSERVATIONS

What are the implications of the dramatic growth of the Internet and the attendant changes in agency costs transaction costs and network externalities for the market system and marketing? Table 3.2 provides a summary of potential impacts on producers, market intermediaries, and consumers. The emerging scenario is that of producers and cybermediaries competing to capture the benefits of Internet-based e-commerce, traditional intermediaries facing some threats, and consumers facing an increasing range of choices (in terms of products and prices) but also rising search costs.

If the growth rates are sustained at high levels, and as commercial applications of the Internet multiply, there will be an intense race to capture the economic benefits arising from the potentially lower agency costs, lower transaction costs, and exponentially rising positive network externalities of the Internet. In this race, the institutions that come out ahead may not be the ones that dominated markets in the Industrial Age. Just as shopping malls and discount merchandisers captured the external benefits of population shifts to suburbia and exurbia, so, too, new "marketspace" institutions are likely to capture most of the economic benefits of the Internet's network externality. The emergent successful players will be characterized by their abilities to understand (1) computer-mediated (rather than televisual) communications, (2) asynchronous, many-to-many (rather than synchronous, one-to-many) communications, (3) interactive (rather than passive) consumer behavior, (4) spontaneous, loose, open (rather than administered, tight) administered, tight channels, and (5) real-time (rather than delayed) market feedback mechanisms.

Table 3.2
Economic Effects of Internet and Impacts on Marketing

Economic effects		Impacts on		
Type of cost/ benefit	Internet- related effects	Producers and Providers	Market Intermediaries	Consumers
Agency Costs and Benefits	Lower coordination and control costs. Potentially greater opportunity costs and risks of delegated agency Greater benefits of wide-ranging agency	Cost savings from flatter organization Potential delegation of agency to customers Ability to reach vast, geographically spread markets at modest costs	Traditional intermediaries face threat of being bypassed New cybermediaries have opportunity to capture agency-delegation benefits by "aggregating" large numbers of repeat-visiting users	Convenience of "self service" available at desktops and in homes With some investment of time, ability to control many aspects of market transactions
Transaction Costs	Faster, more direct transactions Lower transaction costs	Shorter and faster production and order-processing cycles Lower costs and stronger profit margins	Direct transactions threaten traditional intermediaries Cybermediaries may benefit from lower transaction costs	Faster access to desired items at potentially lower prices
Network Externality	Positive externality of large networks Negative externality when networks are intrusive	Frantic race to create large, ubiquitous, user-friendly networks Trade-offs have to be made between reaching out to ("assisting") users and infringing on their private time and (virtual) space	Cybermediaries attempt to aggregate users and to become their "network of networks"–that is, a one-stop site for multiple types of transactions in cyberspace	Incentives available to join networks and to switch networks Greater choices but increasing search costs Standardization (no/low choice) becomes appealing if it lowers search costs without significant price penalty

Uncertain Business Models

In principle, the idea of building an electronic marketing system that lowers agency and transaction costs and that offers rising benefits of network externality is very appealing. By early 1999, about 40 percent of traditional large retailers in the United States had opened e-commerce sites, and the remaining retailers were racing to do so (Grover 1999). Similarly, direct producer-to -customer e-commerce sites and various types of cybermediary sites were also proliferating. While the appeal of e-commerce was evident in these trends, it was not clear if the business models to turn e-commerce into a profitable activity had crystallized. Even in the case of Amazon.com, the most prominent of cybermediaries, the net loss widened from 16.4 percent in the last quarter of 1997 to 18.4 percent in the last quarter of 1998.

For producers with established distribution channels, e-commerce offered an exciting opportunity as well as a major risk–of losing the support of their traditional channels. This has prompted companies such as Compaq to search for business models that would capture the benefits of e-commerce while not alienating traditional channels (Egermann 1997). Similarly, established retailers also faced a dilemma. They could not ignore e-commerce and had to open up transaction-oriented Web sites. At the same time, they risked cannibalizing their own high-margin, in-store business by increasing volumes of low-margin, Internet business (Grover 1999).

It will take many years to establish the specific modalities of converting the *potential* benefits of e-commerce into *practical* benefits in terms of strong and growing profit margins. This is a challenge that needs to be addressed both by strategic marketing practitioners and by researchers studying the nature and operation of electronic markets.

Focusing on Consumers and Marketing Institutions

It should be noted that, after the early euphoria over Internet-based commerce has settled, the pace of changes in marketing systems and methods will be dictated not by the pace of technological change but by the rate and nature of changes in consumer behavior. While in retrospect many changes in the market-oriented lifestyles and behaviors of consumers may appear dramatic, such changes are fairly slow compared to the rate of technological change. For example, after over a century of experience with the telephone and over four decades with the television, consumers' use of these media for shopping is limited and supplementary compared to in-store retail commerce. Similarly, consumers' participation in Internet-based commerce will remain supplementary to established forms of commerce for decades to come. From a marketing systems perspective, in the foreseeable future, we can expect to see the emergence and growth of a significant and parallel set of marketing institutions that offer electronic forms of commerce, in competition with, but also complementary, to established forms of commerce. In selected arenas, such institutions may surpass and supplant established forms of commerce. In these arenas the electronic wheel of retailing will spin the fastest.

Emerging Marketing Research Needs

The question of how widespread and entrenched electronic markets will become is an open one. It is certain, however, that they will play an increasingly significant role in the markets and marketing methods of the future. A great deal of strategic research and practitioner-directed counsel on electronic commerce and Internet-based marketing is already on the bookshelves and newsstands. What we lack are systematic studies of how the marketing system, institutions, practices, and concepts will transform as a result of these changes. We have presented a sampling of economic perspectives that could be used to plan and conduct such research. The changes, however, are not merely economic. Internet-based commerce will have deep political, cultural, and social implications as well (see Brown 1995; Miller 1996). It is, of course, easier to take a historical perspective on such changes and there is no doubt that future historians will find the emergence and growth of electronic commerce a fascinating topic of study. Major public policy changes and mass private investments that will shape Internet and its successors are happening now. To have some influence on such change or at least to prepare the field of marketing as to what systemic changes lie ahead, marketing research that looks at the immediate past, the present, and the immediate future is very important at this juncture. Just as significant studies of how distribution and market systems of a high-level economy operate appeared in the middle decades of the twentieth century, major studies of how Internet-based and other forms of electronic commerce will shape our markets are needed at the dawn of the twenty-first century.

QUESTIONS FOR DISCUSSION

1. In what ways are agency costs for marketers likely to decrease, and in what ways are they likely to increase because of the growth of the Internet and electronic commerce?

2. Why does Internet-based commerce lead to lower transaction costs? Use a transaction cost perspective to explain the rapid growth of b2b (business-to-business) exchanges.

3. Are there instances when the network externalities for a user of the Internet-based method of transacting business stop being positive and turn negative? Discuss why and provide some illustrations.

4. In the long run (over 10 years), which of the three—lower agency costs, lower transaction costs, or rising positive network externality—will prove to be the most influential in shaping the nature of e-commerce?

4

Electronic Commerce and the Transformation of Marketing

Nikhilesh Dholakia, Ruby Roy Dholakia, and Martin Laub

INTRODUCTION

As trade barriers fall and global markets emerge, companies are adopting electronic commerce practices in order to remain competitive or to increase their market share. Although previous forms of electronic commerce such as Electronic Data Interchange (EDI) have been around for years, we are now witnessing the rapid adoption of the Internet as a new commercial medium. The Internet allows businesses to participate in a truly global, electronically mediated marketplace (Auger and Gallaugher 1997; Hoffman and Novak 1995b; Quelch and Klein 1996).

Companies such as Sun Microsystems, Cisco Systems, and Dell Computers have successfully managed the transition of a significant proportion of their business into the electronic medium and, as a result, report Internet-related revenues in billions of U.S. dollars. Many other companies with prosperous businesses in the physical marketplace, however, have found it difficult to translate their traditional forms of marketing into the realm of the Internet. For example, Borders–America's most profitable chain of bookstores and the leader in creating the book "superstore" concept–fell behind its physical and virtual rivals when it came to the Internet ("Borders" 1999). Finding such slow transition to be an opportunity, upstart firms such as Amazon.com, eBay, Priceline.com, and Mobshop have taken the lead in developing marketing strategies that seem to work well on the Internet.

This raises the question: Does the traditional marketing mix no longer apply in the age of electronic commerce? Evidence seems to abound that the time-honored four Ps-product, place, price, and promotion-are increasingly coming under pressure. Several authors argue that virtually every aspect of marketing in electronic marketplaces differs from the way companies used to do business (Cash 1994; Cronin 1994; Hoffman and Novak 1995a; Rayport and Sviokla 1994). New marketing concepts are needed that may help companies successfully deploy electronic marketplaces as a medium for electronic commerce.

This chapter provides a framework for new, emerging marketing theories for the age of electronic commerce. It discusses the logic of electronic marketplaces and gives a definition and typology of the key terms used in the context of electronic commerce. It then looks at the economic characteristics of electronic marketplaces and the implications for businesses. Next, successful approaches to conducting electronic commerce are reviewed. Based on this analysis, a new marketing framework for operations in electronic marketplaces is developed, and the findings are summarized.

THE LOGIC OF ELECTRONIC MARKETS

The concept of electronic markets is not very new. Electronic marketplaces have been around since the 1970s. Consider the computerized airline reservation systems such as United Airlines' Apollo or Sabre (initially a part of American Airlines), which allow customers to book flights on almost every airline via travel agents around the world. Or consider J.C. Penney's Telaction, an electronic home-shopping system that allowed customers to shop via a cable television channel and a push-button phone (Malone, Yates, and Benjamin 1989).

Growth of the Internet

None of these electronic marketplaces, however, created an air of excitement comparable to that created by Internet-based markets. The tremendous growth of the Internet has led hundreds of thousands of companies to set up shop on the Internet, and millions of consumers worldwide are eagerly participating in the global online marketplace. The arrival of easy-to-use Web browsers transformed the Internet from a specialized, text-oriented medium, to a multimedia, massive, and global cyberspace. According to a mid-1995 estimate by Sun Microsystems, the number of Web sites was doubling every 53 days (Cortese et al. 1995). By December 1996, about 627,000 domain names had been registered, and this number exceeded 1.5 million by the end of 1997 (Friel 1997). By early 1999, the registered domain names numbered 5.3 million. By 2000, well over 300 million people were using the Net. In the next few years, the number of people having some type of Net access with a mobile device may approach 1 billion.

Electronic Marketplaces: Various Roles

The Internet has created a new electronic marketspace that no longer requires firms to invest huge amounts in the development and maintenance of task-specific trading systems. This makes it compelling for companies, small and large, to take advantage of the benefits of this new medium. Electronic marketplaces eliminate much of the paper handling and clerical work, driving down the costs of creating, processing, distributing, storing, and retrieving paper-based information. This reduces processing time and allows increased automation, thereby lowering overhead and inventory. Consequently, it permits just-in-time production and payments. Furthermore, companies of every size can now participate in a truly global market and reach customers in remote locations (Schutzer 1995). Electronic marketplaces not only constitute a medium for marketing communication but also offer a means of distribution, especially for digital product categories (Hoffman and Novak 1995b). Software companies such as Network Associates and Adobe use the Internet to offer their products in directly downloadable form. They encourage people to download and test their software on a free, trial basis and subsequently collect site license fees from corporations and individuals that decide to use it continuously (Cronin 1994). In short, in electronic marketplace companies can reduce the marginal cost of interorganizational coordination and handle large volumes of market transactions (Bakos 1991).

Electronic marketplaces provide consumers with a plethora of information and choices, but they also create the risk of information overload. When consumers are inundated with information, they soon get frustrated because they can no longer make a rational decision within the time that they have. Here easy search mechanisms are helpful. Directories and searching tools on Web portals such as Yahoo!, Go Network, Lycos, Excite, and Snap make it particularly easy to locate a company or find information on a certain product or service. Specialized search sites exist for categories such as automobiles (e.g., Autobytel.com, MSN Carpoint) and travel services (Expedia, Travelocity, TheTrip.com). Yet, the problem of selecting among many different offerings often remains. One solution to this problem was BargainFinder, the "mother of all Shopbots," developed by Andersen Consulting (Jasco 1998). Shopbots are shopping robots or agents that take a user's query, visit the shops that may have the desired products, bring back the results, and present them in a consolidated and compact format. Other shopbots followed: Pricewatch for computer hardware, Priceline.com for airfares, and Bottom Dollar for general merchandise categories (Jasco 1998). By decreasing the time and cost of obtaining information and enabling customers to find the products that best match their needs (Bakos 1991), such sites have begun to tackle the problem of information overload.

Electronic marketplaces can facilitate online product trials. Digital Equipment Corporation (now a division of Compaq), for instance, allowed customers on the World Wide Web to "test-drive" its Alpha AXP computer. Such simulated trials lead to reduced uncertainty in the decision-making process and ultimately stimulate purchase (Hoffman and Novak 1995b).

All these benefits of electronic marketplaces translate either directly or indirectly into savings for the customer and increased efficiency for the business. Therefore, some authors argue that the development of electronic marketplaces is inevitable and that ultimately, many, if not most, transactions will be conducted electronically (Malone, Yates, and Benjamin 1989). One leading industry observer, for example, projected that by 2003, half of the U.S. firms will conduct over 80 percent of their transactions by electronic means (Fernandez 1999). The economic and social impact of such a massive transformation is self-evident.

Barriers to Electronic Marketplaces

The growth of the Internet notwithstanding, there still remain some problems associated with electronic marketplaces that need to be addressed before they will find general acceptance. While the World Wide Web is far friendlier than the older interfaces, about 50 percent of the people report difficulties in using computer-based technologies (Katz and Aspden 1997). Many Internet users are still concerned about the risks associated with sending a credit card number over the Internet or using any other form of electronic payment. As with any new direct marketing channel, the risks associated with product delivery and return still constrain a wider use of electronic marketplaces for commercial activities (Dholakia 1995). In addition, research shows that online shopping is perceived to be relatively convenient and efficient but not yet very fun to use. Compared to store, catalog, or television shopping, it is also viewed as a somewhat intimidating way to shop. Such negative hedonic perceptions appear to be another significant barrier to the greater use of shopping in electronic marketplaces (Dholakia and Pedersen 1994). As shopping is still a predominantly female activity, electronic marketplaces might not be able to attract a sufficient number of potential customers as long as there is some male bias in the global Internet user base. Moreover, electronic marketplaces still lack many of the useful services encountered in physical marketplaces (such as ease of return, layaway, alterations) and cannot provide the kind of socialization that people are often looking for when they go to a mall. According to Jarvenpaa and Todd (1997), although shoppers were impressed with the number and variety of online retailers, in most product categories they were disappointed with the depth of product offerings. Even though not all of these shortcomings of electronic marketplaces can be overcome in a short time, it is clear that new methods to effectively deal with these constraints will continue to evolve quickly and lead to an increased acceptance of electronic marketplaces.

ELECTRONIC COMMERCE: DEFINITIONS AND TYPOLOGY

So what exactly does electronic commerce in electronic marketplaces mean? The Federal Electronic Commerce Acquisition Team gave one of the best definitions of electronic commerce. They defined it as "the paperless exchange of business information using EDI electronic mail (e-mail), electronic bulletin boards, electronic funds transfer (EFT), and other similar technologies" ("Electronic Commerce at Bank One" 1995). Electronic data interchange is thereby often seen as the cornerstone of electronic commerce. "EDI is a common industry standard for preparing, processing and communicating business transactions electronically with other companies, regardless of their different computing platforms" ("EDI: Cornerstone..." 1995). Although electronic commerce can be conducted over many different systems, including cable shopping networks, the French Minitel system, or online services such as AOL, none of these mechanisms have the far-reaching scope and potential for transforming the marketing function as the generic, Web-based Internet (Hoffman and Novak 1996).

The terminology used for the environment in which electronic commerce is conducted has been evolving over time, resulting in ever more sophisticated definitions. One of the early definitions for electronic markets was given by Malone, Yates, and Benjamin (1989: ES24), who referred to it as "networks that let customers compare and order offerings from competing suppliers." Later, Bakos (1991: 296) introduced the terms "electronic marketplace" and "electronic market system," which he defined as "an interorganizational information system that allows the participating buyers and sellers to exchange information about prices and product offerings." While these definitions were somewhat vague, Rayport and Sviokla (1995: 75) rendered a much more comprehensive definition of what they called "marketspace." They saw marketspace as "a virtual realm where products and services exist as digital information and can be delivered through information-based channels." This definition reflected, to a greater degree; the rapid development of the Internet, the new global medium that no longer limited the environment of electronic commerce to organizations as Bakos' definition did. Even more precise were Hoffman and Novak (1996), who introduced the term "hypermedia computer-mediated environments" (CME). They defined CME as "a dynamic distributed network, potentially global in scope which allows consumers and firms to 1) provide and interactively access hypermedia content (i.e. 'machine interaction'), and 2) communicate through the medium (i.e. 'person interaction')." While this definition is clearly restricted to hypermedia environments, of which the World Wide Web is certainly the most popular, all the other terms encompass a wider spectrum of platforms for electronic commerce. For the remainder of this chapter the term "electronic marketplace" is used for networks that allow the exchange of digital information for the purpose of conducting business. This includes global networks such as the Internet as well as local, proprietary networks. It also encompasses new networks, such as Internet 2 or mobile networks (IP-based or not), that are likely to become pervasive in the future.

ECONOMIC CHARACTERISTICS OF ELECTRONIC MARKETS

To grasp the implications of electronic marketplaces on businesses, one must first understand their economic characteristics. As consumers obtain easier access to more information about price and product offerings of alternative suppliers, their search costs of obtaining the information decrease. By the same token, suppliers' costs of communicating information regarding price and product characteristics to additional customers also decline. These benefits obviously increase with the number of participants joining the electronic marketplace as long as effective and efficient search mechanisms are in place to deal with the vast amount of information available. Consequently, the average price that businesses charge in electronic marketplaces for certain products-especially commodities-decreases, as the proportion of customers with low search costs increases (Bakos 1991). This clearly empowers buyers, who are able to get a better mix of benefit-price bundles (Sarkar, Butler, and Steinfield 1995).

Decreasing search costs also result in lower profit margins for sellers; businesses can no longer command a price premium (Bakos 1991). In addition, switching costs in electronic marketplaces approach zero, as participation in electronic marketplaces no longer requires large investments of money, time, or skill. This reduces even further the market power of sellers.

Sellers in electronic marketplaces also have the opportunity to substantially reduce their coordination and transaction costs. Although these might not always offset the smaller profit margins, companies may enjoy the benefits of increased volume (Benjamin and Wigand 1995). In addition, electronic marketplaces redefine economies of scale and scope. Even small companies can now achieve low incremental costs for additional product or service offerings. This makes them more competitive even in markets dominated by big companies. Once a product or service is offered in the electronic marketplace, it does not matter whether a single person or millions of users request it. These new economies of scale make it possible for FedEx to allow any individual with access to the Internet to track packages through the company's Web site. This brings a FedEx office into every home with a desktop computer. Or consider the United Services Automobile Association (USAA), an insurance company that makes use of the new economies of scale. USAA found that it could also use its customer information to create new value for its customers by serving a broader set of their needs. The company now offers, for instance, financing packages and shopping services for almost every kind of product in addition to its core business. This results in a loyal customer base for USAA and new profitable business ventures (Rayport and Sviokla 1995).

IMPLICATIONS FOR BUSINESSES

The economic efficiencies of electronic marketplaces can constitute potential opportunities as well as potential threats for businesses. If a company cannot differentiate its products or services on any other basis but price, it is likely to face fierce competition from firms participating in the electronic marketplace. As more and more goods and services are transformed so that they can be offered or even transmitted electronically, the number of companies involved in this new field of competition will increase dramatically. Eventually, electronic marketplaces are likely to become a strategic necessity and part of almost every industry's infrastructure (Bakos 1991; Fernandez 1999).

Companies competing with firms in the electronic marketplace have to appreciate the "law of digital assets." Digital assets-text, graphics, audio, or video stored as digital information-are not used up in their consumption. With digital assets, one could have a potentially infinite number of transactions with variable costs close to zero. One example of a company making use of digital assets is Image Technology Corporation, a company that captures, organizes, selects, manipulates, and distributes photographic images digitally. Image

Technology can create a repeat customer's order far more quickly at a fraction of the costs incurred by companies using traditional techniques. Having created a database of images, the company can take advantage of tremendous economies of scale and scope and price aggressively while still making good margins, rival companies without digital assets have a tough time competing with Image Technology (Rayport and Sviokla 1995). Digital assets, however, have a major disadvantage. They are very easy to copy and retransmit. This raises serious questions of intellectual property rights and commercial protection of these properties, especially in countries where the laws of the firm's home country cannot be enforced readily. Innovative solutions to such problems are being sought worldwide. Examples of this include digital watermarks developed by Fraunhofer IHG, a German research institution, to indelibly inscribe digital documents with an electronic mark.

In cyberspace, producing or service-providing firms also have to stress relationship-based marketing plans in order to achieve customer loyalty. Electronic marketplaces offer a variety of ways to do this through direct technology links (Sarkar, Butler, and Steinfield 1995). Establishing a Web site to advertise products, provide customer service, or elicit comments is just one option. Companies operating in both the electronic marketplace as well as in the physical marketplace have the unique opportunity to "sense and respond" to customer needs rather than to simply make and sell products and services (Bradley and Nolan 1998). USAA, for example, uses intelligent sensing methods to match a customer need to an appropriate source of supply (Rayport and Sviokla 1995).

Successful actors in electronic marketplaces may try to reimpose switching costs in the form of loyalty programs similar to frequent flier accounts. New and innovative switching incentives like the idea of a "cool site," a "sticky" site, or a must-visit portal (such as Iwon.com, which doles out daily cash prizes) have developed rapidly and are playing an important role in attracting new customers in the electronic marketplace. Such categorization may confer power to third parties or cybermediaries designating these sites, especially in a situation of information overload (Dholakia 1995).

As coordination and transaction costs in electronic marketplaces decrease, many companies have to reevaluate the make-or-buy decision. It is now often cheaper to buy than to make a product, and this will ultimately result in more market activity and fewer vertically integrated companies (Malone, Yates, and Benjamin 1989). Several authors argue that in their search for competitive advantage, manufacturing companies will try to bypass one or more of the organizations within the traditional industry value chain (Benjamin and Wigand 1995; Orme et al. 1995). While this may hold true for certain classes of products-especially those where asset specificity is low, those that are easy to describe, or those that can be distributed in digital form-there are also factors that limit disintermediation in electronic markets. Sarkar, Butler, and Steinfield (1995) argued that, contrary to the popular notion of disappearing intermediaries, we would witness the emergence of "cybermediaries." These cybermediaries (electronic malls, electronic trade or auction sites such as eBay and Onsale, electronic exchanges such as eSteel, and portals such as Yahoo! or

Lycos are examples) perform the new role of brokering relationships between producers and consumers in the world of electronic commerce. Cybermediaries, however, will not be able to command a margin as high as that of intermediaries in the physical marketplace will because they do not incur the same costs for retail space and personnel: providers and customers would simply be unwilling to pay much for the services of the cybermediaries. Whether they choose to go direct (such as Dell or Gateway computers) or rely on cybermediaries (such as book and music publishers), companies wanting to be market leaders and maintain market share in the global economy have little choice in terms of embracing electronic commerce ("Managing Electronic Commerce" 1995).

SOME SUCCESSFUL CASES OF ELECTRONIC COMMERCE

One of the older, pre-Internet electronic commerce success stories is from Japan. Prior to 1985, used car dealers had to travel to one of the physical locations where used cars were sold to retailers. A proprietary computer and satellite communication system called AUCNET allowed used car dealers to participate in online auctions without having to travel physically. They could select the cars conveniently on a computer screen that showed the cars in digital formats. Car sellers also profited from the system because they incurred lower costs, as no cars had to be moved from one auction site to another. As subscribed car dealers all over the country logged onto the system, increasing the number of potential buyers, the bidding became more intense and sellers, were even able to command a 6 percent to 7 percent premium over the price that they would get at a physical auction. Buyers in the electronic marketplace were willing to pay more because they enjoyed the convenience of desktop shopping and got a better selection of used cars (Rayport and Sviokla 1994). In the e-commerce arena, eBay has adopted the essence of this idea and created an unexpectedly wildly successful c2c (consumer-to-consumer) business model that it is defending vigorously against all interlopers (Roth 2000).

Digital Equipment Corporation (DEC), now a division of Compaq, used the Internet to publish press releases, product announcements, new services, sales promotions, and other information since the early 1980s. Then on October 1, 1993, it officially launched its World Wide Web server. This was one of the first major commercial Web sites and was registered with the NCSA *What's New* list and the CERN *World Wide Web Servers* list. It provided its entire electronic catalog with product descriptions, pictures, and ordering information-some 4,000 documents. Electronic ads were sprinkled across World Wide Web magazines, which allowed the reader to click through to a specific Digital advertisement. But DEC offered more than just graphics and information. It decided to allow all potential customers to enter an Alpha client-server, load their own software on this server, and take it for a "test drive." The result: some 1,400 Alpha users were recorded daily, each filling out substantial demographic information for DEC's sales force (until it had to terminate the offer in November 1995 due to legal restrictions). This rather unconventional marketing approach resulted in a total of 6.7 million log-ons to DEC's Web site in the first

18 months and made the site one of the most successful of its time, with more that 175,000 "hits" a day (Andelman 1995; Cronin 1994; Jones 1994).

Hello Direct, Inc., a telecommunications products mail-order company in San Jose, Calfornia, put much of its catalog on the Web and used an 800 number to take orders.   Soon thereafter, the company averaged 4,500 "hits" a day, resulting in a growing number of e-mail inquiries. But the advantages of selling online went well beyond eliminating some postage and printing costs. The real benefit was the two-way flow of information between the company and its customers.   While customers drilled more and more deeply into the site, searching for additional information about Hello Direct's products, they were automatically tracked.   When they encountered a problem, they could conveniently use the e-mail buttons on the Web pages to ask for more detailed information, get technical support, or suggest product improvements. This helped the company identify which products were getting the most attention and, perhaps, why that was so, thereby reducing the high expenditures for conventional market research. It also allowed Hello Direct to enter into one-to-one relationships with its customers, which could not be justified in the physical marketplace due to prohibitively high marketing and administrative costs. While Hello Direct's online customers are still a minority, the company's efforts seem to pay off, as online orders are about 10 percent higher on average than the print-catalog orders (Verity, in Verity and Hof 1994; Weston 1995).

TRANSFORMATIONS IN THE MARKETING MIX

Companies wanting to maintain or gain a competitive edge can no longer neglect electronic marketplaces and the Internet. But how can companies make effective use of this new medium? Simply transposing traditional marketing strategies into the world of electronic marketplaces will not work. The Internet is not a place for sending out blatant advertisements to e-mail accounts around the world. This global network has a strong culture of free discourse and a bias against anything resembling a sales pitch (Cronin 1994). Yet it is uniquely suited to develop strong relationships, establish dynamic customer communities, and enter into two-way communication with highly involved lead users of technical products (Cross 1994). Internet and other electronic marketplaces, however, seem to pose opportunities and threats that do not fit very well in the traditional marketing concept of the four Ps (see Table 4.1). What is needed is a new and extended framework. In electronic marketplaces, the boundaries of the marketing-mix elements are getting increasingly blurred.

Products

Products for which electronic marketplaces are feasible can be determined by asking the following question: Can the company help a customer in the purchase process by providing information about the product via an electronic medium?   This is definitely the case for commodities and standardized products that are easy to describe and where asset specificity is

Table 4.1
Marketing Mix in Traditional and Electronic Markets

Traditional Markets	*Electronic Markets*
PRODUCT	
Physical or digital form	Physical as well as digital forms
Standardization in products	High degree of differentiation and customization
PRICE	
Consumer's search costs are high	Consumer's search costs are (often) low
Prices vary according to retail format	Prices and profit margins tend to converge to the minimum possible
Consumers have significant switching costs	Consumers have zero or minimal switching costs
PLACE	
Wholesalers and retailers exist	Disintermediation of many traditional wholesalers and retailers, reintermediation by new breed of cybermediaries or infomediaries
Physical presence of shoppers usually required for transactions and delivery	Physical presence of shoppers not required for transactions and delivery. For digital products, even physical distribution system not required
For retailing, location is very important	Location is unimportant (except for logistical reasons)
PROMOTION	
Promotional costs very high for broadcast and major print media	Substantial savings in promotional costs, especially for early entrants who become dominant
Promotional messages are pushed to the consumer	Consumers pull themselves into a Web site
Communication is one-way	Communication can be interactive
Hard to track consumers' interests, preferences, and decision-making activities	Possible to track many of consumers' interests, preferences, and decision-making activities

Source: RITIM Research.

low. But even products that are somewhat complex in nature can let customers narrow their search according to a few important product features and might, therefore, succeed in electronic marketplaces (Malone, Yates, and Benjamin

1989). In the United States, for example, over 30 percent of car buyers were "shopping" for cars on the Internet before shopping for them in the physical marketplace (Deck 1998). By 2000, the proportion of Americans using the Internet to find car-buying information had crossed 60 percent.

Products with substantial transactional volume in electronic marketplaces include computer software, books, graphical designs, movies, music, and the like because they can be maintained in digital form and are easy to transmit over a computer network without any physical inventory movements. But also all manufactured goods sold through mail order fit perfectly the requirements for being traded in electronic marketplaces (Benjamin and Wigand 1995). For such products, almost everything except the physical entity can be digitized. It should be noted that although digitized multimedia representations of physical products assist the buyers in their purchasing decisions, such representations do not eliminate the uncertainties of electronic markets.

Of course, not all products sell in electronic marketplaces, especially not those that require extensive explanation and face-to-face contact with a salesperson (Lowenthal in Andelman 1995). Before declaring a product unsuitable for electronic markets, however, one has to see the opportunities that the electronic marketplace offers. Who would have thought of selling used cars over a computer network? Having inspected the used cars, collected photos, and verified the information, Japan's AUCNET was able to provide all the relevant information for used car dealers in digital form and stimulated online purchase decisions (Rayport and Sviokla 1994). In the United States, CarMax has adopted this model of selling cars and applied it to the retail market. The content of the transaction, the used car, is replaced by digital information in the electronic marketplace. In some cases this even allows for the complete replacement of a physical product with an information-based service. For example, answering machines, fax machines, and disk storage media are gradually being replaced by phone-based and Web-based messaging and storage services (Dholakia and Venkatraman 1993).

An even greater opportunity arises for companies in service-based businesses. Having produced digital assets, companies can either create their own proprietary electronic marketplace, use their digital assets to expand the scope of their operations, or both. Bloomberg Financial Systems, for instance, offered a proprietary system with all the financial data that an investment professional desired. Having developed a user base, Bloomberg started using its system to expand its scope. Users of the Bloomberg terminal could also display sports scores, purchase opera tickets, or preview vacation destinations. In this way Bloomberg was able to satisfy more and more of its customers' needs in its electronic marketplace (Rayport and Sviokla 1995). With the rapid growth of the Internet and the explosive growth in financial information available on the Internet, however, proprietary terminals became less attractive, and Bloomberg had to reorient its strategy toward the Internet (Kover 1998).

Price

In the electronic marketplace the traditional, cost-based pricing offers little guidance to marketers (Rayport and Sviokla 1994). As customers' search costs decrease, so do prices and profit margins for commodities and standardized products. Eventually, commodity markets may even be destabilized by price wars that eliminate any excess profits once enjoyed in the physical marketplace (Bakos 1991). Other factors may also lead to lower prices in electronic markets. In many cases, sales or value-added taxes may be saved because goods are shipped across state or national boundaries. Elimination of intermediaries can save costs. By conducting up to 40 percent of its business over the Internet, Cisco Systems reduced its annual operating expenses by U.S.$270 million (Ghosh 1998). Some of these savings may be passed on to buyers as lower prices.

This being the case, it will become ever more important to distinguish one's offer from the competition by adding additional value and to position it on dimensions other than price. If a high degree of product differentiation can be achieved in the electronic marketplace (e.g., through added value), buyers are less inclined to settle for anything else than their ideal product. The more that an electronic product offering fits the buyer's ideal preference, the more desirable it becomes for the buyer, and the higher the price that the company may be able to charge for the product and services (Bakos 1991). For instance, commissions for Web-based stock trading services ranged from U.S.$8 to U.S.$30 per trade. Suretrade, a no-frills Web stockbroker, charged U.S.$8 while Schwab and Fidelity, which positioned themselves as a "life goals"– oriented financial sites offering a range of services besides trading, charged U.S.$25 30 per electronic trade (Brooker 1998).

The opportunities to add value to information-intensive products and services in electronic marketplaces are virtually limitless (Cash 1994). Phone companies with their voice mail services, for example, offer greater convenience and functionality than answering machines. This translates into added value for the customer and allows the phone companies to charge–on a discounted cash flow basis–several times the cost of the competing physical product. In the AUCNET system, buyers were willing to pay a 6 percent to 7 percent average price premium because they got a better selection of used cars with greater convenience (Rayport and Sviokla 1994).

Place

Some of the most important structural changes in electronic marketplaces are disintermediation-elimination of wholesale and retail layers and selling directly to consumers–as well as reintermediation by "cybermediaries" that are specialized in electronic commerce. Such changes are most evident for digital products that can be distributed over the Internet itself, obviating even the need for physical distributors.

But how does a company price products that can be delivered right over an electronic network? Distribution is a large cost factor in the physical marketplace but can approach zero for digital products in electronic marketplaces (Cash 1994). One way chosen by Network Associates, the antivirus software developer, is to make its software freely available on the Internet and ask for license fees only after it had been installed and tested on an organization's computer system. New software releases are scheduled every six to eight weeks and are included in the two-year license fee. The combination of free software distribution to individuals and subsequent collection of license fees from commercial customers fits very well with the prevailing culture of the Internet (Cronin 1994). It is also conceivable that customers are no longer charged for product parts that they do not want. Companies can develop custom products–containing only the requested components and features-and price them accordingly (Cash 1994). Dell and Gateway have shown that such BTO (build-to-order) methods result not only in happy customers but also in enormous savings in inventories.

The innovative method that Network Associates and others use to offer and distribute free software is another indication of the disruption of the traditional marketing-mix in electronic marketplaces. Would it make a difference if Network Associates were located not in California but somewhere on the other side of the globe? Not really! In ubiquitous electronic marketplaces physical location becomes irrelevant, and so do large amounts of retail space or shelf space (Bosley 1994). It is as if all stores were at one location (Cash 1994).

This is especially appealing to small companies at remote locations and nichers that do not have a large enough market in their city or region. For companies with digital assets, distance does not even affect delivery costs because their product or service can be shipped electronically (Anderson 1995). It also allows aggregation of widely dispersed niche markets that would need different outlets in the physical marketplace. This has been done successfully by companies such as Virtual Vineyards, which has been offering not only a selection of excellent wines but also a variety of authentic specialty foods from around the world. Businesses offering their products in electronic marketplaces such as the Internet, however, should be aware that they are targeting a global audience. Even the smallest of firms have to be prepared to handle shipping, customs, and international payment problems (Cohen in Orme et al. 1995).

As location in electronic marketplaces becomes irrelevant, the decisive factors of place (or distribution) shift to the creation and utilization of new, boundary-free infrastructures to reach a critical mass of consumers (Zimmermann 1995). Until homes are wired for easy-to-use interactive devices that provide consumers with high-quality video interactions in the electronic marketplace, electronic sales channels will be somewhat limited in their ability to make inroads with the consumer. The technologies required for this, however, are evolving rapidly (Benjamin and Wigand 1995), and high-speed, video-based interactive access will become available in many advanced countries in the short-term future.

For small companies that set up a Web site, this means that they may not necessarily generate enough traffic to their site unless they make some use of cybermediaries. Renting space in an electronic mall, registering the site with key Internet directories, creating a "cool site" that gets listed as such, and trying to get as many hits as possible via the popular search engines–these are just some of the options that smaller companies have to increase volume of transactions on the Internet.

Promotion

Electronic marketplaces also offer endless opportunities to promote a company and its products or services. With its ever-growing pool of middle-to upper-class users, the Internet provides access to the prime target groups for many marketers. In addition, online promotion can be delivered almost instantaneously around the globe, at a fraction of the costs of traditional means such as print, television, or radio. A study by IBM indicated that firms putting forth online catalogs on the Internet could save up to 25 percent in processing costs and reduce cycle time by up to 62 percent (Hoffman and Novak 1996). It is, therefore, not surprising that the biggest market for the Internet is considered to be advertisement and marketing (Anderson 1995).

To be successful, businesses that want to use the Internet as a promotional tool have to be conversant with the rules of this new medium. The old mass-market approach and hype of television, billboard, and magazine advertisement will not work on the Internet, where the audience is far better educated and more upscale than the average consumer (Janal 1995). In fact, almost everything in this new medium is different from the traditional mass communication model, where no interaction between the consumer and the firm takes place.

On the Internet the message is usually not sent to the consumer. Rather, the consumer comes to the message. Consumers control the type and duration of advertising exposure. Web users can link to the site of a company where they are free to explore as little or as much of the information as they want, instead of having it all shoved down their throats (Anderson 1995). This shifts the power completely to the consumers (Gerald O'Connell in Anderson 1995) and reverses the typical, one-to-many communication process to a many-to-one process. The push-type promotional strategies of traditional markets give way to pull-type promotional strategies in electronic markets. Smart companies are even able to go one step beyond and enter into a one-to-one communication process with the members of their target audience by customizing their offers to individual customers. Cookies–pieces of data transmitted by Web servers to client computers–allow marketers to track the users' navigation paths within a Web site (Leibrock 1997). Through such tracking, site visitors' interests and preferences can be learned, and marketers can tailor their offerings and promotional approaches to specific Web site visitors. Such tracking, of course, has raised concerns about privacy (McGrath 1999).

To reach online buyers, marketers have to create an information-rich, interactive form of marketing communication for a personalized sales approach (Janal 1995). The multimedia and interactive capabilities of the Web have the potential to offer exactly this. It is a medium that allows publishing, real-time communication broadcast, and narrowcasting all in one. Information can be updated instantaneously and retrieved 24 hours a day. Most importantly, the interactive nature of the medium makes it possible to engage consumers in asynchronous dialogues that occur at both parties' convenience (Deighton 1997; Hoffman and Novak 1995b).

Businesses can make use of interactive ads, for instance, to give customers exactly the information for which they are looking. Consumers simply click on icons or hypertext to obtain more detailed information on the products in which they are interested and get it in the form of text, picture, audio, or video. This can be a very effective way to reach consumers who generally do not like the mass-market, hard-sell approach and who do not respond to any other form of advertisement. This new way of nonintrusive advertisement is expected to work best on the Web, where users, unlike commercial online services, do not face time charges for accessing marketing information and are, therefore, likely to spend more time reviewing it (Janal 1995).

The Web also offers unprecedented opportunities to tailor the promotion-mix precisely to the individuals' needs and enter into ongoing relationships with the customers. Companies such as Hello Direct or DEC strategically locate e-mail buttons on their Web sites to elicit comments about their products and services from their customers. It is also possible to present sophisticated fill-out forms and other incentives to obtain relevant information from customers in order to serve them more effectively in the future (Hoffman and Novak 1995b). This allows businesses such as Virtual Vineyards, the wine and specialty foods merchant on the Internet, to recommend and customize special offers to its customers (Dholakia 1995). Digital Equipment Corporation (now Compaq) also employed such a strategy. Each of the Alpha computer users had to fill out a variety of demographic information items, which generated substantial leads and became part of DEC's corporate lead-tracking database (Andelman 1995). In combination with the use of small icons as electronic ads in e-zines, this fits right in the culture of the Internet-nonintrusive but available to those who want it (Jones 1994).

But the Internet offers more promotional channels than just the World Wide Web. If used correctly, companies can also benefit from newsgroups or mailing lists. As found by Sivadas, Kellaris, and Grewal (1995), readers of a particular newsgroup are avid consumers of products/services related to the type of the newsgroup. Newsgroups and mailing lists resemble more the traditional media as they deliver the message right into the hands of the users. There is, however, a strong bias in the Internet community against raw sales pitches, and only a few newsgroups do not oppose advertisements. Using electronic junk mail as a means of advertisement has already proven arrogant and unsuccessful (Dinsdale 1995) and might in the future even be subject to legal restrictions.

In order to succeed in these media, companies must strictly adhere to so-called Netiquette and offer information about their products and services only where appropriate. Before starting any promotional program, it is strongly advisable to identify the target audience first. The Internet provides effective means, such as search engines, to find likely groups, and by following the discussions in these groups, companies can find out whether the community would appreciate their information or not. It is essential that the information provided be of high quality and that customers can respond conveniently to the company (Cronin 1994).

An even better way for companies to promote their products and services is to start their own newsgroup, mailing list, or virtual community. Then they can let people know about their offerings, get feedback on what customers like and do not like, solve customer problems, and get a better understanding of the interests and trends in their market (Cross 1994). Companies that have set the standards in these areas are mainly from the computer industry. Adobe or Dell, for example, dedicate several people to monitor their (and competitors') newsgroups in order to respond to customers' problems and suggest new uses of their products. As Internet users are generally early adopters of new product technologies, this gives them a competitive edge in realizing new product opportunities and shifting trends in the market. Additionally, this two-way form of communication offers the opportunity to build strong relationships with a segment that is extremely unwilling to respond to any traditional, one-way form of marketing communication such as mass advertising (Mehta and Sivadas 1995).

Strong customer relationships are paramount for companies that want to compete effectively with businesses offering products of higher quality or lower prices. According to Treacy and Wiersema (1995), "customer intimacy" is a very useful route to market leadership. Customer-intimate companies do not pursue onetime transactions but try to cultivate long-lasting relationships in order to gain lifetime customers. For that, they need detailed customer knowledge to respond quickly to almost any need, which often only they, by virtue of their close relationship with the customer, recognize.

No other medium besides the Internet seems to be so uniquely suited to collect and analyze these huge amounts of customer data at such a low cost. Interactive Web sites allow companies to obtain relevant customer information for the purpose of building customer relationships. Web servers can provide information on which pages are accessed, when and for how long they are accessed, which Web site the user previously visited, and which domain address the user belongs to (Hoffman and Novak 1996). Hello Direct, for example, uses this information to learn about the interests of its customers and find out which products are getting the most attention. Subsequently, the information is used to update Hello Direct's offerings-almost instantly compared to mail-order catalogs (Verity, in Verity and Hof 1994). More sophisticated Web sites also provide the option of user authentication or registration in which the user has to sign in with an ID (identification) to use the site fully. This enables companies such as Virtual Vineyards to use information on new and repeat-visit patterns, thereby tailoring the marketing program specifically to individual customers or groups of customers (Hoffman and Novak 1995b). Businesses using these means can develop extensive customer databases and use them to enter into a new era of low-cost micromarketing. As consumers increasingly demand products targeted to their individual tastes or preferences, companies must customize their offerings to ever-smaller segments, eventually all the way down to the individual consumer. The Internet is an efficient instrument for developing true one-to-one relationships and extract value from them. Companies lacking the capability of reaching the microsegments efficiently might end up with offerings that are designed for everyone but appeal to no one (Cronin 1994).

The Internet offers more than just a low-cost, database-driven marketing approach for achieving new levels of customer relationships. It is an ideal medium for creating and sustaining true customer dialogue (Cross 1994; Deighton 1997). Newsgroups and mailing lists are excellent media to discuss product features, solve customer problems, and suggest new product uses, and get customer feedback. E-mail, as a one-to-one communication medium, is uniquely suited to provide customer support in an asynchronous dialogue that occurs at both parties' convenience. This allows firms to be closer to the customer than ever before and respond faster to changes in its competitive environment. It also offers new opportunities to create stronger brand identities that may translate into brand loyalty (Upshaw in Hoffman and Novak 1995b). Companies engaging in this form of marketing will reap the benefits by building and maintaining customer relationships that promise to be highly profitable in the long run.

SUMMARY AND CONCLUSIONS

Companies that want to stay ahead of the competition can no longer ignore electronic commerce and associated electronic marketplaces. To gain a real competitive advantage, however, they have to understand the logic of these emerging electronic markets. Simply transposing traditional marketing-mix strategies into the world of electronic marketplaces will not yield satisfactory results.

In ubiquitous electronic marketplaces physical location becomes irrelevant, and so do large amounts of retail space or shelf space. Many products and services exist in digital format only and may even be distributed as such. Product offerings, prices, and promotional campaigns are no longer geared toward the mass market but can be customized to the individuals' needs in cost-efficient ways. Electronic marketplaces are also ideal marketing communication media for creating and sustaining true customer dialogue (Deighton 1997). This allows firms to be closer to the customer than ever before and achieve and maintain new levels of profitable, long-term customer relationships.

Although most of the excitement about electronic commerce and electronic marketplaces is based on the tremendous growth of the Internet, sales on the Internet have been relatively slow to develop. Electronic markets outside the United States and Canada picked up steam only in 1999. So far, in the global context, the Internet has served more as a channel for public relations and image building than as a sales channel (Mundorf, Zwick, and Dholakia 1999), but this state of affairs is changing rapidly.

While electronic commerce has exhibited explosive growth in recent years, this method of doing business is still in its infancy. As greater numbers and a wider variety of actors appear in kaleidoscopic patterns of relationships in the electronic marketplace, these types of markets will become more complex, often much more so than their physical counterparts. Success will be increasingly difficult to predict as new types of technologies emerge and transform parts of the electronic marketplace. To survive and prosper in the electronic marketplace, market players will have to be ready with contingency plans based on scenarios that take into account potential technological innovations as well as changes in consumers' preferences and behaviors.

QUESTIONS FOR DISCUSSION

1. In what ways are electronic markets and Internet-based marketing different from physical markets and conventional marketing?

2. Over the next five years, what will be the likely impact of technological innovations on the four Ps of the "marketing mix"–product, price, place, and promotion–in electronic markets?

3. Electronic communities and groups have become a new arena for understanding consumers and markets as well as for influencing them. What are some of the most creative ways in which electronic communities are being employed or used by online marketers today?

Part II

Online Marketing across the World

5

Internet-Based Marketing in Germany: A Comparative Study of the Media, Banks, and Insurance Sectors

Wolfgang Fritz and Martin Kerner

This chapter examines Internet marketing profiles in three different German industries: the media, banks, and insurance firms. The media industry is the pioneer in Internet marketing: they are the Web leaders in Germany. Banks and insurance companies are Web followers. This empirical comparison includes factors such as goals, strategies, and the marketing mix, as well as the success of the companies' Internet marketing efforts.

Internet marketing of the Web leaders is more affected by e-commerce considerations than that of the Web followers. Web sites of the followers are primarily characterized by focus on communications objectives. Even the followers, however, are making a gradual shift towards e-commerce. This shift seems to be stronger in the banks sector than in the insurance industry.

INTRODUCTION

In 1999, the consulting company Roland Berger and Partners published a study on the Internet activities of 102 large companies in Germany. The results show that various business branches use their e-commerce potential very differently. The media industry has on average the highest amount of electronic transactions, followed by the tourism industry. Whereas, banks only appear in the middle of the range, and retail and insurance businesses show only a low level of e-commerce orientation (see Roland Berger and Partners 1999; Preissner 1999: 192).

A major reason for these differences is that not all products are equally marketable in the Internet, and because the Internet users' demands for them continue to be highly varied. It is, therefore, possible for the favored industries to more quickly and comprehensively take advantage of the potential the Internet offers for e-commerce.

Figure 5.1
Number of Internet Users

World total	201.00 Million
Africa	1.72 Million
Asia/Pacific	33.61 Million
Europe	47.15 Million
Middle East	0.88 Million
Canada and USA	112.40 Million
Latin America	5.29 Million
Source: NUA Internet Surveys, November 1999	

According to our own research, businesses in the media industry (content provider, especially publishing houses, radio, and TV-stations) were able to employ the Internet earlier and better than banks and insurance enterprises. Hence, the prior will be referred to as the Web leaders and the latter as the Web followers. Its role as a successful Web leader, in connection with its know-how advantage, are precisely the reasons that the media industry has been better able to exploit the potentials of e-commerce compared to the other industries. The differences that appear between the leaders and the followers shall be analyzed (Section 3). However, first Internet users' behavior affecting the leaders and followers will be briefly examined (Section 2).

THE WEB USER

One can assume that over 200 million people worldwide have been using the Internet since November 1999, over half of that sum in North America, and 8 to 10 million in Germany (NUA Internet Surveys 1999; GfK Medienforschung AG 1999). As illustrated in Figure 5.1, the concentration of Internet users is in the industrial triad of North America, Europe and Asia.

The reasons people have for using the Web favor the media industry. Consequently, this offers an explanation for the differing potential of the three industries under observation. According to the (American) GVU studies as well as the (German) W3B-studies, the reasons for using the Web are the acquisition of current information (GVU: 73.6 percent; W3B: 84.3 percent), and entertainment (GVU: 61.4 percent; W3B: 68.0 percent), which were both more common than the shopping of goods and services (GVU:52.4 percent; W3B:59.1 percent). Aside from the computer industry (software and hardware), the media industry (books, music and magazines) has played a significant role in Internet related services. The willingness to acquire financial services, stocks or

Figure 5.2
Utilization of Web Offers

"Do you use the following Web Offers?"	frequently %	occasionally %	total %
Online Newspapers and Magazines	33,2	45,5	78,7
Online Business Newspapers and Magazines	19,9	37,3	57,2
Web Offers of TV Stations	8,7	41,5	50,2
Regional Online Newspapers	14,3	30,4	44,7
Web Offers of Banks	25,2	22,7	47,9
Web Offers of Insurance Companies	2,3	14,5	16,8
Source: W3B-Survey October/November 1998; Fittkau and Maass GbR 1999			

insurances, and also to practice home banking is relatively less common. (GVU 1998; Fittkau and Maass 1999; GfK Medienforschung AG 1999). This can be seen to a limited extent in Figure 5.2 in which the results from the German W3B survey in October/November 1998 are presented (Fittkau and Maass 1999).

Although online surveys like those from GVU and W3B suffer from several methodological problems that must be considered (see Bandilla and Hauptmanns 1999), one can assume that the services provided by media companies have always been better suited for Internet users' desires than those of banks and insurance companies. This trend has been further developed by the free information that media businesses have made accessible to Internet users at first. In this manner, since the beginning they have employed a strategy referred to as "Follow the Free" (Zerdick et al. 1999: 16). All of this offers an explanation to why the media industry has been a leader in Internet marketing and not the banks or the insurance industry. The next section will examine how this appears in the individual aspects of online marketing on the Web.

INTERNET MARKETING IN THREE DIFFERENT INDUSTRIES

The Sample

In 1996, 1997, and 1998, we surveyed over 800 companies in Germany, who had experience with the Internet, about their online marketing (Fritz and Kerner 1997 a; Fritz, Kerner, and Köennecke 1998; Fritz 1999 a). About a third participated in the survey. In the following, some results of the most comprehensive survey will be presented; 739 companies were asked to participate, and 241 replied (response rate = 32.6 percent). The sample included among others 53 media corporations (publishing houses, radio, and TV-stations), 28 banks, and 24 insurance companies, which had an own website.

Figure 5.3
Objectives of Internet Marketing

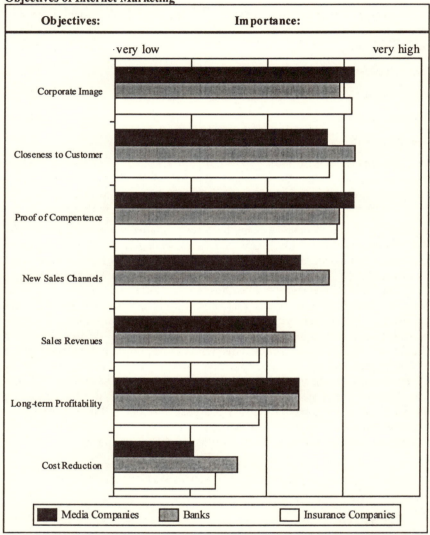

This was about one-third to one-half of all the firms on the Web in these three industries in Germany. However, due to the small sample size, the following may only be viewed as an exploratory study.

Figure 5.4
Strategies of Internet Marketing

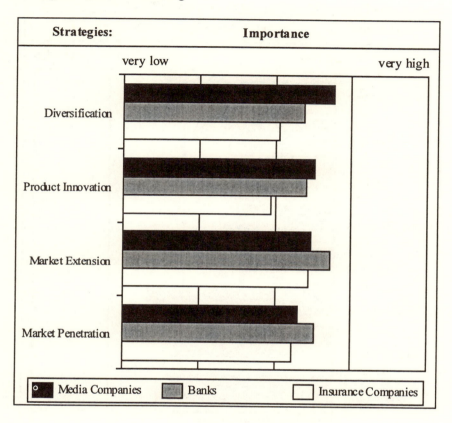

The Media Industry as the Web Leader

Marketing activities of German companies on the Web that are worth mentioning can only be traced back to 1994. Since the very beginning the media industry has been the most active participant. For such companies the Internet since its onset had more relevant implications than it had for others.

The motive, to appear as a pioneer on the Web, has had a great significance for the Web leader's commitment to the Internet. Another important aspect has been the utilization of their early presence on the eb as a means to rapidly react to the inevitable competition.

The specific marketing goals of media companies for their Internet marketing may be viewed in Figure 3. As one can see, corporate image and proof of competency are the most significant, whereas closeness to the customer, new distribution channels, and most notably the classic economic orientations toward sales revenues, long-term profitability and cost reduction,

Figure 5.5
Instruments of Internet Marketing – Their Importance Today

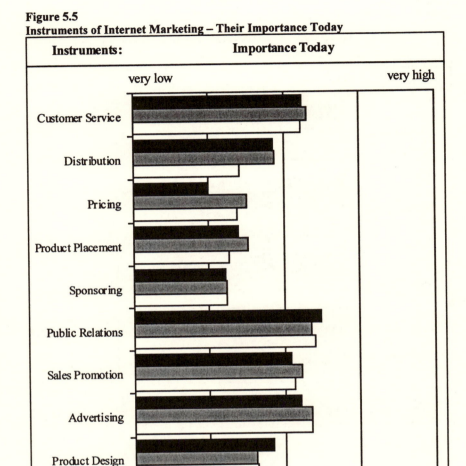

play a less significant role. When comparing these goals to those of the followers, one notices a slightly stronger emphasis on image and competence directed goals. There is also the difference between the followers; the banks place a greater emphasis on closeness to the customer and new distribution channels. Overall, there are only relatively minor differences between the Internet marketing goals of the leaders and followers.

Differences can also be seen in the marketing strategies. Figure 5.4 depicts the comparatively higher relevance of marketing strategies for the media

Figure 5.6
Instruments of Internet Marketing – Future Importance

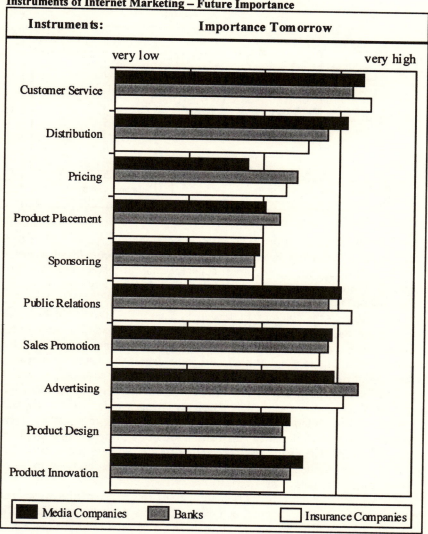

industry. The media industry not only offers conventional services to their given markets, but develops also new online services to capture existing as well as new markets. By doing their strategic emphasis has been on product development and diversification. These findings suggest that the strategic marketing dimensions of the media industry are broader than those of the followers.

The media industry's strong orientation towards service innovations is manifested on the level of the marketing mix, which may be viewed in Figures

Figure 5.7
Success of Internet Marketing

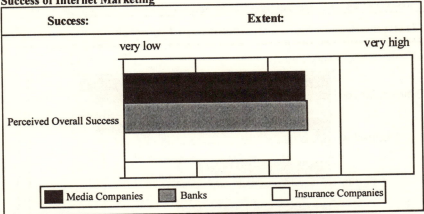

5.5 and 5.6. The current and future situation projects that for the media business product design and product development on the Web are more relevant than for the other branches. But it becomes apparent that all three branches are dominated by communications purposes (public relations, advertisement, and sales promotion) followed by customer services.

According to the findings illustrated in Figure 5.5, there will be some changes in the future. Especially media firms (and also insurance companies) expect an above average increase in the Internet's importance as a means for customer service. The media, but not to the same degree the insurance industry, will also benefit from the Internet's influence on sales and distribution, which outperforms communications. In connection to the increasing relevance of the Internet as a sales tool, the media industry's changes point clearly towards e-commerce. The Internet marketing leaders have more quickly seen opportunities for the development and distribution of innovative online products than the followers. Therewith, they accommodate the Internet users' behavior (see Part 2), and can, hence, develop their Internet marketing early on to serve their profit objectives (see Figure 5.3).

For the time being, media firms are making rather reserved assessments about the success of their Internet activities. On this point the media branch differs only slightly from the other two branches, as can be seen in Figure 5.7. Especially with regard to profits, there appears to be a large discrepancy between the goal's importance and achievement (see Fritz and Kerner 1997b: 26f.). And so, e-commerce's financial success, including that of the leaders, continues to keep us waiting despite a few exceptions. Even though their Internet marketing has not been satisfactory, almost all of the firms surveyed reported that they would act in the same or similar manner as they had been while establishing themselves on the Web.

Banks and the Insurance Companies as the Web Followers

About a year after the Web leaders, banks, and insurance companies began presenting themselves on the Internet in Germany. Furthermore, their adaptation of the Web has been a long drawn out process. And for this reason, they may be viewed as the followers as far as Internet marketing is concerned (see Fritz and Kerner 1997c: 15f.; Fritz and Kerner 1997d: 15f).

The banks and the insurance companies have had more technology and imitation oriented motives than the media businesses. They present themselves on the Web, because they do not want to fall behind the technological developments that everyone is talking about, and of course, because the competitors are there already (see Fritz and Kerner 1997c: 16f; Fritz and Kerner 1997d: 16f.). These are the typical motives of the followers and not of the pioneers.

In view of their marketing goals, there are slight differences between the two followers. For banks, customer service, distribution channels, increased sales revenues, and long-term profitability have a greater significance than for insurance companies, whose primary goals are corporate image and competency (see Figure 5.3). Hence, banks seem to have a more consequent E-commerce orientation (see Preissner 1999: 192).

The marketing strategies of the banks and the insurance companies are more conservative than those of the media businesses. The former have used their established services to expand to old and to new markets via the Internet (see Figure 5.4). Marketing strategies and service innovations on the Web are especially rare in the insurance branch. Internet marketing strategies are of greater importance for banks than for insurance firms.

All this does have a subsequent effect on the marketing mix. There is almost no difference between the two followers' present assessment of the Web's importance for their marketing mix. Only distribution and selling is emphasized more by banks and than by insurance companies (see Figure 5.5).

The emphasis differs slightly when the future significance of the Web for the marketing mix is assessed (see Figure 5.5). Banks stressed Internet marketing as a means for advertisement and customer service. Whereas, insurance companies emphasized public relations, advertisement, and customer service even to a higher degree. However, when interpreting future developments, banks' distribution, and sales have greater prospects than insurances'. In short, the marketing of banks and insurance firms on the Internet today and tomorrow is predominantly applied in customer service and communications. But banks, however, emphasize distribution and sales as well. These results demonstrate the differences mentioned in the introduction; the difference between these two business branches' e-commerce potential, and the differences found in Internet users' preferences of online services from banks as well as insurance companies (see Table 5.2).

Marketing success on the Internet has been slightly higher for banks than for insurance companies. However, both businesses only range in the middle (see Figure 5.7). Despite the apparent lack of success, almost all of the banks and slightly more hesitantly the insurance companies, who participated in this study, stated that they would employ the Internet in the same or similar manner as they have been.

CONCLUSIONS

All three industries, including the innovators of Internet marketing, are not satisfied with their marketing success on the Internet. There are barely any companies that do not want to further expand their activities on the Web. All three branches recognize the Internet as an important tool for their marketing. The media industry is focused on, aside from customer service, sales and distribution, and thus especially on e-commerce. In comparison, the banks and the insurance industry are driven primarily by communications purposes. There is a greater chance of developing e-commerce for banks than for insurance companies, however, even the insurance industry appears to be reevaluating its Internet marketing towards E-commerce (see Fritz 1999b).

QUESTIONS FOR DISCUSSION

1. Compare the findings of this chapter with the Internet strategies of Media, Banking, and Insurance industries in the United States. What are the similarities and differences?

2. In the German companies discussed in this chapter, what is the role of the management in promoting or slowing down e-commerce?

3. Look at some German Media and Banking Web sites and analyze them based on the issues discussed in the chapter.

4. Do you think online banking will become the dominant mode of banking in the near future? Compare and contrast Europe and the United States in this regard.

6

Traditional Retailing and Electronic Commerce on the Internet

Wolfgang Fritz

Traditional retailers are confronted with a new challenge: Internet-based e-commerce. The Internet will probably increase the intensity of competition in retailing, because it enables new competitors to enter a given market and to compete in the global marketplace more easily. Furthermore, a reconfiguration of the value chain in retailing is often assumed. New electronic intermediaries will emerge and take over important functions of conventional retailers. Because the Internet can connect producers and consumers directly, traditional retailers as well as wholesalers can be bypassed and thus be affected in their existence (disintermediation).

Although electronic transactions are concentrated only within a certain number of product categories, and therefore the threat is limited, conventional retailers should react by choosing a double strategy. On one hand, they should build on their core competence and extend their unique closeness to the consumer. On the other hand, they should build a new electronic competence. This must include the development of a comprehensive online marketing program.

The results of an empirical study conducted in Germany are presented to illustrate how German retailers utilize the Internet as an instrument for their marketing mix. According to the respondents, the Internet is of considerable importance only for public relations, advertising, and sales promotion but of less importance especially for the assortment of goods. These findings indicate that the Internet marketing of German retailers is not sufficiently affected by e-commerce considerations. Obviously, German retailers have not realized the relevance of the Internet for their marketing management in full measure, and they do not yet react to the challenge of e-commerce in an adequate way.

The Internet is on the way of becoming one of the most important media for communications and e-commerce transactions. Within the next decade, the number of Internet users will reach 1 billion worldwide, and the commercial use of the Internet will become more and more popular. Studies conducted by Forrester Research and IDC predict that the total sales revenues from e-commerce transactions on the Web should rise to more than U.S.$ 500 billion worldwide by the year 2002 (Fritz 1999e).

Figure 6.1
Reconfiguration of the Value Chain in Retailing

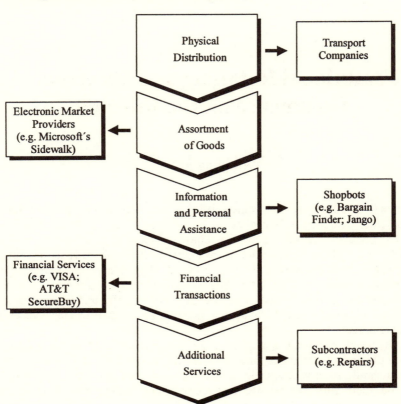

INTRODUCTION

The rising Internet economy may cause some fundamental changes in the structure of markets and firms and in the distribution system. "Virtual" or "borderless" firms may emerge, and organizational hierarchies may be replaced by informational "hyperarchies." Furthermore, a reconfiguration of the value chain in many industries is often assumed (Evans and Wurster 1997; Dholakia and Dholakia 1999; Picot, Reichwald, and Wigand 1998). Internet-based e-commerce is often regarded as a serious threat, especially to traditional retailers (Fritz 1999c; Fritz and Kerner 1999).

In this chapter, some impacts of the Internet on the competitive environment of traditional retailers are examined. Furthermore, the results of an empirical study conducted in Germany in 1998 are presented to illustrate how German retailers utilize the Internet as an instrument for their marketing mix.

IMPACTS OF THE INTERNET ON COMPETITION IN RETAILING

In principle, the Internet can change the rules of competition in retailing in three ways:

- It can enhance the intensity of competition in retailing (Fritz 1999c).
- New electronic intermediaries may emerge and take over important functions of conventional retailers (Albers and Peters 1997).
- The existence of traditional retailers and wholesalers may be affected, because the Internet can bypass them by directly connecting producers to consumers (disintermediation) (Wigand and Benjamin 1996).

Growing Intensity of Competition

It is argued that the Internet will intensify competition in retailing, because it enables new competitors to enter a given market and to compete in the global marketplace more easily (Quelch and Klein 1996). Those companies eager to take advantage of the Internet on a global scale can utilize the Internet's opportunities for international business without any physical presence in the international markets. Traditional barriers to market entry, like physical stores, lose their significance. Coupled with the fact that the Internet lowers the mobility barriers and hence the loyalty of the consumers (Dholakia and Dholakia 1999: 31), it seems to be evident that the intensity of competition will increase.

Reconfiguration of the Value Chain

Among the new competitors of the traditional retailers are companies from other industries such as computers, telecommunications, media, and consulting. These new competitors can provide at least some if not all of the classic functions of a retailer both better and more cheaply electronically (see Figure 6.1). By doing this, they reconfigure the traditional value chain in retailing (Albers and Peters 1997). For example, software companies or online services might provide assortments of goods by running cybermalls on the Internet (e.g., Microsoft's Sidewalk, America Online's Shopping Channel) (Little, Cowles, and Kiecker 1997). New electronic intermediaries, like online brokers and intelligent software agents or shopbots (e.g. Andersen Consulting's BargainFinder, Amazon's Shop the Web), can take over the functions of providing information and personal assistance to the consumer. They also allow for a quick and comprehensive inspection of an expanded set of options. Furthermore, new electronic competitors will take over retailers' full range of financial services by providing consumers with the opportunity to conduct their own financial transactions through easy and convenient access via the Internet.

Disintermediation

Not only will new electronic intermediaries emerge and take over important functions of traditional retailers, but they, as well as wholesalers, may be bypassed and their existence thereby affected. In other words, the Internet can directly connect end users with producers and bypass the traditional intermediaries (disintermediation), both on the supply and on the demand side (Brandtweiner 1997; Brenner and Kolbe 1997). Hence, buyers can purchase their goods via the Internet directly from the producers. Astounding examples of how manufacturers use the Internet's direct marketing capabilities can be found. The success of Dell Computer Company, one of the most important direct marketers of computers, is, to a high degree, due to its Internet-based direct selling competence. Disintermediation as well as reintermediation by cybermediaries that are specialized in e-commerce are some of the most important structural changes caused by the Internet in the distribution system (Dholakia et al. 1999: 69).

Online Shopping

For conventional retailers, such scenarios are threatening. However, the threat is based on several assumptions, that are at least questionable (see Peterson, Balasubramanian, and Bronnenberg 1997: 331). Such scenarios can take place only if the Internet is widely accepted, and if there is generally a high degree of online shopping. Until now this has not been the case, and it is not expected to be within a midterm perspective. According to corresponding research conducted in the United States and Germany, electronic shopping isn't close to being the preferred use of the World Wide Web. However, the results do show a tremendous difference concerning the segment size of online shoppers. In the United States the use is much more than in Germany (see Fritz 1999e; Fittkau and Maass GbR 1999; GVU 1998).

Depending on the product category, the role of electronic shopping varies. Almost all of the research on Internet usage shows that computer products, books, magazines, music, and, to a growing extent, services like travel are among the most popular items to be purchased on the Web. The interest in groceries, electronics, furniture, pictures, and other art objects is much smaller. These findings implicitly identify those product categories in which the threat to conventional retailers is relatively high (the former) and those where the challenge is limited (the latter).

INTERNET MARKETING OF TRADITIONAL RETAILERS IN GERMANY: AN EMPIRICAL STUDY

Basic Orientations

Although the Internet's potential to be a serious threat to traditional retailers is often overestimated, it does exist for a certain number of product categories (e.g., computer hardware and software, books, compact discs, travel services). In order to adequately react to the challenge that the Internet presents, conventional retailers should choose a double strategy. On the one hand, they should build on their core competence and extend their unique closeness to the customer, and, on the other hand, they should build a new electronic competence. Retailers can create a greater closeness to their customers by providing improved personal assistance from well-trained salespeople and by adding more entertainment events, ambience, and social interaction to the shopping experience. However, to a certain extent, conventional retailers, especially those in Germany, are far from addressing all these needs. They ought to make a serious effort, for example, in improving the friendliness and qualification of their service personnel, which are often criticized. Shopping in physical stores must become much more convenient for the customer, because convenience is reported to be one of the most important reasons for the customer to shop online. The given potential for traditional retailers may be illustrated by the following examples:

Ogden Corporation created American Wilderness, a nature preserve located in a shopping mall, with 160 wild animals, a restaurant, and a shopping boutique. Land Rover dealerships built offroad test tracks so customers can experience the thrill of driving sport utility vehicles. Athletic shoe stores have installed basketball courts and rock-climbing walls. Some grocery stores have scheduled "single nights," with contemporary music, name tags, food samples, and flattering lighting to emphasize the social aspects of shopping. (Burke 1997: 357)

It is not enough for conventional retailers to build only on their strengths. In order to overcome their potential weakness with respect to their electronic competitors, these retailers need to build their own electronic competence. This is suggested by Burke (1997: 357) in a similar way: "As a starting point, retailers can improve shopping convenience, emphasize knowledgeable and personalized service, and enhance the entertainment value and ambiance of their stores. Creative retailers will go far beyond this list of suggestions, developing both high-tech and high-touch selling approaches."

Today, only a minority of conventional retailers in Germany have developed such far-reaching approaches. For example, in the early 1980s big mail-order houses, like Quelle, Neckermann, and Otto-Versand, began building their competence in new online media by entering the German BTX-system (today called "T-Online"). But for the majority of the small and medium-sized German retailers, the adequate use of the Internet remains a problem even today. Nevertheless, building a new electronic competence implies for all conventional retailers, among other things, that they have to develop a comprehensive and professional online marketing program. This would include, for example, the creation and maintenance of cybermalls and virtual communities in cooperation with software companies, telecommunications providers, and online services. Some big retailers in Germany, like Karstadt AG ("My-World") and Metro AG ("Primus Online"), and even a few small ones, like "onkelemma.de," have already established such electronic offerings successfully. But in many cases, the integration of the Internet into the marketing program of conventional retailers is still needed.

In order to illustrate how and to what extent German retailers utilize the Internet as an instrument for their marketing mix, the results of an empirical study (n = 241 firms) conducted in Germany in 1998 are presented. Among the respondents were 16 big retailers (including mail-order houses) that belong to the most important in Germany and Europe (e.g., Karstadt AG, Metro AG, Quelle AG, and Neckermann AG). Due to the economic power that these companies represent and also with respect to their role as innovators for e-commerce in German retailing, the results of the study can be seen as relevant, although the sample size seems to be small (see Fritz 1999c).

Marketing Objectives and Strategies

Figure 6.2 shows that German retailers as well as firms from other industries reported image- and consumer-related goals as the most important objectives for their Internet marketing ("better corporate image," "greater closeness to customers," "increasing customer loyalty"). However, differences between retailing firms and the rest of the sample were reported concerning the assessment of less important marketing goals (e.g., "market share," "sales revenues," and "cost reduction"). Retailers tend to assess them as even less important than the other firms. Especially in view of the widely predicted boom in e-commerce, the relatively low ratings for classic economic goals like market share, sales revenue, long-term profitability, and cost reduction are astonishing. This confirms leading German managers' remarks concerning electronic retailing: with only a few exceptions, they emphasize the companies' philosophy that in the near future traditional sales channels will continue to have priority over the electronic offering systems in retailing and that the Internet activities are still not measured against their profits.

The strategic orientation of Internet marketing in German retailing is relatively weak in most cases. As far as marketing strategies on the Web are pursued, they are aimed to a higher degree at a better penetration of the given markets with the given assortments of products, than to develop new assortments for new markets (see Fritz 1999c). This rather weak strategic attitude is embodied in the marketing mix as well.

Figure 6.2
Importance of Objectives for the Internet Marketing of German Retailers

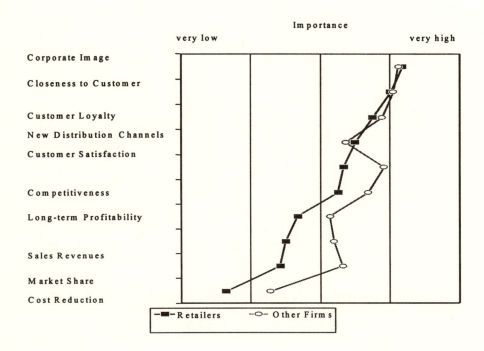

Marketing Mix

In order to examine the impact of the Internet on the marketing instruments of German companies, the respondents were asked to assess the importance of the Web for their marketing mix today and for the next two to three years (for the latter, see Figure 6.3).

According to the respondents, the importance of the Internet for product or assortment design and product or assortment development today is relatively low. From the retailers' point of view, this restrained judgment will also hold true in the near future. In contrast, managers from the rest of the sample were more optimistic about the future impact of the Web on companies' product policies. Compared to the retailers, they see a much higher potential. On the other hand, retailing firms reported the importance of the Web as average for customer service today, but of considerably higher importance in the future.

Retailers were very reserved when rating the importance of the Web for distribution. They continue to depend on their traditional local stores. However, the importance of the Web for distribution is expected to increase.

Concerning pricing, retailers as well as the other companies in the sample see the importance of the Internet at its present state as relatively low. It is expected to be only slightly higher in the future.

Figure 6.3
Future Importance of the Web for Selected Marketing Instruments

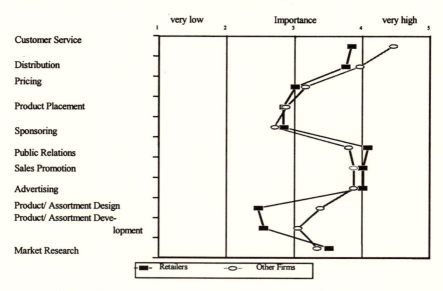

The main emphasis has been put on the Internet's role as a means of communication for German retailers. According to the respondents, the Web today is of considerable importance, especially for public relations and advertising, and is slightly less important for sales promotion. When the respondents were asked to assess the importance of the Web for the future, all of these instruments were rated considerably higher.

One unique characteristic of online communication is that it provides a powerful means of building a one-to-one relationship with the customer. As a consequence, retailers can offer customized product-assortments based on individual shopping patterns.

However, according to the results of our survey, this form of interactivity is far from being realized on a broad basis. For German retailers, the Internet is currently of considerably higher importance for public relations, advertising, and sales promotion but of less importance for the assortment of goods.

Marketing Success

The respondents were asked to assess the overall performance of their companies' commercial Web activities. Having been measured on a five-point scale (1 = very poor, 5 = very good), the ratings were not overwhelmingly positive, but slightly positive with an average of 3.5 for the sample without retailers, and 3.1 for retailers (see Figure 6.4). Retailers are obviously less satisfied with their online marketing efforts than companies foreign to the retail industry. Moreover, a further causal analysis has shown that the retailers attribute the success of their online marketing program only to advertising and

Figure 6.4
Success of the Internet Marketing of German Companies

Measure of success	Retailers (means)	Other Firms (means)	t-test p
overall success (1 = very poor; 5 = very good)	3.1	3.5	0.07
Index of success (max. 387)	144.9	198.0	0.01
r = 0.54; p = 0.00			

public relations on the Web. Utilizing the Web as a means of product-assortment decisions is rather regarded as a failure factor of online marketing. Nevertheless, German companies are going to adopt the Web as a means for e-commerce, although this will take place at a rather slow pace.

SUMMARY AND CONCLUSIONS

As we have shown, Internet-based e-commerce is not always a threat to traditional retailers. It depends to a large extent on the product category and the industry. Therefore, many undifferentiated predictions regarding the impact of the Internet on conventional retailing are overstated. Nevertheless, the Internet and electronic shopping will give new electronic intermediaries the opportunity to compete with existing retail formats. Therefore, store-based retailers should react in time to defend their territory. This includes the development of a comprehensive online marketing program.

As the findings of our empirical study show, German retailers have not yet realized the full potential of the Internet for marketing management, and in many cases they have not been managing the challenge of electronic commerce in an adequate way.

Recent research conducted in Germany supports these conclusions. Even some of the biggest and most important German retailers show deficits with respect to e-commerce: only 7 out of 10 have their own Web site, and only 6 out of 10 offer online shopping to their customers (Kienbaum 1999). Even the biggest mail-order house in Germany and worldwide, Otto-Versand in Hamburg, earned only U.S.$50 million sales revenues in e-commerce in 1999, which is only 0.3 per cent of its total sales revenues of U.S.$16.5 billion.

Other research shows that German firms in general neglect mass customization strategies in e-commerce to a great extent (Piller and Schoder 1999). Especially the mass customization of products and product-assortments—as it is performed, for example, by Streamline, an online supermarket in the United States (see Peppers and Rogers 1997: 159)—seldom occurs in most of the German industries, including retailing.

QUESTIONS FOR DISCUSSION

1. In what specific ways does the Internet pose a serious threat to traditional retailing?

2. What can traditional retailers do to counter the threat created by the Internet?

3. What are some relative strengths of traditional retailing, and how can electronic retailers acquire similar advantages?

4. E-commerce companies often have difficulty achieving brand recognition. Do you think that opening or buying physical retail stores is a solution?

7

The Internet as a Grocery Store: Observations from Sweden

Solveig Wikström and Maria Frostling-Henningsson

INTRODUCTION

In Sweden consumers have been able to shop for groceries on the Internet since 1996. During the years that virtual grocery shopping has been an alternative for Swedish consumers, the number of companies offering the service has grown significantly. At present there are approximately 50 Swedish grocery stores supplying groceries virtually. The virtual grocery store with the largest number of online consumers is Prisextra (http://www.prisextra.se). Prisextra currently has nearly 20,000 Swedish online customers, all in the Stockholm metro area.

Even though this kind of service has been of enormous interest for several constituencies ranging from Swedish grocers, to the media, to consumers, the rate of adoption has been much slower than initially expected when the first virtual grocery shops were launched. Only a small proportion of Swedish consumers has actually changed its behavior and is now shopping groceries in front of the computer screen. The number of consumers shopping groceries online varies, due to some unreliability and sometimes unavailability of data. At the current rate of adoption, however, online grocery sales are estimated to amount to fully 1 percent of the total grocery sales, virtual shopping is successfully spreading to a wider range of consumers. Initially, urban, dual-income households with children dominated the online shopping landscape. Now, increasingly, dual-income households without children as well as small companies, advertising agencies, day care centers, and service centers for the elderly are joining the online grocery market.

But what does the future hold? The benefits of online shopping for the consumers are obvious, but what are its shortcomings? Is it just a matter of time before online shopping takes off? Are there still some significant barriers to overcome? In this chapter we analyze the experience of some early adopters of grocery online shopping. The results will be helpful for firms developing virtual grocery stores. Swedish consumers are a useful population for acquiring insights into online shopping behavior because Sweden was among the pioneers of Internet shopping services and is, for several other reasons discussed later, a suitable test market.

SWEDEN: FERTILE GROUND FOR VIRTUAL GROCERY MARKET

Sweden, a homogeneous country with a well-educated consumer base, seems to provide perfect conditions for adopting virtual grocery shopping. Moreover, Swedes tend to adopt new information and communication technologies (ICT) quickly. This has been the case for the telephone, the fax machine, the mobile phone, and the computer. Technology orientation is part of the Swedish culture. In fact, the rate of adoption of these devices is among the highest in the world. As a result, Sweden has a high and homogeneous diffusion of ICT. The technology has been integrated in workplaces, homes, schools, libraries, and senior citizen homes. Even in preschools and day care centers, computers are an essential part of the furnishings. A special boost came when trade unions in 1998 put programs in place offering attractive loans for computer purchases for employees (Sundelin 1999; Höij 2000; Bohlin 2000). Unlike many other countries, access to computers in Sweden is no longer a matter of social class (Höij, 2000). In fact, measures like these and the genuine interest in technology have resulted in computer access for close to two-thirds of the Swedish population between the ages of 18 and 74. At this point the estimates are that about half of the population has access to the Internet.

The fact that the adoption rate of mobile phones is one of the highest in the world indicates that not only the government push but also the technology pull trigger the interest in Net shopping in Sweden.

Cultural and social realities in Sweden reinforce the country's favorable disposition toward the adoption of ICT and, by extension, toward online shopping. Women increasingly reject traditional gender roles and confidently leave their homes to join the workforce. Because of a higher female working percentage (close to 100 percent), the country has made a spot in a day care center a statutory right for Swedish parents. Despite these facilities, however, families where both partners pursue their careers do face a serious time crunch. Such families could be expected to be positive about the added convenience of online shopping. In addition, to enable individuals willing and qualified to pursue higher education to do so, the Swedish government provides loans to students regardless of their socioeconomic situation. Consequently, many young Swedes pursue a college degree, which prepares them for the challenge to adapt successfully to a fast-moving and fast-changing workplace and living environment. Pursuing such college programs creates further time pressures.

Time pressure is a topic that is receiving more attention than ever (Jönsson 1999). Many households are struggling in their everyday lives to reconcile a growing shortage of time with job, household duties, family, and leisure. In this time-pressured context it is not surprising that there exists a need for services that help save time. Maids, baby-sitters, cleaning services, and personal dressers have gained considerable currency as of late. Of course, virtual grocery shopping emerges as a logical addition to the list of time-savers in a service economy. In sum, Sweden seems to hold a lot of promise for the rapid spread of virtual grocery shopping.

EMPIRICAL DATA

The purpose of this chapter is to create a better understanding of the benefits and shortcomings that early adopters in Sweden experience with virtual shopping of groceries. We carried out research on a set of early online consumers in order to understand what aspects are important for them in choosing this new form of shopping and what might hold them back from doing so.

Data were collected over a period of three years, during which we followed 22 Swedish households. We interviewed the household members at several times, using a method based on storytelling. Several researchers emphasizing the qualitative research approach have inspired us in using storytelling as a method (Brown 1998, 1999; Gudmundsdottir 1996; Marton 1981; Mishler 1986; Woodruffe-Burton 1998). We also engaged in introspective research because one of the researchers' own household was included in the study. Introspective data were collected in diary form over a period of two and a half years. Introspection has been used successfully by earlier marketing researchers such as Brown (1998, 1999), Holbrook (1995), and Zaltman (1997). In our study introspection proved helpful in interpreting the data and in identifying themes and reactions among the interviewees.

Household Characteristics

The households included in the study consist of dual-career families with above average combined income. Household size varies from three to seven, except in one case of a single woman. All families live in or around Stockholm. Average level of education is high among the adults, with the majority of the parents holding a college degree. All participants possess superior knowledge of computers, and the diffusion of high-tech appliances among these households is high. Many of the households own several computer systems. Among the professions represented in the study are medical doctor, researcher, computer consultant, head of trading, controller, vice president, general manager, management consultant, entrepreneur, engineer, and a graduate college student. We conducted the majority of our interviews with women and only five with men.

Selecting the Respondents

In qualitative studies, to find a representative sample of participants in order to generalize the study's findings is not a central aim. But the way in which the respondents are chosen is crucial for the quality and results of the study (Miles and Huberman 1994). We included 22 households, 16 of which we contacted by letter to explain the aim of the study. The letters were put in shopping bags that were delivered to online customers in May 1998 and September 1998. Out of all the households contacted, we decided to follow four very closely for the next two years. Later, two additional households were included in the study because of their potential to provide valuable information. One of them consisted of a single mother with two children; the other, of a single person. We had monthly, sometimes even weekly meetings with the families and thereby gained a deep understanding of the circumstances under which they managed their lives.

THE CONCEPTUAL BACKGROUND

What concepts are useful for understanding consumers' experiences and shortcomings in shopping groceries on the Net? We started our analyses with a conceptual framework called the TIMES-model developed by Kaufman and Lane (1996a, 1996b), which was originally designed to understand the traditional shopping situation. As a starting point, it proved helpful, but we anticipated the need to incorporate other concepts as well to fully understand the consumers' perception of the new shopping format with all its new qualities.

The TIMES-model, developed from a rationalistic point of view, is based on the idea that a household has limited resources that must be allocated to achieve an optimal shopping experience. According to the TIMES-model, the resources that are needed to form a shopping experience are:

- Time: the limited time that a household has to engage in shopping.

- Information: information about opening hours and assortment.

- Money: a household is constrained by a limited budget available for shopping.

- Energy: physical energy and mental energy spent on shopping.

- Space: the distance that a shopper has to travel to complete a shopping trip.

These resources–time, information, money, energy, and space–can be combined or traded for or can supplement each other according to the individual consumer preferences.

When following the 22 Swedish households, we felt that these resources are insufficient to understand the nature of the online shopping situation. Thus, based on the stories told by the Swedish online consumers, an improved conceptual framework for virtual shopping was constructed. In addition to all the dimensions of the TIMES-model, experiential and emotional aspects were also found to be important for our respondents. The improved framework therefore includes rational as well as experiential aspects of shopping. They fall into several categories, which are discussed and illustrated next.

Flexibility in Time and Space

This aspect was of crucial importance for changing our participants' behavior in favor of online shopping. Many of the consumers interviewed had chosen to become online consumers in order to save time. "If we go to a supermarket it takes a lot of time. I think it could easily take three hours to go around and look for things. And you are much more effective when you shop from home too. If you go to a supermarket you walk around and look for everything else like special offers. It takes much more time"[8] (male, department store manager, two children).

After trying to buy groceries in the virtual grocery stores, however, many consumers realized that the timesaving was only minimal. Long download times as well as arduous order and checkout systems almost entirely offset the timesaving achieved by staying at home. But consumers still preferred shopping groceries online, because more important than timesaving per se is the possibility to gain time flexibility. Virtual grocery shopping provides the consumers with an alternative to the ordinary opening hours in the grocery store. Shopping can be shifted to times when the alternative cost for time is low, such as late at night when the children are asleep. "And I can shop whenever I want. I can even shop at midnight" (female, controller, five children).

Besides time flexibility and savings, the possibility to shop from anywhere, regardless of location, was stated as another important advantage of shopping for groceries in front of the computer screen. Our household members shopped either from their workplaces or from their homes.

Information

The Internet makes it possible for consumers to handle great amounts of information. Virtual shopping allows for information and price transparency. This enables consumers to search deeply as well as widely for price and other information. The way that the virtual grocery stores are presented on the Web sites today, however, makes it difficult–sometimes simply impossible–to compare information such as list of contents, nutritive value, calories, or other information that is of importance for consumers. One of our participants provides a good example of the difficulties that consumers face when trying to find the information in the virtual grocery store that they are used to finding in the traditional store; "We have this problem with our son who is allergic to eggs. You don't get information about the items we know usually include egg when we are out on the Internet. Then you have to order that item just because you know you can use it, otherwise you guess or you just don't order it" (male, engineer, two children).

In general, the information that the consumers can find in the virtual store today is not sufficient. To cope with the lack of information, consumers in the study often take a chance and order items that they think are the ones that they wish to order. Often these items turn out to be something other than what they expected.

The consumers in the study also complained about insufficient information regarding weight and package size. A translation problem exists between the way in which consumers are used to choosing items in the physical store and the way they are forced to choose in the virtual store. In the physical context, visual impressions are important. In the virtual counterpart, consumers have to make their decisions based on written descriptions. Blunders are inevitable during this transition period but nevertheless very aggravating for the consumer. "Once I was going to buy eight bananas and then I got eight kilos instead. I had to accept I made a mistake and then I had to give away bananas to family and relatives. It is quite a pile when eight kilos arrive" (male, department store manager, two children).

In our interview data, we find many similar stories concerning the challenges of mastering the new "language" of online grocery shopping. No doubt, it is very easy to make mistakes when ordering from a text-based Web site. There is much room for improvement on both sides of the exchange.

Financial Resources

For our households, the fee for the service is not perceived to be a barrier to adopt virtual grocery shopping. On the contrary, many are well aware of the price of their own time. Time for these consumers is a scarce resource with significant opportunity costs. A general conception is that the value of the time that virtual shopping "saves" is greater than the fees that the virtual grocery stores charge for this service. "We are probably prepared to pay quite a lot for this service" (female, medical doctor, three children). "So it is the time and the carrying [of bags of groceries]. I am more than willing to pay for that" (female, controller, three children).

Thus, these mothers have an explicit awareness of the cost of time, so they value it. "I think one could say that it started when we both began to work. We are of the opinion that we now have more money than we have time at this time it is quite all right if it costs a little more if we save some time. I'd rather work than shop, and I'd rather work one hour more and shop like this and by doing this I can pay the fee they charge" (female, engineer, two children).

Human Resources

Another important reason for these households to shop from the virtual grocery store is the physical relief provided by virtual shopping. Online consumers do not have to pick the groceries, go through the checkout, pack the items in shopping bags, load them in the car, and take them home as required for a traditional shopping trip. No doubt, for some consumers, grocery shopping represents a heavy activity that demands a lot of physical strength. Especially women in the study emphasized the benefit of physical relief as a justification for turning to virtual grocery shopping:

You save energy because you are pretty exhausted when you have been away and rushed around that supermarket, trying to find things and then you have to go home, so you are going to pack everything in the car, you go home, you unpack the car, and then I have this long flight of stairs to our house, so physically it is really strenuous. And it is this joy when the doorbell tolls, you open the door, and there are all your shopping bags. So just the fact that it has come up to the door is an important thing (female, area manager, three children).

I do not have to carry it up three flights of stairs as I used to do before (female, occupational therapist, three children).

Many of the consumers stressed the importance of not having to carry heavy bags as a reason for changing behavior. This makes sense because the majority of households in our study consist of big families. One participant, a father of two teenage sons, even checked the weight of each delivery. Just the dairy products in this household add up to an astonishing 30 liters (8 gallons)!

To carry home all this heavy stuff it's several kilos you carry home. In the beginning when we shopped at Foodexpress you could see the weight when the groceries were delivered. You do not think about it but it was 60 to 70 kilos (male, department store manager, two children).

I think it is both boring and tiresome to shop for food in the store. It has to be bagged, loaded and stowed, into the car and out of the car. I do not like supermarkets (female, secretary, two children).

Technology as Status Mediator

For a household, online grocery shopping not only implies a way of facilitating the everyday life of consumers but also demonstrates a positive relationship with technology in general and to the Internet in particular.

For consumers who have turned to grocery shopping on the Internet, the transition implies that a well-known behavior has been replaced by a completely new behavior. When this study started in 1997, virtual grocery shopping was not a widespread phenomenon. To be able to shop virtually, a certain amount of computer literacy and access to the hardware and software and willingness to adopt novel ways were the prerequisites. Thus, for some consumers, virtual grocery shopping signifies a feeling of being on the "cutting edge" and pioneering: "It is somewhat modern And then it is hard to put it in words but to be able in discussions with colleagues, you can appear as pioneer and tell them that you shop on the Internet" (male, vice president, one child).

For the men in the study, virtual grocery shopping implied a way of enhancing their status as modern and proactive guys. Clearly, men were concerned about personal reputation when considering adopting the new behavior. Several of them expressed that it was important for them to be perceived as advanced in relationship to new technology. For the vice president just quoted, who deemed it important to be considered a pioneer, shopping groceries virtually was a way of enhancing this desired image. Campbell (1994), Livingstone (1994), and Wheelock (1994) report similar evidence in their studies. Here are some more quotes from men in our study:

I have been a computer nerd for some time so I considered it a fun thing to do. There is some I think it is typically boyish you want to have the latest equipment. It was in those days (male, engineer, two children).

And then I find it cool too it is cool to be able to say–I shop on the Internet. It is foolish but that is the way it works if I am to be perfectly honest. It shows that you are modern in a way. You are part of your time (male, engineer, three children).

The women interviewed have quite different reasons for changing behavior in favor of virtual grocery shopping. For them practical reasons are far more important. The essential reasons that they shop online are the ability to allocate time in a flexible way and to avoid having to carry heavy shopping bags. They feel that technology can serve as a facilitator in the pursut of everyday life duties.

Stimulation of the Senses/ Variation

A widespread conception of virtual grocery shopping is that it is difficult to create variety. Especially after having shopped online for some length of time, it becomes difficult for consumers to find new products in the virtual store. Consumers' shopping strategy in the virtual store is based on efficiency and on rationality. The range of variation is stated to shrink as a result of the so-called "Expresslis". The Expresslist is based on the items that a consumer purchased during the previous shopping trip, and many consumers simply use the list as a reference to streamline their shopping. After some time, grocery shopping becomes routine, repetitive, and monotonous. "Every week we have bought the same products, and that is not much fun after a while. And of course, you can choose in the list whether you want roast beef or ham, but it does not look so nice when you see it like that. You are so used to see the meat in a counter in front of you and make the choice based on what looks nice" (male, engineer, two children).

Many consumers find it difficult to visualize the desired products when they have to shop from text-based categories. The visual stimulation that consumers derive from the real "object of desire" is hard to replicate online. The challenge for consumers to "get a feel" for the product when represented virtually and to gauge its quality is considerable:

It is really hard to buy to buy whatever it can be, like a loaf of bread, that you have never bought before and to believe it can be good. You want to see it being good (female, own company, three children).

What I thought was difficult in the beginning was that you do not have the faintest idea of what you eat. You know what the package looks like, but at least on Prisextra, they only have the name and brand (female, supervisor, living alone).

Initially, the consumers shopped for all their groceries on the Internet. They happily found that fresh products were of even better quality than when they had picked the items in the store themselves. Thus, it was not the poor quality of delivered products that led some consumers to purchase fresh produce and other experience-oriented products from the supermarket or the specialty store. Rather, we suggest that a lack of sensorial stimulation is the reason.

To solve the problem of reduced sensorial stimulation, consumers divide the goods according to the demands that they wish to satisfy. During our interviews we detected a tendency to divide the purchases of groceries into utility shopping and experiential shopping. Utility shopping occurs in the virtual grocery store and includes staples such as rice, canned goods, diapers, soda, and detergent. Experiential shopping occurs in the physical store, often a local store or a delicatessen shop, where the purpose is to gain inspiration and stimulation and to acquire information about new and exciting products.

Social Interaction

The consumers in the study are not driven by a need to socialize with other human beings in the grocery store, observing them in the act of shopping, or getting inspiration from them. On the contrary, they appreciate the ability to shop for groceries on their own. The grocery store is not a place where they wish to meet other people. The households that are part of the study consist, with one exception, of at least three people, so loneliness is not a big problem for these consumers. The possibility to shop for groceries virtually provides these households with an opportunity to make more time available to be able to socialize with friends and acquaintances. Paradoxically, the possibility to shop for groceries alone in front of a computer screen provides these households with an opportunity to be more social in other contexts:

I never liked shopping I think it is terrible with all these people [the crowds] (Woman, entrepreneur, three children).

I think it [physical grocery store] is so much filled with agony and it is often crowded where I live the grocery stores are small and everything is so crowded and crammed and you can never pass, you almost have to pass on a line in the right order. If you forget anything you can hardly come back again. It is so much people. I find it stressful (Woman, supervisor, living alone).

Many consumers who were interviewed share the same feeling of discomfort that these women expressed:

Otherwise it is this herd instinct I have a little bit of a problem with that supermarkets usually enforce. You are one in a big crowd who is supposed to fall for a lot of cheap tricks. I was the one who was often doing the shopping. It was awful. Terrible. You met all your neighbors there and it was always the men that went to the supermarket and they were completely broken when they came with their shopping carts. And when they went home, they were shining like the sun. When they had done that the raid to the store Awful experience (male, department store planning, two children).

Even though shopping in supermarkets has been expressed as a tedious and boring activity, the need for social interaction in the physical store is stated to be of importance under certain circumstances. Basically, interaction is seen as a useful way to ask the staff questions and to get advice. Social interaction with physical people is considered to be important as a way to make better decisions. The social interaction in this context has a reason–to get advice and to help the consumer to make better purchase decisions.

Figure 7.1
A Conceptual Framework Applicable for Virtual Grocery Shopping

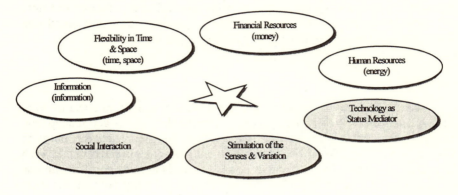

The consumers that have been studied appreciate the integrity as well as the possibility to choose physical store trips when social interaction with the staff is desired. These consumers have a very active life, and they do not suffer from lack of social contact with other people. ICT gives them possibility to make time available to socialize with relatives, friends, and acquaintances.

The opposite situation might be the case for people who are lonely. For them the grocery store can serve as an important location to meet other people. For the elderly, people living on disability pensions, or for people living alone, the grocery store, the post office, and the library may represent important social meeting places. Under such circumstances, the prospect of shopping for groceries virtually can imply both isolation and loneliness.

However, for active families the loss of interaction with other customers occasioned by shopping groceries on the Internet is perceived as a benefit. They appreciate not to be disturbed by others and to be able to shop efficiently. In certain cases, however, they may miss the possibility to interact with the sales staff, to ask questions, and to get advice.

The Conceptual Framework in Summary

Based on the in-depth study of the 22 households in our research project, virtual shopping of groceries can be understood in a conceptual framework that includes the seven resource and experience variables illustrated in Figure 7.1. These variables are, in one way or another, of importance for assessing the future adoption of virtual shopping of groceries. These variables are also of importance for e-retailers that are considering developing a grocery retail format for the Internet.

When shopping on the Internet, consumers tend to combine, trade off, and supplement variables in the framework in Figure 7.1 in different ways in order to attain efficiency. While the recourse variables in the framework are about increasing efficiency, the experience variables are about feelings. When switching from the brick-and-mortar store to the virtual store, the main driving force is the search for efficiency. In this search consumers' expectations are high. They seem to base their decision to shop or not to shop via the Internet on some sort of implicit cost-benefit analysis. They continue to shop as long as the benefits are greater than the cost relative to the traditional way of shopping. But efficiency is not enough for all types of grocery shopping and all types of consumers. There is also a demand for fulfilling emotional needs. Because of limitations in the digital technology, the e-retail format has difficulties in terms of meeting the consumers' need for experience. Thus, there are restrictions to be noted on the emotional side, particularly in the case of creating experience.

Let us discuss the importance of each one of the conceptual variables in Figure 7.1. What are their strengths, and what are their limitations? What limitations are of temporal character, and which ones seem to be more enduring?

- *Flexibility in time and space.* This variable seems to be the most important variable as it provides the greatest benefit. With further improvement in hardware and software, it should be possible to do the shopping even more time-efficiently.
- *The information on the Web site* and the layout of the site are still an undeveloped area. The way that the offerings–the products and the services-are presented is inferior compared to the brick-and-mortar store. Some of the weaknesses could be eliminated by further development of software programs and by bringing consumer needs and wants into Web design. Other weaknesses relate to the media's limitations in terms of reproducing the real world.
- *Financial resource.* In many online shopping categories, consumers expect discount prices on the Net compared to in the physical store. For online grocery shopping, consumers don't seem to expect lower prices than in the physical store. In fact, consumers don't hesitate to pay extra for the benefit of getting time and convenience in return. Thus, consumers trade money for convenience.
- *Human resources.* In terms of saving physical effort, Internet grocery shopping offers a valuable benefit. While physically easier, because of deficiencies in technology and information provision on the Web, online shopping is mentally more demanding than shopping from a traditional store. In due time, it should be possible to eliminate most of these mental "costs" by improving the e-shopping systems.
- *Social interaction.* Most of the grocery shopping today is perceived as an arduous routine activity that should be carried out fast and efficiently. In such a context there is no need for social interaction. The consumers don't seem to feel alone at the screen when shopping. What they sometimes miss out on at the screen is the opportunity to interact with the sales staff. Interactivity is clearly an item that developers of e-shopping formats should seriously consider.
- *Technology as a status mediator.* Initially, this variable was important for understanding the early adopters' interest in shopping for groceries on the Internet. But status is an ephemeral driver for adoption of new e-commerce behaviors. We can already see how its importance is fading. Being an online shopper of groceries is no longer creating attention at the coffee table in the office.
- *Stimulation of the senses and stimulus variation.* The weight of this variable is much greater than we expected. Stimulating the senses while shopping seems important in two ways. First, when the consumers can't see the product display in the store, they lose inspiration, and the whole shopping "basket," that is, the product

choice, is affected. Consumers don't get the variety in consumption that shopping in the physical store provides. This is the reason, after a while, that consumers need to go shopping at the supermarket to get inspiration for more variety and to try new products. "Stimulation deficiency" on the Internet is a rather difficult challenge to overcome at present. Further improvements of hardware and software enabling the reproduction of the physical store should be helpful. With a mirror model of the physical store, "as real as the real store," consumers should regain much of the inspiration provided by the brick-and-mortar store.

Second, for certain product categories and for certain shopping occasions, it is important to see, smell, and touch the products. This is particularly the case for fresh products and for those occasions when consumers want to prepare a special meal. It is less about distrusting the picker of the goods and the quality of the products than about which products should be picked, how to cook and serve them, and so forth. It is a mix of a need for seeing, touching, smelling, and talking about the product with a knowledgeable person. In this case the digital channel most probably has an enduring limitation that cannot be overcome with more technology.

RECENT TRENDS

In our ongoing study, some recent changes have become noticeable regarding virtual grocery shopping. For example, consumers who, for some length of time, have been shopping for most of their groceries online are now changing their shopping behavior. The monotony and boredom associated with text-based Web sites force consumers to devise two distinct shopping strategies. To create product variety and arouse their senses, consumers spice up the rational shopping practice of the virtual store with experiential shopping that occurs outside the virtual store. Experienced online consumers now, to a greater extent, limit their online product range to convenience goods and also cut down on the number of virtual shopping sprees. If, in the beginning, online shopping was a weekly activity, consumers now use the Internet once a month or every third week for grocery shopping purposes. Consumers return to the local grocery and specialty stores for perishables and do so more often in their search for novelties and "sensual stimulation."

Even though most e-commerce sites force consumers to search for items by their brand name and category, thus creating a minimum of visual engagement, some positive developments can be observed. Pictures are used more frequently now than at the time that virtual grocery shopping was introduced. In an attempt to satisfy consumers' experiential motives, recipes are now sometimes included. Furthermore, at some Web sites consumers get easy access to specific information regarding product ingredients and other specifications critical for special-need customers. Allergic consumers can now find Web sites that allow them to search for products free of lactose or gluten. Consumers concerned about health issues can search for health foods. The most advanced e-commerce sites, of course, assemble information about the consumer's personal profile.

When virtual grocery shopping was initially introduced, a majority of consumers still preferred the option of picking up the selected and packaged items at the store. There is now a tendency for consumers to prefer to use the whole service package of selecting, picking, packing, and delivery, thus extending and adding value to the service.

ISSUES FOR FURTHER RESEARCH

One of the most urgent issues to be addressed in future research is to learn how attitudes and behaviors regarding e-shopping develop over time as consumers move from innovators, to early adopters, to early majority. For this to happen, more process studies and more longitudinal studies are needed in order to follow the consumers' reactions and responses. By the same token, we need to explore how the supply side is developing and how technology, applications, and Web sites keep improving. In fact, the diffusion of online shopping is dependent on the interplay between both the demand side and the supply side.

Another important issue is to study e-shopping in an everyday life context, where the new shopping behavior actually takes place. What kind of shopping and how much of the shopping do different categories of consumers and households perform over the Internet? Conversely, which types of consumers object to using the e-shopping format? On what grounds do they object? Further, what are the characteristics of the heavy, light, and nonusers of e-shopping services? Is it possible to discern any patterns that separate users and nonusers over time? Finally, we have identified in our recent research consumers who purposefully disconnect from e-shopping. They do this in the same way as some people purposefully get rid of their e-mail and cell phone. Could this be an emerging pattern of reaction from some parts of the population? If so, how is this reaction to be understood?

SUMMARY AND CONCLUSIONS

Sweden as a market has many prerequisites for virtual grocery shopping. It is a useful laboratory for understanding how new e-commerce behaviors are adopted. In retrospect the diffusion of virtual grocery shopping, as a new way of shopping, has been slower than expected. The question arises as to why this is the case. We have used a qualitative method to find out the benefits and shortcomings experienced by the early adopters when they shop for groceries in a virtual context. Some aspects of importance have emerged. These aspects emerged in the interviews as decisive in one way or another for shopping for groceries on the Internet. The different emerging aspects can be woven together into seven generic concepts that are helpful for understanding why people turn to the Internet to shop for groceries and what turns them off. These conceptual variables are presented in Figure 7.1.

Based on the stories told by consumers, two aspects have emerged as particularly important for shopping for groceries virtually. The first is flexibility (in time and space–ability to shop when and where you want to), and the second is convenience of having the groceries delivered directly to the home (saving efforts–conserving human resources or energy). Initially, the new technology per se was a driving force, specifically for men. To be able to apply the new technology to grocery shopping was considered challenging and exciting (technology as status mediator). This is no longer the case.

There are also certain "costs" involved for the consumers in shopping on the Internet compared to the traditional way. Consumers have to pay for the picking, packing, and delivery (financial resources). This is, however, not a barrier since people are willing to trade money for time and convenience. Other "cost items" are the insufficient information on the screen (information) as well as the fact that there is no sales staff available to answer questions and to get advice from (social interaction). Shopping on the screen is also considered more mentally demanding (human resources) because of the immature shape of the e-shopping format and the technology. Online shopping is also more demanding in terms of planning the shopping episode. When one shops at the store, much of the planning occurs right in the store where the product displays remind the consumer of what is needed.

The most decisive "cost" of e-shopping is on the emotional side, not on the rational side. Shopping for groceries on the screen provides very little stimulation of the senses (stimulation of the senses). You can't see, touch, or smell the products. The lack of visual stimulation also leads to insufficient variety in consumption. All this implies that consumers have to combine their virtual shopping in varying degrees with shopping in the supermarket and the specialty store.

The framework presented here for understanding why people shop on the Internet and what holds them back from doing so should be helpful for firms entering grocery e-retailing and those already in the e-business.

As has been pointed out, there are ample opportunities for providers of e-retailing services to improve their efficiency for consumers. More efficient e-shopping formats would most probably speed up the adoption of online shopping of groceries since there are huge categories of consumers who are time-pressed and need convenience of the type that e-shopping could offer.

On the other hand, there are limitations that are of a more enduring character. These are emotional limitations inherent in the digital channel. It may take time before the virtual grocery store can offer the same stimulation for the senses as does the physical store. This caveat brings us to the question: Will there be a need for modifying the total grocery shopping system (physical and electronic) as a consequence of the emerging e-retailing format? According to the reactions from our interviewees, the e-store has certain competitive advantages in the case of basic products, while the physical store has an advantage when it comes to different kinds of fresh produce and specialties. There is also a need for a showroom function as well as an interactive consultant, both provided by the traditional store but not yet by the online supermarket. What new combinations could satisfy these needs in an efficient way?

QUESTIONS FOR DISCUSSION

1. Based on the Swedish experiences with Internet grocery shopping, what lessons can be drawn for (1) the United States and Canada, where most people drive to the grocery store and where packing services are provided by the store, (2) Japan, where people use a combination of supermarkets and convenience stores, and (3) emerging countries, where the affluent consumers can often get hired help for grocery shopping?

2. As the e-tailing format gains wider acceptance for groceries, what changes is it likely to induce in physical formats of grocery retailing?

3. In technological terms as well as design and human terms, what can be done to make grocery shopping Web sites more interactive in terms of providing advice, answers to customer questions, special assistance, and other services that a physical store could provide?

4. What are some of the possible ways to reduce the monotony of online shopping for groceries, to build some excitement into such shopping, and to introduce new products and ideas (such as recipes) using the online format?

8

Evolution of Web-Based International Marketing: Patterns Exhibited by Danish Companies

Morten Rask

Companies that act internationally do not usually make the transition from traditional marketing to full-blown Web marketing in one step. In a study of Web strategies of Danish firms, it was found that Danish companies go through three evolutionary stages: (1) the electronic brochure, (2) the electronic manual, and (3) the electronic store. moving from the brochure, to the manual, to the store stage entails an increasing intensity of interaction between the company's Web site and its customers. To handle the rising degree of interaction intensity, companies go through a learning process. The corporate organization has to evolve to meet the demands of increasing Web-based interactions. These demands are discussed in terms of automation, formalization, integration, and evaluation.

INTRODUCTION

What is Web-based marketing? It is as much about relating to customers as it is about staying competitive. In this chapter marketing is understood as the process of managing effective interactions with current customers and initiating interactions with new, potential customers. Today, such interactions take place via traditional methods (face-to-face, phone, fax) as well as through the Web. As a general rule we can state that the more interactive the corporate Web site, the more opportunities that it offers for implementing the firm's marketing strategy. Numerous authors have classified Web marketing strategies. Many of these classifications are in terms of the technology that makes different types of interactions possible. For example, Quelch and Klein (1996) classify Web sites according to whether they offer information, support, service, or transactions. Others have categorized Web sites according to whether they create Internet presence, provide content, or constitute an online storefront (Hoffman, Novak, and Chatterjee 1995; Peters 1998).

In this chapter, the categorization of corporate Web sites is not based on technological differences but on the level of interaction intensity offered by the site and the demands that such interaction places on the internal organization of the firm. A Web site's interaction intensity is characterized by its primary purpose, which ranges from the electronic brochure (minimal interaction), to the electronic manual (moderate interaction), to the electronic store (maximum interaction). A firm can follow several of these Web site strategies at the same time. In such a case, the dominant purpose is used to characterize the interaction type and Web strategy of the firm.

Web-based interaction is a two-way street. Customers learn about the company, its products, and its policies. Simultaneously, the Web marketer learns what the customer learns while browsing the Web site. In an international setting, effective Web-based marketing should encourage customers to learn about the company in a "proper" way. For example, an appropriate learning sequence for international customers would be one where they first read about the company's profile, then learn about its products and services, and finally contact the firm to set up a sales meeting. When we look at this process from the perspective of the company that establishes a Web site geared to its international markets, the critical task is to learn what the customers have learned. This can be done by Web site traffic analysis. Such an analysis generates reports that provide information about the visitors of the Web site, answering questions such as, When do they visit, where do they visit from, and what do they do during the visit to the site?

In Scandinavian countries, internationalization of companies has traditionally been seen as a learning process about international markets and international operations (Johanson and Vahlne 1977). The Internet provides new strategic as well as new learning opportunities during the internationalization process. The following sections explore some of the implications of the Internet for the internationalization process.

Instant Internationalization

The internationalization process is traditionally seen as an incremental process of global expansion. A company that is internationalizing moves from its home market to a geographically or psychically proximate market. Subsequently, it advances farther and explores distant markets and at last may become a global company. With the Internet, the process looks different. When a company establishes a Web site in a widely spoken international language, it becomes, in principle, a global company. However, the company cannot be everything to everybody: it needs to focus. The Internet-based internationalization process can be characterized as *decremental*. Such a process starts in the global arena, focusing on "being everything" to a limited number of customers. In a sense, then, the conventional process and the Internet-based internationalization process form total opposites. In an incremental internationalization process, the company decides how it should expand from being a local player, to being a global player. In the decremental process, it has to decide how to come down from a global, all-encompassing position (represented by the first Web site), to a well-targeted, specific market position.

The Internet alters the perception of distances and thus directly influences a company's internationalization process. Earlier, physical distances in time and space were key dimensions in defining what international business was all about–a company became international when it began to transact with customers across national borders. Today, even for companies that do not (or do not want to) make cross-border transactions, the reality of globalization is inescapable: the Web knows no boundaries. Furthermore, because collecting market information at a low cost is now feasible, knowledge about promising markets outside the home market is created, thereby leading to an increase in international transactions. For example, in the mid-1990s, a college bookstore in California started selling books on the Web even before Amazon.com, and it found a ready market in Japan for its collection of *Manga* comics and books on Japanese prints.

Distances, however, are not merely geographic. Cultural differences and differing national regulations also create "distances," even when two countries are in geographic proximity (as in the case of the United States and Mexico, or Italy and Slovenia). Such borders do not disappear when the Internet enters the scene. The psychic distances in terms of differences in language and cultural background and differences in political-economical contexts continue to remain barriers to Internet-based internationalization. Even in the age of the Internet, international actors have to understand such differences in order to manage the company's internationalization process.

This chapter focuses on how Danish companies use the Web as a new marketing tool. On one hand, the Web makes their internationalization process different from what they were used to in the past. On the other hand, Danish companies may still face the old barriers to international expansion and have to work hard to eliminate such barriers. The Internet assists in internationalization, but it is not a magic bullet.

THE DANISH CONTEXT

The Danish economy is small and open–and Danish companies have always been forced to have an international orientation. Exports and continuing internationalization of the company are the preconditions for growth and survival. Therefore, it is no surprise that the first Danish companies that used the Internet and the World Wide Web had a strong international orientation. According to the Global Digital Marketing Index, Denmark scores very high and ranks number 7 just after the United States (Bishop 1999). Approximately 50 percent of all Danish Web sites have English as the primary language (Economist 1999; OECD 1999). Because of their deep commitment to internationalization, Danish companies can provide us with some valuable insights for understanding the evolution of Web-based international marketing.

The remainder of the chapter presents the findings of two empirical studies–a longitudinal study and a cross-sectional study.[9] The longitudinal study monitored 43 Danish companies and their use of the Web at four times, starting from November 1996. It was repeated in October 1997, July 1998, and July

1999. These 43 Danish companies were representative of Danish firms using the Web for international marketing. On a global scale, Danish companies are relatively small, and so are the companies in these two studies, with a few exceptions. The median size of the companies was 400 employees; the smallest had only 1 employee, and the largest had 217,000. In terms of annual sales, the median was $168 million. Their Web sites were in English or another foreign language, and their addresses and phone/fax numbers were represented in an international way, that is, with a definition of their country and the international dialing codes. The Web sites of the 43 companies were downloaded and described. In 1996, the sample contained 43 Danish companies, but because over the years some companies had gone out of business, were bought up, or ceased their international Web-oriented activities, only 37 were retained for the final monitoring process in 1999. The study concerns both industrial and service companies, from the private sector as well as the public sector. The companies studied can be classified as Internet service providers, IT-services, Web design, industrial machinery, beverage, banking, magazines, cleaning solution, power supply, medicine, consulting, ports, hearing aid, commercial councils, pumps, shipping, credit cards, toys, pipelines, modems, network cards, software, weather forecasting, directory publishing, dating agency, telecom, museums, airports, and records.

From this longitudinal study, the three main interaction types–electronic brochure, electronic manual, and electronic store–were developed. These interaction types were used in a cross-sectional study of manufacturing companies in the North Jutland region of Denmark (Rask 1999). The questionnaire was sent to 110 Danish industrial firms in January 1999. The response rate was 47 percent. There was a wide dispersion in terms of size of firms and in terms of exports as a percentage of total sales. The average size of the firms was 118 employees. The smallest company in the sample consisted of 3 and the largest of nearly 1,000 employees. In terms of export share of total sales, the average was 62 percent; the smallest export share was 5 percent and the largest was 98 percent.

A Typology for International Web-Based Marketing

Based on these studies, we can derive three types of learning. First, these studies allow us to develop the three-category typology for Web-based international marketing. Second, the three interaction types represent stages in the expansion of the companies' international marketing on the Web. Third, these studies allowed us to assess the priority of these interaction types for various firms.

After analyzing the 43 Web sites over the three-year period, it was possible to outline three ideal types of *interaction* for international marketing on the Web: the electronic brochure, the electronic manual, and the electronic store.

When using the *electronic brochure* strategy, the company's aim is to inform its potential customers about its strengths. The company expects the customer to pick up the message and hopes that the customer will contact the

Table 8.1
Evolution of Interaction Types over Three Years

Brochure 99	Manual 99	Store 99
3D-Video Produ.	Berendsen COM	CapaCity Soft.
Araneum	Cabinplant	Copenhagen Airport
Belle Systems	Carlsberg	CTW
Den Danske Bank	GRUNDFOS	DataCompagniet
Engineering Weekly	ISS	DMI
Kampsax	Jyske Bank	Hugin Expert
LEC	Lasat	Kraks Forlag
NESA	Nordisk Wavin	LEGO
PBS	Olicom	Maersk Line
Port of Aalborg	Oticon	Novo Nordisk
TofKo	Port of Aarhus	Tele Danmark
	Ramboll	Tycho Brahe Planetarium
		Voices Of Wonder
		Aalborg Commercial Council

company. The Web furthers the internationalization of the firm as information about the company disseminates all over the world.

When using the *electronic manual* strategy, the company tries to guide the customer in using the company's products and services. The company expects that Web-based product and service guides will enhance the customer experience and engender a great deal of satisfaction with the company and its products and services. In the traditional setting, the internationalization process can be very resource-intensive–demanding a lot of communication effort and travel. The Web site relieves some of these pressures and thus allows the company to project a more global presence without the customer's feeling that the company is "far away."

When using the *electronic store* strategy, the company aims at persuading the customers to use (or buy) its products and services. The Web site of the company is its global store, and the company is usually thoroughly globalized. With a Web-based global store, the market possibilities of the firm are not constrained by its geographical localization.

The intensity of Web-based interaction between buyers and sellers varies across these three interaction types. Interactions at the electronic brochure type of Web site are primarily based on giving information about the company and its products. With the electronic brochure strategy, the interaction ends when the current or potential buyer has read the information, unless the buyer chooses to contact the company. The electronic manual strategy is based upon guiding the buyers in solving their problems. The level of interaction intensity is higher than with the electronic rochure strategy but not as complex as with the electronic store strategy. Web-based guidance implies that buyers actually depend on the assistance provided by the company's Web site. If the explanations on the Web site are inadequate, then buyers' problems can get exacerbated. The electronic store has the highest intensity of interaction. Such interactions entail a very complex process to persuade and enable a customer to buy and/or use the product.

RESULTS

In 1996, approximately 50 percent of the 43 firms used the electronic brochure strategy. The electronic manual and the electronic store strategies each accounted for about 25 percent. In July 1999, the picture had changed. Table 8.1 shows that in 1999 each of the three types of interactions represented approximately a third of the sample. Many of the companies using the electronic manual or the electronic store strategies in 1999 had upgraded their Web sites from a lower level of interaction intensity. It is remarkable that only one company had ratcheted down its interaction intensity.

One would expect that the companies would start by using the electronic brochure strategy and over time increase the interaction intensity as they learn how to handle the new Web-based marketing channels. However, not all companies are able to use the electronic store strategy because they have products that cannot easily be sold on the Web, if at all. Overall, Table 8.1 shows that, over time, companies gradually increased their interaction intensity. This is a natural consequence of the learning process. The complexity of the learning process varies from company to company, and such learning makes varying demands on the companies. It is also important to observe that many companies did not change their Web interaction type before 1999. This shows that it takes time to overcome the challenges of Internet-based international marketing and to assemble the resources to upgrade to a higher interaction level.

Priorities Assigned to Interaction Types

The prioritization of the interaction types was studied in the cross-sectional study, which showed that 8 out of 10 companies intended to have a

Table 8.2
The Companies' Purpose with the Web Site Compared to the Results

If the purpose is ↓ - then the result will be →	Increased company recognition	That the company is not perceived as "far away" by the company's contacts	Better customer service	Increased sale	Number of Firms	Frequency	Interaction type
A business card on the Internet	89%	70%	68%	68%	37	84%	
An information channel for customers, because it increases recognition	91%	74%	69%		35	80%	Bro-chure
An image-creating effect, because the company's Internet address is used in advertising	91%	76%	70%		33	75%	
To relieve the pressure on the company, in a way that the customer does not feel that the company is "far away"	92%	81%	77%		26	59%	Manual
That the customer can easily use the company's products or services	100%	81%		81%	16	36%	Store

Web site by the end of 1999, which corroborates the findings of a nationwide survey of Danish firms (Forskningsministeriet 1999). The cross-sectional survey also showed a positive relationship between the level of experience with a Web site and the size of export share: the more Web-savvy firms had greater export shares. Interestingly, the size of the company did not have any obvious relation to the degree of experience with a Web site. Smaller firms, thus, could outdo their larger rival by being more Web-savvy.

When the companies were asked about the purpose of their Web site, the consensus was that Web sites were not merely a way of advertising the company and its offerings. The purpose was also to relieve the pressure on resources. With a good Web site, a company could project a more global presence without its customers' feeling that the company is remote. These companies were also asked about the results that they obtained from their Web sites. The consensus was that the Web sites had very positive impact in terms of customer service, customer satisfaction, and sales and that the Internet had resulted in a strong expansion of the market opportunities abroad.

To probe the relationships between the purpose and the result of the companies' international Web marketing, two descriptive factor analyses were carried out. Tables 8.2 and 8.3 show the results of these analyses. These tables show how the "five purposes of Web sites" relate to the "four results from websites." In table 8.2, the percentages reflect the number of companies that reported a given "Web site purpose" as having high or some importance and at the same time strongly or partly agreeing with a given "Web site result." In Table 8.3, the percentages reflect the number of companies that strongly or partly agree with a given "Web site result" and at the same time had given the states "Web site purpose" a high or some importance. In both tables, 60 percent was the limiting value: the "Web site purposes" and "Web site results" scoring lower than 60 percent are not listed. The column named "Number of Firms" in table 2 shows the number of companies that explained a given purpose as having high or some importance. In Table 8.3, the "Number of Firms" gives the number of companies that strongly or partly agree with a given result. The frequency column presents the number of firms as percentage of the total number of companies in the analysis.

Table 8.2 shows five purposes grouped in three interaction types. It appears that the electronic brochure is the most important strategy, as 8 of 10 companies recognize the related purposes as having high or some importance. The electronic manual is the second most important strategy, recognized in 6 of 10 companies. Finally, the electronic store strategy is recognized in only 4 of 10 companies.

This priority of the interaction types in a purpose perspective can also be found when comparing results and purpose, as shown in Table 8.3. However, a smaller difference is found between the purposes and the results of the Web sites. Actually, 5 out of 10 companies had experienced increased sales based upon their Web site, where only 4 out of 10 had that same purpose.

Organizational Impact of the Web Marketing Strategies

The findings showed that the electronic brochure, electronic manual, and electronic store are prototypical concepts that capture the companies' strategies in international marketing on the Web. The concepts are also expressions of the stages that the companies go through when they expand their international marketing on the Web. Finally, it is shown that the companies prefer interaction types with a low, rather than a high, level of intensity. International marketing on the Web is a learning process, and the Danish companies are still in the initial phases of the learning process. Table 8.4 summarizes the findings of this chapter and outlines the demands that the three prototypical stages make on the corporate organization.

Table 8.3
The Companies' Results from the Web Site Compared to the Purpose

If the result is ↓ - the company had the purpose→	To have an information channel to customers	To relieve the pressure on the company	To have an image-creating effect	To have a business card on the Internet	That the customer can easily use the companies' products or services	Number of Firms	Frequency	Interaction type
Increased company recognition	91%	69%	86%	94%		35	80%	Bro-chure
That the company is not perceived as "far away"	93%	75%	89%	93%		28	64%	Manual
Better customer service	89%	74%	85%	93%		27	61%	
Increased sale				100%	62%	21	48%	Store

In Table 8.4, "action, expectation, and result" address the definition of the interaction type. "Automation and formalization" refer to the processes involving individuals within and outside the company. "Integration" is a condition for automation and refers to the degree of cooperation between the various departments of a company. "Evaluation" refers to the possible methods for understanding the actions of the Web site users. Table 8.4 shows that the three interaction types make very different demands on the corporate organization:

- When using the electronic brochure strategy, the marketing department should be able to routinely collect the needed information from the rest of the organization and to publish such information in a hypertext format on the Internet. Understanding the impact of this strategy is made possible by Web site traffic analysis reports: information about the patterns of who visits the Web site, when they visit, where they visit from, and what they do during the visit to the site.
- When using the manual strategy, the marketing department should coordinate and the competence centers (i.e., customer service, technical support, etc.) should create added value by automating and formalizing the customer contact processes. The evaluation of this strategy's impact is based upon comparing the customer's inquiries with the profile of the same customer as well as compared with the customer's satisfaction with the product and general performance of the company. These data should be understood in the perspective of the amount of resources used on the current customer.

Table 8.4
International Marketing on Web–Concepts for Awareness and Action

	Brochure	**Manual**	**Shop**
Intensity of interaction	Low	Middle	High
Action	Information	Guidance	Usage of product/service
Expectation	The customer acquires information	Increase in customer satisfaction	The customer uses the company's product/service
Result	Increase the company recognition	The company is not "far away"	Market opportunities are independent of geography
Automation and Formalization	Routine promotion in hypertext format	Parts of the company's customer contact (except sales)	Existing and new sales process focusing on product or service descriptions and ordering
Integration	Marketing/sales function	Marketing/sales coordinate the contributions from the centers of competencies	The whole company
Evaluation	Simple interaction analyses by statistical tools	Comparison of customer inquiries, profiles and the used resources plus customer satisfaction analyses	Actual sale combined with evaluation as the two other interaction types

- When using the electronic store strategy, the marketing department should coordinate the sales process, and the rest of the company should support this process. Especially, obtaining support from the finance departments and logistical units could be very important. The main understanding of this strategy's impact is measured in Web-based turnover and return of investment. These figures can be compared with the evaluation results created in the electronic brochure and manual strategies.

Given the complexity of the organizational learning process, especially for the electronic store stage, it is understandable why Danish companies were still in the initial phases of a Web-based internationalization strategy in 1999. First of all, the interaction type with a lower level of interaction intensity places fewer demands on the internal organization than interaction types with higher levels of interaction intensity. Second and maybe even more important, feedback possibilities are not as developed in the electronic brochure strategy as in the electronic manual and the electronic store strategies. Thus, it can be difficult to show the value of the Web development work. The recognition of the importance of international marketing on the Web is not easily visible to the rest of the organization. Therefore, it can be difficult to gain the organizational support and the needed resources for expanding the strategy to interaction types with a higher level of intensity. In addition, it can be even more difficult to get the whole organization's interest and participation in the learning process.

MANAGERIAL IMPLICATIONS AND FUTURE RESEARCH

The chapter has shown that, in terms of international Web marketing strategies, Danish companies use three types of interactions: electronic brochure, electronic manual, and electronic store. Danish companies have been going through a learning process as to how to handle the challenges and opportunities of international Web marketing and how to increase the intensity of Web-based interactions over time. It is, however, still the electronic brochure strategy–the one with the lowest level of interaction intensity–that has the highest priority. The second in terms of priority is the electronic manual strategy, and the final one is the electronic store strategy. One reason for this could be that the three types of interactions entail an escalating set of internal requirements in terms of automation, formalization, integration, and evaluation. Another reason could be that the companies are only in the early stages of getting a grasp of the new decremental, Web-based internationalization process.

More research is needed to understand the organizational learning required for Web-based internationalization and how such learning occurs in different situations. In the meantime, companies can initiate discussions on these issues. Such discussions could focus on the following:

- Which types of products/services are appropriate candidates for international, Web-based marketing?
- What kind and amount of resources are the companies willing to put into Web-based marketing activities?
- How do you benchmark your company's performance on the Web against the best practices in your industry?

One approach to determine the industry "best practices" standard is to create a better understanding of country, competitor, and customer conditions related to Web-based international marketing activities. Taking the typology presented in this chapter as a starting point, it is possible to create international Web-based marketing activities that incorporate the interaction type most suited to the firm's resources, products, and prevailing competitive situation. Last but not least, if companies are to learn from their experiences, they need to create systems for continuous monitoring and evaluating of the use of their Web sites.

SUMMARY AND CONCLUSIONS

Generalizing from this study of Danish companies, it is clear that the internationalization process for companies in cyberspace is different from that in physical space. Unlike the physical world, where major investments are required to build international offices and facilities, Web-based internationalization can occur quickly and can be scaled up to rather high levels quite fast. In doing so, however, companies may realize that while they can *reach* a global market through the Web they, do not necessarily have the organizational resources to *serve* a global market in effective ways. This may lead to some scaling back, a kind of decremental process of internationalization. This is especially true for new start-ups: they are born on the Web and start with the view that they are global companies from day one. In time, they have to adjust their international strategy to match their resources and capabilities. The framework of "brochure, manual, and store" orientations presented in this chapter would be of help in adjusting the internationalization strategy of both start-up firms and established firms attempting to internationalize their Web-based activities.

QUESTIONS FOR DISCUSSION

1. What distinguishes the "decremental" process of internationalization from the more conventional incremental process of internationalization?

2. Discuss whether interaction intensity is a good concept for developing a typology of firms' Web strategies. Can you think of alternative approaches?

3. Assuming that globalization will keep accelerating, could you conceive of any reasons that a firm might want to *reduce* its internationalization efforts?

9

Online Auctions:
The Emerging New Electronic Agora

Tobias Lührig and Nikhilesh Dholakia

INTRODUCTION

In the burgeoning world of electronic commerce, a new breed of Internet-aided activity has been gaining momentum. Consider the following:

- From a housewife who dabbled occasionally in part-time jobs, Pamela Corezon has turned into an eBay entrepreneur. She scours the antique shops, yard sales, and flea markets of Southern California looking for interesting items and then puts them up for auction on eBay. On average, the United Parcel Service (UPS) truck makes two stops at her home every day. Pamela–affectionately called "eBay Queen" by her friends–nets about $7,000 a month from her Internet auctions.
- Retro Printworks, a small, high-quality printing company, found that many of its key customers kept asking whether Retro belonged to the new Web-based vertical exchanges in the printing business. Traditional customer relationships that Retro had developed over decades were in the danger of unraveling unless Retro quickly formulated a clear strategy to bid on printing jobs through various "forward" and "reverse" auctions on the Web.
- Steel industry's red-hot portal, e-Steel, was launched as a neutral site that offered a combination of e-commerce services and personalization software. It enabled users to check product availability, post orders, and buy and sell steel–one-to-one, one-to-some, or one-to-all.

The common theme in these examples is the ability of buyers, sellers, or both to engage in an Internet-aided bidding process.

THE IMPACT OF THE INTERNET ON AUCTIONS

Like the physical counterpart, Internet-based auctions come in many flavors. Forward auctions are seller-controlled electronic markets in which the seller seeks bids from multiple buyers. The antiques and collector section of eBay.com is a good example of such a marketplace. These items are rare, and the desire to buy is high. There are buyer-controlled sites where the buyers receive bids from many sellers. In the automobile and computer industries, many "exchanges"–sites that are controlled by groups of companies and offer auctions and other means of transacting to their suppliers–are growing. There are also so-called reverse auctions. On www.demandline.com small businesses can request a product or service and state the maximum price that they are willing to pay. The site aggregates the demand nationwide and runs a reverse auction in order to achieve the lowest price possible. An auction site for restaurant supply and services–www.restaurantmarket.com–does the same but aggregates the demand on a local level. The difference here is that the buyer receives the company profiles of the five best bidders and can choose one of them. Finally, there are neutral Internet sites, such as e-Steel, that facilitate buyer-seller interactions, including bidding and auctions.

AUCTIONS

The fastest actions in auction in the world is often not at the places where we expect it. It is not at Sotheby's, it is not at eBay, it is not at FreeMarkets, it is not even online, yet! Consider the following (van Heck 2000). Nearly 60 percent of the world's cut flowers are sold each year in a large complex near the airport in Amsterdam, Holland. Almost 34 million flowers and 3 million potted plants are traded in 60,000 transactions each day. Most flowers are flown to one of the several auction arenas. The largest could cover 100 soccer fields and host 2,500 buyers. After change of ownership the flowers are rushed back to the airport and shipped to the destination specified by the buyer. The key process is an auction mode called "Dutch auction." Unlike the more common English auction, in which bidders push the price in increments from a low opening bid, no actual bidding is involved in a Dutch auction. When a large quantity of easily evaluated goods must be sold quickly, the Dutch method is ideal. In the flower auction halls, big "clocks" are installed, with a needle pointing to the price at any time. In front of each bidder's seat is a big button. The first bidder to signal with the button can stop the needleand, fix the price, and the auctioned lot is shipped to its new destination. Behavioral researchers have shown that this auction mode tends to generate higher prices. Because everybody has only one chance to bid, the desire to avoid losing a particular lot motivates bidders to stop the "clock" at a higher price than they would have offered in a competitive bidding like the English style. Besides generating higher prices for the seller, the Dutch auction is extremely fast.

Other companies have recognized this advantage of the Dutch auction and adopted it. E-businesses like FreeMarkets run Dutch auctions several times a day in *seller-controlled markets* with many buyers. Intermodalex.com sells free container space for oceangoing vessels. Like flowers, container space is easy to evaluate. Only four dimensions need to be known for bidding on container space: destination, departure, space, and price. Besides the Dutch auction, several other auction modes can be found (see Figure 9.1). In a reverse auction, which is particularly interesting for *buyer-controlled markets*, the buyer names the ceiling price of the item to be sold, and the sellers bid for the lowest price under the specified ceiling that they hope will get them the item.

Figure 9.1
Types of Auctions and Marketplaces

English Auction: Starting from a low opening price, bidders push the price in increments until only one bidder remains who wants to take the item at the bid price. Given:

Dutch Auction: An auction mode in which the price starts with a high price set by the auctioneer and drops in increments until a buyer signals that he or she will take the item. Given:

Reverse Auction: Buyer names the item and its maximum price. Sellers bid for the lowest price to get the deal. Given:

Seller-Controlled Marketplaces: A single vendor seeking many buyers usually sets these up. The aim of such a marketplace is to create or retain value and market power in any transaction.

Buyer-Controlled Marketplaces: These are set up by one or more buyers with the aim of shifting power and value in the marketplace to the buyer's side. Many involve an intermediary, but some particularly strong buyers have developed marketplaces for themselves. Example: GlobalNetXChange, set up by a group of American and European retailers.

Why the Internet Is Ideal for Auctions

Until about 150 years ago, most trading took place in open marketplaces or bazaars in which prices moved continuously, and it was easy to check up on competitors by peeking over to the next retail stall. Physical and information barriers, however, prevented a transparent national or global market. Outside of small local areas, price abnormalities existed, and market price could not reach equilibrium. Now the Internet seems to be creating the possibility of a permanent, worldwide bazaar in which no prices are ever fixed for long, information is instantly available, and buyers and sellers spend their lives haggling to get the best deals. The Internet makes it possible to generate different pricing mechanisms. In particular, it allows price and product comparisons to be made and various kinds of auctions and exchanges to take place! Any believer in Adam Smith's ideas must welcome the kaleidoscope of different web-based auctions that are becoming available the world over.

LESSONS FROM eBAY

eBay has nearly 20 million registered users bidding for some 5 million items. Each user spends nearly two hours a month on the site. In late 1999, eBay boasted a brand recognition of 91 percent in the United States. It attracted 10.5 million unique visitors to its site. From 1998 to 1999, the growth rate of traffic in terms of unique visitors was 141 percent. eBay's charges are typically no more than 7.5 percent, compared with over 25 percent for offline auctioneers. Within three years eBay has become the world's leading auction company, in the offline as well as the online world. It took 3.5 years after founding of the company to reach the $100 million sales barrier, and there is no end in sight.

McKinsey's Three Cs–Fundamentals for eBay

We can examine the success of eBay using the three Cs–fundamental success factors that McKinsey & Co. believes all successful e-businesses should have. The three Cs are:

- **Content:** Whatever appears on the Web page should be dynamically pinpointed to demands and expectations of the individual page visitor. On the site of MLP, a German financial consulting firm of academics for academics, all individual financial details of a client such as health insurance rate, car insurance, liquidity, and retirement plans are viewable. Individual interests and demands are employed to filter news items. Clients fix their strategic and tactical financial goals with the help of an MLP consultant and an "electronic assistant" that offers products and services matching the client's needs and rate comparisons. Automatic alert functions allow the client to change the insurance company if other providers start offering better rates or services.
- **Community:** Through site-to-user and user-to-user interactivity, the provider can create a dedicated community of mutually supporting members. The British site vavo.com is specialized on people over 45 years. The site enhances user-to-user interactivity in various ways. Members can build their own Web pages, open and join their own interest groups in a chat room, and use various news boards. Vavo.com also boosts site-to-user interactivity by offering help with family or class.
- **Commerce:** The Web site provider must synergistically manage all activities that generate incoming cash flow, be it through selling goods, subscription revenue, or advertising. Classical examples of such sites are search engines or Web catalogs like Excite or Yahoo! After entering the searched word the first lines of the output are links to preferred partners or own commercial activities. Entering the search word, "Beatles," for example, generates the first set of links to books, comact discs (CDs,) or auctions about "Beatles." Clicking and buying products or services "behind" these links generate revenues for the portal as well as for the merchant to whom the link takes the user.

In case of eBay, not only the three Cs of McKinsey but also several other success factors associated with e-commerce are evident.

Content

eBay offers a huge and eclectic variety of categorized items for auction (Poole 2000). This content is dynamic and contributed by millions of sellers. eBay needs only a relatively small staff to manage this content. Most of the categories are filled with many items so that it is always interesting for a visitor to look for desired items, to check out market values of various items, or simply to browse. With My-eBay, a personalization tool is provided for those who visit eBay frequently.

Figure 9.2
The Five Digital Promises

Promise of Convenience: Brands that promise to get the best products, at cheapest prices, and fastest delivery. Examples: Major eBrands such as Amazon.com and Buy.com.

Promise of Achievement: Brands that let the customer feel like a winner. Example: E*trade.

Promise of Fun and Adventure: Games or spectacular events employing "immersive" technology thrill the users. Example: Quokka Sports.

Promise of Self-Expression: Provding the customers with opportunities to express and display themselves and their interests. Examples: GeoCities and Epinions.

Promise of Belonging : Creating a community with vibrant user-to-user. Examples: iVillage.com and Mercata.com.

Source: Adapted from *Net Business* (April 2000: 10)

Community

All auction eBay participants create the huge eBay community. eBay provides feedback functions on its site for each participant. For example, besides the user name of every eBay member, information about how experienced and trustworthy the participant is and the number of successful auctions by the member is provided. A second tool is a rating system. After a successful transaction, the buyer and the seller can rate their transactional partner by awarding quality points. This average quality point score is displayed close to the member name, accessible to everyone.

Commerce

The business model of eBay is simple but powerful. Revenue comes from two main sources. eBay generates cash flow with 7.5 percent commissions on successful auctions. The second source of revenue is banner advertising on its site.

Digital Promises of eBay

Successful e-brands are based on some digital promises (see Figure 9.2). Out of the five digital promises in Figure 9.2, eBay delivers at least two. Many features of the eBay system make it easy to set up an auction and sell off unwanted belongings or auction off desired collectibles. eBay fulfills not only the promise of convenience but also the promise of achievement.

Table 9.1
Emerging Range of B2B Transaction Systems

Business Model	Characteristics	Examples of Firms
Business Portals	Firms that pool resource to create industry-focused content, community, and trading systems	VerticalNet, Earthweb
Procurement Solution Vendors	Provide software or portal-based solutions to help streamline the internal and external work flow of client companies, including procurement tasks	Ariba, CommerceOne, Oracle, SAP, MRO.com
Catalog Aggregators	Create searchable databases, trading systems, and online catalogs focused on specific industries or niches	Chemdex, Netbuy, PlasticsNet, SciQuest
Reverse Auctions	Allow buyers to post RFPs and let sellers bid on buyers' needs	FreeMarkets, Visteon
Vertical Auctions	Focus on particular industries and allow sellers and buyers of post their trading needs and facilitate bidding	Adauction.com, FastParts, CattleOfferings.com
Vertical Exchanges	Create neutral, real-time, two-way negotiation process for companies dealing in commodity or near-commodity goods	Altra energy, e-Steel
Horizontal b2b Sites	Firms specializing in transactions focused on specific business processes (buying, shipping, project management)	BidCom, iShip, Celarix

Source: Adapted from b2b articles by Nathan Beckford on RagingBull.com (1999)

Critical Mass

One of the most important goals for an auction-based business is to achieve a critical mass in terms of users and revenue. This is doubly so for an Internet auction since the competition is intense, and the window of time available to reach a critical mass is rather short. Reaching the critical mass requires a sufficient supply of interesting auctions as well as a sufficient cash flow to cover operating, marketing, and customer acquisition costs. By creating the world's largest online, one-to-one trading community, eBay has been very successful in grabbing a nearly 10 percent share of the online auction market.

First-Mover Advantage

As in any other business, market players who enter a market first have the so-called first-mover advantage, long-term studies have shown that first movers are, on average, more successful than second movers. With its 1995 launch, eBay was one of the first e-commerce sites focused on consumer-to-consumer transactions. Later entrants in this field, such as OnSale, have had a hard time countering eBay's first-mover advantage.

Market Leadership

Auction sites like eBay have reached such a magnitude that it will be very difficult and expensive to pass their market share. Because of its high market share, a market leader such as eBay can enjoy the biggest scale effect and benefit the most from market growth. Long-term studies have shown that market leaders generate the highest value on average.

Network Effect and Attractiveness of Scale

Another strong factor affecting the performance of Information Age and e-commerce firms is the phenomenon of positive network effects. For most such firms, each new user gains from the existence of the previously established network of users. Also, the value of the network for each existing user increases as new users join in. In the case of eBay, the more people who use its auctions, the better the site becomes. The rising numbers of eBay users generate a growing tide of content for the site. This growing content, in turn, attracts more people to the site.

BUSINESS-TO-BUSINESS AUCTIONS

Business-to-business auctions are part of the evolving multitrillion-dollar b2b (business-to-business), Internet-based market systems. Table 9.1 shows the range of b2b, Internet-based business-to-business transaction systems. Auctions are either explicitly or implicitly a feature of many of these b2b systems. FreeMarkets is one of the leading b2b marketplaces. The company lets buyers post requests for proposals (RFPs), and allows vendors to bid for the business. By streamlining the information flow and assisting with RFPs and vendor prequalifications, FreeMarkets cuts the buyer's cost by 2 percent to 25 percent. The transaction volume at the FreeMarkets site was U.S.$ 2.7 billion in 1999. FreeMarkets conducts online auctions for industrial parts, raw materials, commodities, and services. But what differentiates a b2b auction from a c2c (consumer-to-consumer) auction?

Besides reducing the need for printed promotional material, two main arguments can be made as to why b2b sites such as FreeMarkets are useful for their business users:

- **Supply chain management** Enterprise Resource Planning (ERP) systems like SAP, PeopleSoft, and Baan are already used by many businesses to monitor order flow, stock on hand, and the billing process. b2b auction sites can provide additional help in terms of analyzing and optimizing the supply chain. b2b auction sites and "exchanges" can provide an interface to vendors through the whole supply chain. Using such interfaces, many buying procedures can be automated via the Internet. An Internet-based front-end and back-end in such an ERP not only saves labor cost but also makes the buying processes more transparent and faster. SAP, for example, promises that 25 percent of administration costs can be reduced, on average through the introduction of itssystems. Links to b2b auction portals can augment such savings.

- **Price reduction.** Depending on the market type, buyers can realize lower prices in buyer-controlled markets, or vendors can realize higher prices in seller-controlled markets. Such price improvements will have an immediate and direct effect on the bottom line of either buyers or sellers. Of course, because of higher price transparency and enhanced competition, there will be more instances of price reduction than of price improvement in b2b marketplaces.

In the b2b markets, auctions have taken root very rapidly. A main reason– at least in the initial phase of such developments–is the cost savings that both sellers and buyers are able to realize in comparison with the old, expensive, pre-Internet ways of doing business. In the future, b2b auctions may become the dominant way of doing business, pushing prices and margins to the bare bones, and sellers will have to be very creative to extract premiums for brands or superior service.

IMPACT OF INTERNET AUCTIONS ON BRICK-AND-MORTAR WORLD

The more people who are attracted by Internet auctions, the more such auctions will affect business practices of the brick-and-mortar world. But the magnitude of the impact will be much bigger for the b2b than for the b2c (business-to-consumer) world. This is because in the b2b sectors, there are immediate and very substantial costs savings achievable through auctions and exchanges (Krauss 2000). Electronic auctions will alter the physical marketplace in various ways. In the paragraphs to follow, we provide some thoughts about the impact of Internet auctions on the physical world of commerce.

Rivalry in the Industry

In businesses where an easy-to-evaluate product or service is offered, the transition to electronic marketplaces with various kinds of auctions (or exchanges) will occur fast. In such cases products, services, and prices will become increasingly transparent, and therefore the rivalry in such industry sectors will very likely intensify.

Prices

Because prices in such cases are variable, and the speed of change is very fast, the price of a product or service will come to depend on basic supply-and-demand conditions, and approach the ideal of a perfect market.

Prices in Seller-Controlled Marketplaces

In such marketplaces, Dutch and English auctions will be most popular. Prices will probably evolve toward supply-and-demand equilibrium. The strategy of the buyers will be to accumulate their buying power into bigger entities in order to reduce prices and gain some market power.

Prices in Buyer-Controlled Marketplaces

Reverse auctions will be the most popular in such marketplaces. The rivalry among the suppliers will intensify, and the price and cost pressures will transmit all the way to the production process and the rest of the supply chain. In order to gain greater market power, we will likely see greater merger and acquisition activity among the suppliers in industries such as automobile and computer component makers. Many companies will exit the market or shift their focus to new areas. Relationship management and after-sales markets will be more important for such players in order to generate sufficient revenue.

Prices in Neutral Marketplaces

Because of an approximate balance in buyer and seller powers, prices in neutral markets may be governed, to some extent, by brand identities and reputations of sellers. Bidding in such markets would be more selective. In case of eSteel, for example, buyers and/or sellers can specify the number, types, and even names of the transacting parties from which they wish to entertain bids. In such cases, relationship management methods will continue to coexist with auctions and price competition.

Shift of Power

In the first wave of the newly evolving, giant Internet b2b and b2c marketplaces, the power is shifting toward the players that already are very powerful. For example, in the automobile industry, General Motors, Ford, and DaimlerChrysler have formed a giant, buyer-controlled marketplace. Suppliers to these automobile companies will obviously be at some disadvantage in the initial phase of such a marketplace. In the second wave or auctions and exchanges, underpowered players would be able to use the same technology to enhance their power. Overall, all these developments would increase competitive rivalry, and the end customer will win. In these new auction-oriented marketplaces, unfocused and inflexible companies will not be the winners and will lose out to nimble and focused rivals.

Strategies for Companies

Increasing rivalry, transparent prices, and bigger markets will lead to market niches' becoming narrower and of great importance to companies. The main challenge will be for each company to develop its individual core competencies in a narrow and focused niche. The upside of the Internet technologies will be that in that niche the company can reach a lot of customers all over the world and enjoy more economies of scale and scope.

SUMMARY AND CONCLUSIONS

With the evolution of c2c online auctions, the classic, informal, c2c activities such as "flea markets" and "yard sales" are facing tremendous new competition. One effect of sites like eBay is to "drag" a large sector of the submerged, informal c2c economy into a mainstream market economy. eBay.com and similar sites show that the transaction inefficiency of these old bazaar like informal markets can be reduced and that new, vastly bigger, formal markets can be created in their place. These effects are dramatic but yet minimal compared to what will happen in the b2b and b2c arenas. Why should potential car buyers not use an Internet auction in order to get their new sprot utility vehicles (SUVs) at the lowest price? Why should somebody go to an antique store or show to sell an heirloom if she or he can auction the same item with less effort and obtain a higher price online? In early 1999, some b2c sites used auctions to attract traffic to their sites. Sometimes businesses sold their products at a loss and declared this as a marketing expense for the Web site and the product. In this way, these firms tested the price-demand curve on a new product before they introduced it to "real" market. With the use of new technologies, the power is shifting increasingly to the powerful market players. Many Internet-driven markets are becoming transparent, more efficient, and faster. Will large numbers of customers buy big-ticket items without aggregating the demand and let vendors bid for their custom? With the Web, more and more products will be traded like commodities, with the consequences of unstable, but transparent, prices. Sellers need to differentiate themselves from their competitors more and more in order to minimize the threat of demand aggregators or underbidding competitors. The upside is that companies can serve bigger markets and utilize their competencies to the fullest extent. These global markets will react faster, but the price volatility will be greater than today. An Internet auction was once a marketing gimmick, but auctions will be a significant component of the future Net-based economy.

QUESTIONS FOR DISCUSSION

1. What strategies should small and medium-sized companies use to avoid the threat of demand aggregators?

2. Can an Internet start-up auction house gain competitive advantage and significant market share in markets where companies such as eBay and FreeMarkets already have pioneering and leadership advantages? If so, how?

3. What are the main reasons that people either use or do not use c2c auction sites?

4. Besides pure auctions, what kinds of other value-added services can c2c and b2c sites provide to enhance their appeal to users?

5. What kind of risks does a company take if buying and selling prices are variable and highly volatile because of extensive use of auctions in its supply chain? What can it do to insulate against such risks?

Part III

Frameworks for Understanding Online Marketing

10

Building Loyalty to Online Stores through Design of Store Attributes

Ruby Roy Dholakia, Kuan-Pin Chiang, Detlev Zwick,
Michele Abbott, and Jerry Paquin

What factors make people loyal or disloyal to online stores? Traditional models of store loyalty provide a good starting point for the understanding of store loyalty in an electronic environment. Because of the uniqueness of the virtual marketplace, however, consumers place a different degree of emphasis on various store attributes as they develop satisfaction with online shopping that leads to online store loyalty.

INTRODUCTION

The Internet has evolved into a hypercompetitive global marketplace. Consumers are the winners because with a few clicks of the mouse they can conveniently compare prices, products, and services across a wide variety of store sites. With such easy and convenient movements across sites, online stores are quite concerned about retaining customers who come to their site and about building consumer loyalty. Online retailers face some critical questions:

- How can store loyalty be achieved and sustained in an online environment?
- What are the dimensions of online store loyalty?
- Are these dimensions different from those found in physical, brick and mortar retailing?

LOYALTY IN A TRANSFORMING RETAIL SECTOR

Over the last century, several developments transformed the retail sector (Christensen and Tedlow 2000). As a result, several types of retail formats today mix electronic and physical store properties in various combinations. There are pure-play Internet retailers such as eToys. We have click-and-brick stores such as Gateway.com and Vitamins.com, as pure-play Internet stores build physical facilities to compete in the total marketspace, not just Internet space. From the other direction, brick-and-mortar stores such as Macy's and Wal-Mart rush to transform themselves into brick-and-click stores. Some predict that fewer and fewer pure brick-and-mortar stores of any substantial size will remain (Fetto 1999).

In the short term, the transforming retail sector offers consumers an expanded choice. In buying books, for example, a consumer can shop at a neighborhood bookstore, at a superstore such as Barnes and Noble or its Internet affiliate, barnesandnoble.com, or at the pure-play Internet retailer Amazon.com. In this dynamic environment, attracting and retaining customers have become a major challenge for existing as well as new retailers.

The Internet, with its low entry barriers for competitors and low searching and switching costs for consumers (Auger and Gallaugher 1997; Klein 1998), is accelerating some of the transformations toward nonphysical store formats (Mulhern 1997). While the costs of searching and switching are low for shoppers in an online environment, attracting customers to shop online for the first time is difficult and expensive. The cost of attracting a new customer can be as much as five times the cost of retaining an existing customer (Peters 1998). Customer acquisition costs are often higher for pure-play, Internet retailers compared to multichannel retailers. Gottlieb (1999) estimated the acquisition cost at U.S.$42 per customer for the online retailer versus U.S.$22 for the multichannel retailer.

To get customers to come back repeatedly is even more imperative. Repeat buyers not only spend more on their subsequent purchase trips but are a primary source of customer referrals. According to a consulting report (Mainspring 2000):

- An average repeat customer spent 67 percent more overall in the third year of his or her shopping than in the first 6 months. For groceries, customers spent 23 percent more in months 31-36 than in the first 6 months.
- On average, each apparel shopper referred 3 people after the first purchase; 7 people after 10 purchases; for consumer electronics, the average customer referred 13 people after 10 purchases.

As online retailing moves into its next phase, where profits become important, repeat customers and loyal customers are even more critical to the success of the online retailer. According to the same research (Mainspring 2000):

- An average customer must shop four times at an online store before the store makes a profit from that customer.
- For online grocers, a customer must continue to shop for 18 months before the online store can break even on that customer.

Store loyalty, therefore, is one of the most important concerns of online retailers. It is not surprising that more than one-third of experienced online retailers are focusing on repeat buyers–the ultimate prize for all retailers (Gottlieb 1999)–and focus is shifting away from transactional metrics like number of visitors, number of shoppers, or number of eyeballs. To emphasize metrics reflecting loyalty and profits, we must first define loyalty and then implement it appropriately within an online environment. While the concepts and experiences from the physical retail world provide some help, in general we have to rethink many of the key concepts of marketing for the online environment (Hoffman and Novak 1997). In this chapter, we discuss ways of extending the ideas of store loyalty to online environments. We highlight the processes by which perceived store attributes affect satisfaction and loyalty in an online environment.

Store Loyalty

When customers show consistency in their feelings toward, beliefs about, and behaviors toward market offerings and suppliers, they strive to maintain exchange relationships with these suppliers (Gilmore and Czepiel 1987). Store loyalty is a result of such attitudinal *and* behavioral consistency. In the physical world, store loyalty is characterized by:

- A favorable disposition toward the store;
- A tendency to visit the preferred store repeatedly, over extended time periods;
- Selection of the preferred store over others when choice exists;
- Psychological commitment to the preferred store based on processing and evaluation of information about that store and its competition.

According to Bloemer and de Ruyter (1998), loyalty to a physical store evolves along the following lines:

Store Attributes → Store Image → Store Satisfaction → Store Loyalty

We discuss each of these constructs that lead to the development of store loyalty in greater detail later. We distinguish two types of processes among customers of online stores–those that *precede* the first purchase and those that *follow* the first purchase.

CREATING THE FIRST PURCHASE

With the diffusion of the Internet to a more broadly representative sample of the U.S. population, shopping has become one of the fastest-growing uses of the Internet. In 1997, 19 percent of the U.S. online users had shopped online; it jumped to 31 percent in 1999 (Crockett 1999). The increasing Net population and the proliferation of Internet sites suggest that the first problem of online retailers is to attract initial shoppers to their site.

Let us look at the process of creating the first purchase depicted in Figure 10.1 in some detail. A consumer may reach a particular online site because of search behaviors that are purposeful (e.g., to buy a specific music compact disc) or nonpurposeful (e.g., Web browsing). The route may be direct and deliberate as a result of seeing/hearing the URL on television, print, or radio advertising or because of a keyword search on AOL. It may be more random and nondeliberate

Figure 10.1
Process of Creating the First Purchase

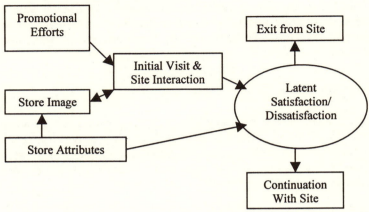

when a user responds to cues online such as banner advertisements, offers for sweepstakes and prizes, and so on.

Promotional Efforts

The initial visit is influenced by the quantity and quality of promotional efforts undertaken by the online retailer as well as by its store image. Promotional efforts-banner advertising, keyword searches, and so on–that successfully lead a consumer to an online store influence subsequent behaviors. Broken links, bandwidth-hogging, media-rich ads can be extremely frustrating and create problems for consumer visits to online stores. A recent survey by Zona Research estimated that e-commerce companies are losing more than U.S.$58 million per month from customers who grow frustrated with Web pages that do not download (Millard 2000). Andersen Consulting found that almost 25 percent of all attempts to purchase an item failed because sites crashed, order forms were corrupted, or goods never arrived. A survey by Software & Information Industry Association found that up to 10 percent of even veteran online shoppers abandoned attempts to purchase online due to a lack of product information (NUA Analysis 2000).

Once consumers enter an online store, they begin forming/strengthening a store image based on the perception of store attributes. A positive experience with the online store site leads to initial or latent satisfaction. This initial or latent satisfaction motivates the consumer to stay at the site and make the first purchase. A negative online experience, on the other hand, leads to rejection of the store and exiting from the online site.

Store Image

The image of a store is a major determinant of first visits; store images are also refined and redefined as the visit continues. Because the consumer regards shopping as a "total experience," it is not just the tangible store benefits (e.g., lower price, greater assortment) that draw consumers to stores; they are also drawn by intangibles (e.g., friendly atmosphere, service experience). Such tangible and intangible attributes, when they are positive, create a favorable image (Martineau 1958).

Store Image = Tangible store attributes + Intangible store attributes

Research suggests that store image affects store loyalty in two ways:

- directly, in the sense that people are more loyal to stores with stronger positive images, and
- indirectly, because a strong store image creates store satisfaction, which, in turn, engenders store loyalty (Bloemer and de Ruyter 1998).

The basic idea is that if consumers have a favorable image of the store, they are likely to develop a certain degree of loyalty (Hirschman 1981; James, Durand, and Dreves 1976; Osman 1993).

Store Attributes

Store attributes or characteristics are a part of a store's retail mix and contribute to the store's image. Store attributes such as accessibility, atmospherics, and product assortment are part of the store's positioning strategy and influence advertising content and style. Macy's and Wal-Mart combine these and other store attributes in different ways; when successful, it leads to differentiation and distinct identities. A great deal of overlap in the store attributes can lead to a blurring of images.

In a regression analysis of selected online store attributes, Lohse and Spiller (1999) found some attributes affecting traffic and a different set of attributes affecting sales. For instance, size of product assortment positively impacts store traffic, but an improved product list has a tremendous effect on sales. It is important to distinguish relevant store attributes and implement them appropriately in an online environment.

COMPARISON OF ATTRIBUTES ACROSS RETAIL FORMATS

Online stores incorporate many of the same attributes as physical stores. Over the years, numerous studies have examined the attributes that are the most critical to the *physical* retail mix and found 8 attributes to be critical: location, store atmosphere, customer service, price, merchandise, personal selling, advertising, and sales incentive programs (Ghosh 1990). Because of the unique nature of the online environment, we have a modified list of 10 attributes critical

Table 10.1
Comparison of Perception on Store Attributes across Retail Formats

Store Attributes	Physical Store	Catalog	Online Store
Geographics and Physical Presence	• Actual geographic location, e.g., mall or stand-alone, suburb or city. • Benefits from physical relationship to other stores.	• Not Applicable (Exception: Catalog retailer has some physical presence. Example: Sharper Image or Brookstone)	• Not Applicable (Exception: Online merchant has some physical presence. Examples: Gateway Country Store, CVS.com and CVS)
Accessibility	• Regional • Affected by distance and available physical infrastructure. • Not always open	• Via telephone • National, even global • Customer must exist on company database • Once on certain databases, likely to receive wide variety of catalogs. • Can "shop" anytime.	• Via computer • Global. • Most commonly found using search engines. • Benefits from hyperlinks and exposure on major portals. • Can "shop" anytime.
Atmospherics	• Store design, store space	• Catalog layout, design and content.	• Site design, site content.
Service/ Experiential Convenience	• Varies - affected by physical display, store traffic, service policies (e.g., lines at check-out, return policies).	• High - can be done from home. • Typically good service policies (e.g., good return policies, search assistance and check-out). • Speed of order processing.	• High - can be done from home. • Typically good service policies (e.g., good return policies, search assistance and check-out). • Speed of communication and order processing.
Speed of Acquisition	• Immediate	• Delayed delivery	• Immediate for digital, delayed for other products.
Price Across Brands	• Relatively difficult to compare prices across stores	• Relatively easy to compare prices across catalogs.	• Exceptionally easy to compare prices across sites.
Assortment	• Varies	• Typically deep selection within narrow categories.	• Typically deep selection within narrow categories.
Security	• High	• Moderate	• Currently lower, but over time people should be more confident.
Information Availability	• Varies	• High	• High
Customization/ Personalization	• Varies - low in discount store, can be high in specialty store	• Some - past purchases affect catalogs sent and future interactions on phone	• Some -past purchases and database record affect interactions. • Very high potential.

to the development of online loyalty: geographics, atmospherics, experiential convenience, price across brands, assortment, accessibility, speed of acquisition, information availability, customization/personalization, and security. Advertising and sales incentive programs are included separately as promotional efforts.

How do store attributes from traditional shopping formats relate to online retail stores? Table 10.1 compares the attributes that are important to the development of store image across three retail formats: physical stores, catalogs, and online stores. The purpose of including catalog shopping is to provide an intermediate shopping format between the two extremes–physical and online. Some attributes are difficult to measure and characterize in online retail stores. Other attributes are still applicable and affect consumers' shopping behavior in an online environment.

ELABORATION OF PERCEIVED STORE ATTRIBUTES

The specific attributes noted in Table 10.1 are described above.

Geographics and Physical Presence

These refer to the specific location of a physical store. Location is a very important attribute for physical stores. Some have suggested that geographics can include the electronic links to online stores. We include such "electronic proximity" in a separate attribute: accessibility. In general, physical location is not a meaningful attribute for an online store and does not affect consumers' perception of the online store. There are exceptions, however. For the catalog and online formats, geographical factors become relevant when some have related physical stores (e.g., Barnes and Noble) and others do not (e.g., Amazon.com).

We have expanded geographics to include physical presence to take into account the variety of retail formats. Consumers may have more awareness and confidence in an online entity with a physical presence. Egghead.com, which had abandoned its physical locations, subsequently rebuilt some of its brick facilities to regain physical presence. When two competitive online retailers differ on this attribute of physical presence–for example, Amazon.com and barnesandnoble.com or CDNow and TowerRecords.com (in both cases the former without a brick component)-they will differ on their respective store image.

Accessibility

This is the ease of reaching the retailer. For traditional stores, accessibility is affected by hours of operation, distance from consumers, and available transportation infrastructure. Catalogs and online stores are accessible in entirely different ways since consumers do not have to leave their homes and can usually reach the retailer at any time. For traditional stores, accessibility is a relatively static attribute. Online stores, on the other hand, can more easily change their accessibility by increasing the number of links or portals through which the consumer can reach them. ArtiSan gifts.com increased its accessibility by being part of Yahoo! Shopping. PalmPilot, for instance, has over 200 links via Web rings, which provide access to its site. Borders bookstores are placing kiosks inside their stores to increase accessibility to its site.

Atmospherics

Atmospherics refer to the store space and design. Retailers use atmospherics to evoke positive emotional reactions among buyers (Solomon 1996). The virtual online shopping environment cannot take advantage of the traditional physical atmospheric qualities. Therefore, atmospherics in this environment consist of the layout and design of the Internet store site. In a report from *Creative Good* (Tedesehi 2000), too many online stores have poor page design, including too much information on individual pages, mandatory filling out of lengthy questionnaires before allowing users to browse through the site and poor or nonexistent product labeling. The report criticized marthastewart.com, for instance, for letting customers add out-of-stock items to the shopping cart without informing them until reaching the final checkout that the items are unavailable. One of the successful examples is provided by DVD Express (dvdexpress.com), a contemporary and cleanly designed Web site offering music and video DVDs. Registered users can navigate the site rapidly, select 'and make their purchase easily, and depart the site once the consumer objective has been achieved (Gottlieb 2000).

Service/Experiential Convenience

This refers to the consumer's perception of the store services, including search assistance, and ease of order processing and returns. In a virtual environment, experiential convenience would also include speed of communication and the nature of user interfaces. While online services excel in terms of search assistance and fast, convenient ordering, they experience problems when customers want to return ordered merchandise or have questions that go beyond the scope of the Web site's database.

Autobytel.com is an internationally branded, Internet-based purchasing program that has successfully addressed the issue of experiential convenience. Since its inception in 1995, Autobytel.com has assisted over 2.5 million car buyers. An easy-to-read user interface helps the automotive shopper navigate the site with very little effort, and e-mail is effectively used to link the shopper with a member of the dealer network (Gottlieb 2000). CVS.com allows online prescription orders to be picked up at stores in addition to delivering directly to the home.

Speed of Acquisition

This is the actual time that it takes to receive the products once the order is placed. In a traditional retail format this is generally immediate, with the consumer walking out of the store with the selected merchandise. There is generally a time lag for catalog and online store orders. For digital products such as news, music, and financial services, online stores can provide immediate delivery.

Speed of acquisition includes time, accuracy, and quality of the order fulfillment program. A customer will never return to a site or refer the site to others if he or she must wait too long for the purchase to arrive, if the incorrect item arrives, or if the product is damaged or never arrives. This need for speed has motivated Amazon.com to use Kozmo to deliver books, music, and toys within 24 hours of order placement in selected markets (Sandoval 2000). Although online store attributes such as accessibility and experiential convenience attract traffic and even generate the first purchase, these are not enough. Order fulfillment, as part of speed of acquisition, is one of the most important aspects of e-commerce (Midgette 1999).

Price across Brands

This refers to the ability to compare prices across brands and between retailers. This is more difficult in traditional formats since it requires significant search time and effort. It is slightly easier for catalog shoppers when they receive multiple catalogs, a common feature given the nature of list management and data sharing among direct marketers. Price comparisons are particularly easy in an online environment since consumers can easily move within and between sites. Priceline.com, for instance, offers grocery shopping with participating retailers. Prices of at least two brands are displayed along with the probabilities of acceptable bid prices. Moreover, there are specialized sites–shopbots–designed to provide price comparisons on the Internet such as zdnet.com or mysimon.com.

Transparency of price has become a major issue of online retailing. When and how the price information is displayed are important; customers are inconvenienced when the prices are viewed only after the product is added to the shopping cart. Taxes and shipping charges have also become more salient in online shopping. According to Forrester, 66 percent of shopping carts were abandoned in 1998 due to complicated instructions or hefty shipping and handling charges. Many cancel the order when they see how much tax and shipping add to the total (Gottlieb 1999). These negative experiences impact the overall image of an online retailer.

Assortment

This refers to the consumer's perception of the range of products carried by the retailer. This varies widely for physical stores, from megastores at one end to specialty stores at the other. Catalogs and online stores typically have deep, but narrow, selections. Lids.com carries only caps. Ross-Simons.com emphasizes jewelry, tableware, and selected gift items. Studies have found that consumers prefer larger stores to smaller ones (Lohse and Spiller 1999) and express disappointment with limited product offerings (Jarvenpaa and Todd 1997). It is understandable why Amazon.com, originally a bookseller, has expanded its product line to include music, video, and toys.

Security

This is the consumer's perception that the transaction is secure and that there is no financial risk associated with the retail transaction. Currently, consumers feel somewhat insecure with all online transactions; perception of unsatisfactory security on the Internet is one of the primary reasons hindering online purchasing (Zellweger 1997). But that perception may change as online retailers reduce these fears by offering clear guidelines to consumers on their online security and privacy policies.

Information Availability

This is the amount of information offered about specific products. Typically, catalogs and online stores offer more detailed information for the products that they sell than do traditional physical stores. Travelocity.com, which is owned and operated by the SABRE Group, a major player in travel and travel-related services around the globe, provides reservation capabilities with more than 420 airlines, representing 95 percent of all airline seats sold, more than 40,000 hotels, and more than 50 car rental companies. This reservation capability is paired with access to a vast database of destination and interest information. Travelocity.com succeeds as an online Internet resource because of its thorough travel information and comprehensive menus of services (Gottlieb 2000).

Customization/Personalization

This refers to the interaction between retailers and consumers. This varies widely for physical stores, from virtually none at a discount store, to significant customization at specialty stores. Catalog stores such as Lands' End and L.L.Bean offer ideas regarding related products based on customer choices. Online stores can project this further by customizing their interactions based on past interactions and customer "cookies," or electronically gathered and stored information located on a consumer's computer. For example, online stores can greet repeat customers by name and suggest products based on prior purchases or questionnaires.

Figure 10.2
Process of Online Store Loyalty Formation

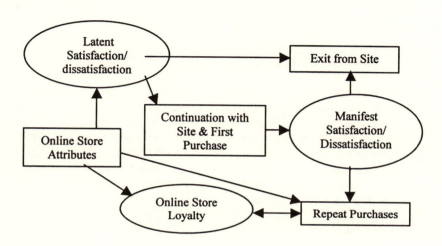

Another potential method of achieving personalization is through real-time, live interaction. Interacting with a customer via browser sharing, text chat, or immediate phone callback presents an intimacy of support that is beginning to rival the more traditional Internet methods (Willk 1999). Such live customer service is effective. At HomeTownStores.com, a hardware site, sales rose 30 percent within a month after a new personal-greeter service was launched in the fall of 1999. The site's chat operator individually greets all 14,000 daily visitors. Cameraworld.com reports that 25 percent made a purchase after it added a service that allows people to talk to reps via Internet phone calls (Mullaney 1999). Customer satisfaction also increases. At Consumer Financial Network, which makes loans and sells insurance, e-mail automation software routes questions from customers to service representatives with just the right expertise to answer them. Its customer satisfaction rate rose 5 percent after the features were added.

BUILDING LOYALTY TO ONLINE STORES

Once the visitor has stayed at the site and made the first purchase, the building blocks are available to build loyalty to the particular online store. Getting the customer to revisit and repurchase is the beginning of the process of loyalty formation. Figure 10.2 continues the process of loyalty formation after the initial visit. Satisfaction with the initial interaction leads to purchase and offers an opportunity for satisfaction to be further defined and strengthened. Repeated purchases lead to loyalty and reinforce the entire process. In this model we distinguish the concept of satisfaction and consider the role of store attributes in greater detail. Starting with Bloemer and de Ruyter's (1998) model of physical store loyalty, our model incorporates store attributes as factors not just affecting the store image but also directly influencing latent and manifest satisfaction and separates the role of first and repeat purchases as factors creating satisfaction and cementing store loyalty.

Store Satisfaction

Actual interactions with the online site during the initial visit lead to an important consequence-store satisfaction. This satisfaction determines whether the online customer stays within the site or exits to another site. We also know that customer satisfaction is a precondition for consumer loyalty toward a store (Bloemer and de Ruyter 1998; Surprenant and Solomon 1987). Consumers are satisfied when their expectations toward a product, a service, or a store match the performance of these entities. Satisfaction with a store cements the consumers' loyalty to that store.

Two types of store satisfaction can be identified-latent satisfaction and manifest satisfaction (Bloemer and de Ruyter 1998).

Latent Satisfaction

This occurs when the consumer is not fully aware of his or her satisfaction because of lack of motivation or ability to evaluate the store. This occurs primarily during an initial visit while the consumer is still navigating the site and becoming familiar with the online retailer. Consumers are not yet capable of, or interested in, evaluating the online store's service performance (e.g., product delivery, easy of ordering) until they make the first purchase. They have only the favorable halo of an overall store image because of prior familiarity with the store name (e.g., Macy.com) or prior exposure to advertising (such as by eTrade) or because they are developing an image as they navigate a site. This type of satisfaction is required to convert consumers from "browsers" to "buyers."

Manifest Satisfaction

This requires an explicit comparison between consumer expectation and store performance. It generally occurs after the consumer has engaged in a very specific interaction, such as placement of an order (e.g., for a CD on CDNOW) or a very specific request (e.g., a bid on Priceline.com). Manifest satisfaction is necessary for consumers to repeatedly purchase from an online retailer and eventually develop loyalty to the store. Manifest satisfaction can develop only after consumers have made a very specific transaction (e.g., interaction with Priceline.com whether or not the offered price has been accepted).

Latent and manifest satisfactions differ from each other according to the psychological process of elaboration. Latent satisfaction results from a low degree of elaboration because of lack of experience with a site. Latent satisfaction can be positive or negative, strong or weak. When latent satisfaction

Table 10.2
Impact of Perceived Online Store Attributes on Latent Satisfaction, Manifest Satisfaction, and Loyalty

Store Attributes	Impact on		
	Latent Satisfaction	Manifest Satisfaction	Loyalty
Accessibility	High	Medium	Low
Atmospherics	High	Low	Medium
Service/Experiential Convenience	High	High	High
Speed of Acquisition	Low	High	High
Price across Brands	High	High	Low
Assortment	High	High	High
Security	High	Medium	Medium
Information Availability	High	High	Medium
Customization/ Personalization	Low	Medium	High
Physical Presence	High	Medium	Low

is positive, it motivates consumers to make their first purchase. After the consumers experience the first transaction, then elaboration–in the psychological sense–occurs because consumers are now motivated and have the ability to evaluate online stores. This elaboration compares the experience against expectations. If the results of such elaborate information processing are positive (in favor of the online store), then the manifest satisfaction leads to repeat purchases and ultimately loyalty toward the online store.

MANAGERIAL IMPLICATIONS

Online stores need to implement store attributes that accomplish two conversion processes–turning "browsers" to "buyers" and "buyers" to "loyal" customers. In the next section, we discuss how different weights of the various online store attributes contribute to latent and manifest satisfaction and affect the two conversion processes.

Likely Effects of Online Store Attributes

Not all attributes are equally important at the various stages of satisfaction and loyalty formation. As consumers progress from latent satisfaction, to manifest satisfaction, to loyalty, specific store attributes are likely to increase or diminish in importance. In Table 10.2, we suggest that speed of acquisition and customization/personalization are likely to be less important for latent satisfaction than the other attributes. Manifest satisfaction will be particularly influenced by service/experiential convenience, speed of acquisition, price across brands, assortment and information availability. For loyalty, customization/personalization emerges as being very important while price across brands and accessibility diminish in importance.

From Browsing to Buying

In order to convert consumers from browsers to buyers, several store attributes are important in this early development of the relationship between consumers and online retailers. Accessibility is critical because it is the point where the consumer initially finds the site. Hyperlinks from other sites or promotional efforts can provide additional store entrances for consumers to access the online store. Atmospherics, assortment, information availability, and price across brands determine whether the consumer continues to stay at the site. Security and physical presence influence whether the consumer completes the order process.

Physical presence involves more than just name or brand recognition. Instead, it provides a sense of security and confidence for customers who may be leery of the cyber-retailer and derive some comfort from the ability to connect to a physical place with a return, a question, or a complaint. It is likely to influence a consumer's awareness and confidence in an online store during the "look-to-buy" process. Each successive purchase reduces the consumer's reliance on physical cues.

While research is limited, some evidence seems to suggest consumers' look-to-buy conversions are influenced by (1) easy site navigation, (2) reduced first-time purchase risk, (3) rapid checkout processes, and (4) rewards for loyal customers (Gottlieb 1999). Lohse and Spiller (1999) analyze the impact of functional store attributes and find that store traffic is affected by additional products (assortment), FAQ (information availability), and promotion on the cybermall entrance screen (accessibility), while a feedback section (service/experiential convenience) and improved product lists (information availability) influence sales.

From Buying to Loyalty

While speed of acquisition is important, customization/personalization is particularly important for the consumer to progress to loyalty. There is a host of techniques used to customize/personalize the relationship. CDNow sends regular, customized e-mail to introduce new CDs. Opt-in programs offer products, deals, and services specified by consumers.

Service/experiential convenience and assortment remain important for the conversion of "buyers" to "loyal" customers. Consumers are likely to evaluate assortment of the stores during each visit, making it a critical variable to all stages of loyalty development. If they cannot find the merchandise for which they are looking, they will go to other stores. Service/experiential convenience never diminishes in importance; it is an attribute that needs continuous improvement to increase customer satisfaction and loyalty.

Two online attributes diminish in importance during the loyalty conversion stage–accessibility and price across brands. Accessibility becomes less important as a positive interaction with the site leads the consumer to remember or bookmark the site for direct visits in the future. Amazon.com is a heavily bookmarked site. Saving money draws shoppers online (Burke 1997), but the effect of price diminishes as consumers move through the conversion process. Once they are satisfied about the fairness of the price, consumers are less likely to engage in extended price comparisons across sites. Amazon.com continues to draw many repeat and loyal customers even if it does not offer the lowest price.

SUMMARY AND CONCLUSIONS

The Internet has intensified retail competition, and traditional as well as online retailers are increasingly concerned about customer loyalty. In cyberspace, there are fewer entry barriers for competitors, and switching costs are rather low for consumers. Such conditions lead to a volatile cybermarketplace in which retailers increasingly struggle for customer retention. In this chapter, we elaborate on the relationships between online store attributes and the processes of satisfaction and loyalty formation.

The electronic commerce environment is still very new, and very little research provides reliable insights into online store and consumer behavior. We have offered a modified list of online store attributes and described some of the ways these attributes are being implemented by various online retailers. More research and substantiation will provide stronger support for the approach suggested in this chapter. In the meantime, online retailers can follow the suggested store attributes that lead to both behavioral and attitudinal components of customer satisfaction and loyalty.

QUESTIONS FOR DISCUSSION

1. In terms of store attributes, how will pure-play online stores distinguish their competitive advantage from other pure-play online stores as well as from stores with both online and physical presence?

2. As consumers gain increased experience with online shopping, how will the role of store attributes change during the process of creating store satisfaction and loyalty?

3. As the consumer profile of online shoppers becomes more representative of the population, what changes have to be made in online store attributes?

4. How will the implementation of specific online store attributes be affected by developments in technology, changes in consumer behavior, and experiences of online retailers?

11

Shopping on the Net:
From the Real World to a Mirror World

Solveig Wikström, Camilla Carlell, and Maria Frostling-Henningsson

In this chapter an assessment of retail offerings on the Net is carried out, using two well-established perspectives in consumer buying behavior–a cognitive decision-making perspective and an emotional experience-seeking perspective. Three models of virtual representation are discussed–the mirror model, the synergy model, and the virtual model. In conjunction with illustrations of Swedish consumers' virtual buying behavior, these models indicate which aspects of a virtual representation the consumers perceive as crucial for engaging in electronic buying behavior and which aspects may turn them off. Managerial implications of the assessment are discussed, and questions for future research are posed.

INTRODUCTION

The transition from traditional, physical offerings in retail stores to virtual offerings on the Net implies not only a change in the offering itself but also a change in the context in which the offering is embedded. In the virtual world, physical representation is abandoned for a new kind of representation. This raises several questions. In this chapter we aim at providing answers to the following questions: What are the constraints in the virtual marketplace compared to the traditional marketplace? Which aspects of the virtual representation consumers perceive as crucial for their participation in new, Net-based buying behavior? Which aspects of the virtual representation do might consumers reject?

MODELS OF REPRESENTATION

Physical representation implies some sort of familiarity; that is consumers know what they can expect. Consumers are not as acquainted with virtual representations as they are with physical representations. Therefore, in the virtual marketplace, consumers do not quite know what to expect. By physical representation we mean offerings that are presented in a well-known traditional and physical environment such as a brick-and-mortar store, a travel agency office, or a bank. By virtual representation we mean some sort of mirror image of the same store, travel agency, or bank as it is presented on the Internet.

MIT Media Lab director Nicholas Negroponte (1995) states that virtual reality can make the artificial as real as reality itself, maybe even realer than real. Virtual reality is aimed at creating a feeling of "being there" by giving a visual impression of what one might be able to see in a real situation. Steuer (1992) refers to this feeling as "presence." However, virtual offerings can also be constructed without any reference to the real world. Virtual representation then refers to all kinds of offerings presented on the Internet. It should be clear that virtual representations have many constraints relative to the physical representations. For instance, sensorial values such as smell, touch, and taste are not possible to convey via the Internet, although technologies to communicate such sensorial values are in the works.

There are different ways of constructing the virtual space compared to the physical space. When it comes to alternative representations, such as moving from a physical to a virtual representation, Venkatesh (1997) distinguishes three different ways in which representations are designed:

- **Mirror Model.** Following Negroponte's lines of thought, this model shows that the representation of the virtual space is designed to resemble the physical space as closely as possible. Thus, the mirror model conceives virtual space as a *replication* of its physical counterpart: the virtual *mirrors* the physical. This could mean that virtual representations include images of physical structures such as shelves or buildings similar to those we find in the physical world. To reassure its customers, a major online pharmacy in the United States, for example, was compelled to include a picture of its physical pharmacy store in its home page.
- **Synergy Model.** This model suggests that the virtual space and the physical space be integrated with each other. The model is a hybrid that combines two different settings by fusing the best elements of both spaces in the virtual representation. For example, physical elements such as shopping carts and cash registers are included in the representation of an otherwise virtual grocery store. Examples of representations constructed according to the synergy model can be found at sites such as www.nk.se or www.peapod.com.
- **Virtual Model.** This model propounds that the virtual space is constructed completely from virtual elements without any reference to a physical world. Virtual elements are symbols constructed on their own premises; that is, no physical representations exist. This approach implies that all the potential benefits of the virtual world can be exploited without any considerations of the real world.

THE ONLINE-SHOPPING FAMILY–A CASE

This is the story of how the Andersson family in Sweden experiences Net shopping and related activities.[10] The family consists of four members. Carl, 39, is a computer consultant, and Lisa, 36, is a physiotherapist. They have two children, Eric, 6, and Sarah, 4. Both children are enrolled in public day care. The family lives in a house in a suburb of Stockholm. With both parents pursuing careers and with two small children, there remains little time for the daily household chores. Both parents work long hours and thus have trouble picking up the children from day care while shopping for groceries on their way home. In sum, Carl and Lisa have a very busy schedule that leaves precious little time for activities belonging to the private sphere.

In 1996, when it became possible to shop for groceries on the Internet in the Stockholm area, the Andersson family saw it as an attractive way to ease their time-pressed routine. NK-hallen, a department store in downtown Stockholm, offered this opportunity. Initially, the family believed that they could buy only standard products such as milk, dried foods, and canned goods. Amazingly, they found that they could buy everything for their household needs such as meat, fish, fruits, and vegetables. They quickly noticed that the store pickers often selected even better items than they did themselves. However, Carl and Lisa had problems finding the items that they wanted on the Web page, which was constructed just like a library catalog. The items were in lexicographic/alphabetical order. It was difficult to figure out under which category a product was filed. Since the Andersson family had no prior experience with NK-hallen, no image of the physical store existed in Carl and Lisa's minds. When shopping from the store's Web page, the Anderssons struggled to visualize its physical structure. To solve this problem, Lisa made a shopping trip to the physical store to create a mental image of its layout. The mental image of the store's physical structure proved very helpful for her when she was sitting in front of the screen. We argue that Lisa's strategic move to familiarize herself with the store's physical layout and product display follows what Venkatesh (1997) calls the mirror model. By making the special effort to go to the physical NK-hallen store, Lisa created a virtual replica of the store in her mind. The mirror representation helped her make sense of the images that she encountered on the screen.

The virtual shopping cart, an icon where customers "placed" their purchases, emerged as a solution to the Anderssons' problem of not being able to find the desired items. With the shopping cart, product selections could be saved and retrieved for later purchase. Now, when the family had to do their grocery shopping, they started with a *full shopping cart*. They simply deleted the items they did not want this time around and added new items as needed. This way of shopping is, of course, the exact opposite of what happens in the physical store. There, the customer starts with an *empty shopping cart* and gradually fills it.

Soon this procedure resulted in a very routine buying behavior where almost the same items were bought every week. As a result the family longed for variation, stimulation, external inputs about sales and featured items, and information about other (possibly new) products. Carl and Lisa solved this problem by going to the physical store every once in a while. They also made some supplemental purchases of items that they ran out of at the convenience store attached to their neighborhood gas station. For special occasions they went to Östermalmshallen, an exclusive delicatessen market offering a wide selection of gourmet foods.

The Andersson family also started Internet banking at about the same that time they started shopping for groceries. After a "teething period" of experiencing some technical problems, the online banking service proved very useful in consolidating the family's everyday financial errands. Despite continuing usage of online banking, however, questions still persisted regarding security, accurateness, and trust associated with this form of banking.

Of all the items to shop on the Internet, flowers turned out to be a popular one. Online flower shopping was convenient, well organized, and visually adept in presenting choices of flower arrangements. As a result, an increasing proportion of the family's gifts to distant friends and relatives became flowers and floral arrangements.

Last April, the family decided to go on vacation. Initially, they didn't exactly know what they wanted to do. They considered options like going skiing in the Alps or going swimming on a sunny Mediterranean beach. After surveying different alternatives, they decided to go to the beaches of the Canary Islands. The information on the Internet, however, was not detailed enough to enable the family to make an informed purchase decision. As a result the family turned to the telephone and ordered their complete tour through the brick-and-mortar travel agency.

The Andersson case, supported by further empirical data on consumer Net-shopping activities, serves as the backdrop for the following theoretical discussions. The empirical illustrations and theoretical deliberations help answer the question: Which aspects of the virtual representation do consumers perceive as crucial for participating in new, Net-based buying behavior? Two well-established theoretical perspectives on buying behavior are used. First, a cognitive, decision-making perspective (Becker 1965; Bettman 1979; Howard 1989) and, second, an emotional, hedonic, experience-seeking perspective (Hirschman and Holbrook 1982; Holbrook, and Hirschman 1982; Holbrook, 1986) are employed.

COGNITIVE PERSPECTIVE FOR EVALUATING THE VIRTUAL AND THE PHYSICAL

Which criteria might be beneficial in assessing the mirror, the synergy, and the virtual models from the perspective of a consumer family such as the Anderssons and other online shoppers like them? One approach is to look at Net-based retail offerings and their representations from a cognitive and rational perspective. This implies reviewing different kinds of offerings, keeping in view the limited resources that a consumer has in carrying out her or his daily life.

Time as a Resource

When the mode of transaction changes from a physical interaction to a digital interaction, the consumers' resource-mix is affected in certain ways that might have implications for how consumers perceive the offerings. The basic set of consumer resources–time, information, money, and energy (Kaufman and

Lane 1996)–seem to attain a new meaning in Web-based shopping and shed light on consumer perception of the new, Net-based offerings. The *time resource* changes, for example, from clock time to technological time, and time becomes more flexible (Kaufman and Lane 1997). Hence, time can be used more efficiently, and more of it may be available when needed. What kind of implications might this have for designing the offering? Some consumers demand only great efficiency in their time use on the Net. This means that the offerings have to be well structured so that they can be easily and quickly grasped. Other consumers, who have very special demands, may be more interested in extensive, precise, and accurate offerings that require more time to review and compare and to complete the shopping task. Therefore, the representation of the offering has to take into account simplicity as well as complexity. From the standpoint of market segmentation and product differentiation, the representations of the offerings should be differentiated to accommodate various consumer buying situations.

When online retailing first started, initial consumer expectations were that shopping online would be timesaving, efficient, and easy to carry out. It is clear that time is a resource that is particularly important for many consumers: "There are times when every minute is booked, then it is most helpful not to have to go downtown for your shopping, because it takes hours for whatever you want to shop. You have to find a parking lot, park the car, and then go to the shops. All that takes time. On the Net you can do your shopping in just a few minutes" (Male, 26).

Other consumers experience a different situation. They find *shopping online* time-consuming and not very easy. Though it may take less time to do the grocery shopping on the Internet compared to shopping in the store, the time in front of the computer is *perceived* as long. Consumers think that they save time while at the same time complaining that it takes too long. This contradiction may be understood using Kaufman and Lane's (1996) "situation-bound time" concept. "I think it takes too much time when I sit there in front of the screen and wait for new pictures and new information to come up" (Male, 64).

Rifkin (1996) shows how information technology changes people's perception of time. When it comes to speed, their expectations increase. This may explain why consumers perceive the technology to be "slow" while, in fact, it may be quite fast. In our research we have repeatedly found support for Rifkin's observations when it comes to consumers' perceptions of time in front of the computer.

Consumers, however, learn how to handle the difficulties. They find shortcuts. In grocery shopping, for instance, they use their shopping cart as a shopping list and as a method to organize their search for needed items. This strategy helps them save time and make their shopping more efficient: "With this shopping cart as a 'shopping list' you have just to go in and click, and this way it goes fast. But if you don't have this shopping cart list and you have to sit there and search around, then it takes time, more than twice as long time, up to 50 minutes. Then you don't save that much time" (Male, 39).

For more complex shopping activities–travel arrangements, for example–technology itself proves to be a problem. Even to computer-literate individuals, such as the Anderssons, the perceived wait appears to be too long, with frequent session termination during peak times and slow connections. These conditions and perceptions resulted in no online buying when the Anderssons were planning their vacation trip. Initially, the Anderssons believed these to be passing problems, but as they continued, the Anderssons grew increasingly dissatisfied. The online shopping service simply did not meet their expectations.

Information Processing

Consumers see *information*–in terms of knowledge about available options and access to such information–as an essential basis for buying decisions. In a virtual context the importance of information has grown immensely. Digital technology is far superior to physical methods when it comes to information processing and storing. The enormous amount of information to which consumers have access, however, needs to be structured in ways that enhance the consumers' ability to use it. In short, the more structured the information about the offering, the easier it is for the consumer to comprehend and evaluate it. With greater amounts of information, the offerings become more transparent. Many people believe that the Internet is an excellent source of information. Access is unlimited and easy.

Observations of how consumers search on the Internet, however, suggest the opposite. Access is far from easy. The huge amount of information available to consumers causes more confusion than clarification. Consumers find it difficult to locate the right Web pages that contain the information for which they are looking. Moreover, consumers struggle to make sense of the information provided on poorly structured pages. When a search is difficult and time-consuming, consumers stop their search and turn somewhere else. A consumer searching for travel arrangements complains: "I'm getting tired of all this. The home pages are too difficult and messy and the search too slow. I'll go somewhere else" (Male, 27, computer system sales representative).

When the Anderssons planned their vacation trip, they realized that the content of the information was too shallow and not detailed enough to enable them to make an informed purchase decision. As a result, they gave up on the Net and phoned their travel agent.

Money as a Resource

When it comes to *money* as a key resource, consumers are likely to benefit from digitization because competitive offerings and transaction flows become transparent and simplified in the virtual world. Well-informed consumers realize that digitization increases market efficiencies and puts pressure on producers' profit margins, resulting in "good prices." As price transparency opens up price competition, firms need to find ways to make their offerings attractive in ways that go beyond the appeal of low prices. This has effects on the design of the Web site as well as the offering itself.

The Internet makes it possible to compare prices across a much larger set of market alternatives than what is feasible in the physical world. On the Net, consumers perceive issues about money and prices differently than in the physical marketplace: "When you are out on the Internet, you can compare prices in the whole world, in any case in Europe because there are no customs. Then you feel that the market has expanded, which means that you know that you can find the best price available" (Female, 42).

The Andersson family states that they have become much more price-oriented after they started shopping online. The way that prices are presented on the Web stimulates consumers to reflect on prices in a new way. For example, price comparisons for groceries are easy to conduct on the screen: "I learn much more about prices when I see them in print in front of me. The price per kilo is much more visible now. I look much more at the prices now, and also at the bottom line. I haven't been as interested in prices before as I am now. Now I know that the price of that juice that our son loves to drink en masse, is up to SEK 19.90 (U.S.$ 2.20). I didn't know that before. I thought that the price was about SEK 10 to 11 (U.S.$ 1.20)" (Female, 49).

Initially, the Anderssons paid very little attention to the cost for the online service. In the beginning they mentioned only the fairly high connection fees. After a while, however, they started to reflect on, and even object to, the banking fees. The Anderssons perceived the banking fees as unjustified because they did most of their banking themselves. In other words, the Anderssons expected some discounts because they banked online. "I find it strange that I should have to pay more when I do more of the work and the bank does less" (Male, 42, bank customer). "We found out that we pay twice as much for our bank services now when we do most of the work ourselves. That is not right!" (Male, 36 and Female, 32, bank customers).

One of the more important benefits for the consumers is the fact that they can use less expensive time to carry out their errands on the Web. The Anderssons conduct their shopping and banking activities after the children have been put to bed. "You can sit down and order when you have the time. And that is hopefully when the children are sleeping. Otherwise you have to do it when the children are awake and then you miss out on that time with the children" (Female, 34, head of direct marketing activities).

Physical and Mental Energy

Various levels of *physical and mental energy* are required to carry out shopping-related tasks. While the demand on physical energy seems to decrease in a virtual context, the need for mental energy may actually increase. The great challenge for firms seems to be how to make the virtual offering attractive to consumers. This involves designing easy-to-comprehend offerings that do not burden the consumers in terms of effort spent in shopping. This may entail the design of software in the sense of visualizing the offerings and the design of hardware that makes electronic shopping as effortless as possible.

Consumers appreciate not having to spend too much physical energy when they shop on the Web. On the other hand, they often point out the increased demand for mental energy that is needed in the new environment. Consumers particularly mention the patience required for constant learning and the tolerance for boredom and routine, as well as the feeling of ineptness: "How many more buttons do I have to push in order to find the thing I am looking for? If you want to order, then you click until a new screen appears, and you go further and further and further now I have pushed ten times, and I wonder how many more times I have to push before I get my stuff?" (Male, 28).

Consumers also encounter more and more advertising, which takes up time and conceals the message (or stands in the way of the information for which they are looking):"There is more and more advertising on the screen, too much needless Java junk that disturbs the search and takes time. When you do the search from home all of us have modems with limited speed, which makes it even slower. It goes even more slowly if you then have to receive a huge mass of banners which you didn't ask for" (Male, 24).

EMOTIONAL PERSPECTIVE FOR EVALUATING THE VIRTUAL AND THE PHYSICAL

In terms of reviewing virtual offerings, are there criteria other than the rational, resource-based criteria discussed in the preceding section? What more can we learn if we focus on aspects other than the rational use of resources? What insights can be gained by turning our attention to basic emotional needs and qualities of human beings? The experiential perspective on consumer buying proposes that in some instances consumers do not make their purchases according to a rational decision-making process. Instead, people sometimes buy products and services in order to have fun, create fantasies, and trigger certain emotions and feelings (Hirschman and Holbrook 1982; Holbrook and Hirschman 1982). Be it in the physical or the virtual world, the consumers make some emotional demands is part of their existence. A variety of such demands are discussed in some detail later. Two aspects are deemed very important when discussing an experiential perspective: social space and physical space.

Social Space

Social space provides an opportunity for social interaction with other individuals. It also provides an understanding of the social context in which an individual leads her or his life. Social space manifests itself in the individual's interest in seeing other individuals and having a social connection with other individuals. Social space also deals with feelings of closeness, safety, security, and social relationships. In today's society there are at least two types of social relationships among consumers as individuals and between technology and the individual. It has been argued that in a technology-driven world, the latter becomes of greater importance (Baudrillard 1988).

A key aspect of social space is learning. We learn by interacting with, and observing, others in a socially constructed world (Berger and Luckman 1966). The world or reality consists of a dialectal interaction between a subjective and an objective element. That is, we receive information on how to act and interact both from within ourselves (past experience) as well as from outside ourselves. Both our past experiences and the reactions from those outside ourselves guide us in our actions. They can be used as a means of sense-making in terms of information received. Sense-making in this case means organizing the information in ways that not only provide guidance on how to act but also help us learn what additional information might be needed.

Our research clearly shows that early Web shoppers operate in a poor learning environment. The way that their learning takes place can best be described as "learning by doing." In the beginning they face a lot of difficulties. Shopping is time-consuming, very arduous, and mentally demanding. Consumers struggle to make sense of what they see on the screen. This is perhaps due to the fact that several important dimensions of information–such as the presence of other consumers and store personnel–are missing. Observing others provides stimulation, orientation, and inspiration that may lead to emulation. Thus, in brick-and-mortar stores consumers are more likely to emulate other consumers' buying behavior: "It is fun to watch other people while they shop and get some inspiration. If they have two choices, you can always think–that looks nice–and you get a few tips on stuff you haven't noticed yourself. I think I go blind sometimes, if I look for one thing I get so caught up that I miss everything else. If you then look at what someone else has picked out, you get some ideas" (Female, 30).

In an ideal case, interactions with the store personnel might provide deep and detailed information about products. Such in-depth information, of course, is valuable for the consumer: "Well, you can't get more information than is presented there (on the screen). In a store you can talk to one of the staff and then you can ask if you need more information" (Female, 39).

The Web page is still not capable of providing either information from other consumers or deep and detailed information from store personnel. A related issue is whether chat groups and virtual communities (Turkle 1995; Hagel and Armstrong 1997) could provide the social interaction between consumers and staff. Well-developed chat groups and virtual communities should be able to enhance social interaction and thus provide a more suitable virtual shopping environment.

Physical Space

The physical surroundings of brick-and-mortar shopping are the concrete physical and spatial aspects of the environment in which the consumers' shopping-related activities take place. Some examples of the elements of physical space are buildings, other individuals, and physical structures such as checkout lines to stand in, buses to ride, and so on. Consumers lose important sources of information in a virtual environment, such as, the information available from the physical elements of a store. Instead, they have to rely on sources of computer-mediated information such as text, pictures, and sometimes sound. A study on knowledge acquisition from pictures and text (Hegarty and Just 1989; Janiszewski 1998) showed that individuals have difficulties with too much text, too many pictures, and too little coherence in the text as compared to the pictures. The same problems seem to occur in the usage of Web pages to convey information to users.

Why did Lisa go to NK-hallen to look at the real store? Just as the social space provides information on how to make sense and understand the environment, so does the physical space provide inputs still missing in the virtual context. Sensorial values, for example, like tasting, smelling, touching, and the possibility to alter perspectives are yet to be incorporated into the virtual space.

When consumers interact in a virtual environment built on fewer dimensions than the physical one, they experience frustration, confusion, insecurity, and anxiety: "Even if I can book my ticket at amadeus.com (the industry's own booking system), it makes me feel more secure to go to a travel agent and let them do it. I want to make sure that I will be able to get my trip!" (Male, 28).

Some consumers experience discomfort in terms of not knowing what to do if something goes wrong with online shopping: "Who can I call on the Internet if something goes wrong? In the physical world I can go to the store and complain. On the Internet it is impossible for me to know who took my information. Who have I talked to? A computer! What if I have entered personal data and they tell me: no you haven't been here" (Female, 26).

SUMMARY AND CONCLUSIONS

In summarizing our results, we would like to draw some conclusions. First of all, the synergy model is the prevalent mode of representation in today's virtual shopping environments. When we review digital representations from a cognitive, rational decision-making perspective, the synergy model seems to be the most appropriate. In the synergy model, elements from a real physical environment are present, helping consumers orient themselves. At the same time new virtual elements help make the environment more efficient by structuring information and making it easier to find information. From an emotional, experiential perspective, the synergy model is deficient. This model does not provide consumers with enough inspiration, variety, and stimulation. Representations according to the synergy model induce boredom and routine behavior.

The virtual model, which is constructed completely from virtual elements without any reference to a physical space, doesn't seem to be a realistic option for the foreseeable future. It is possible that new virtual elements will be increasingly introduced on the Web sites, but the frame of reference will still be physical, which is more in line with the mirror model.

We do not perceive the mirror model as capable of satisfying both consumers' rational needs as well as their emotional needs in a buying situation. We therefore propose a hypermirror model that develops elements more real than reality itself. Thus, the hypermirror model combines both physical and virtual representations to create virtual environments that are more beautiful, exciting, accurate, and precise than any real representation. Should the hypermirror model be able to convey easily retrievable and well-structured information, which a rational consumer-buying situation requires, it would be able to stand alone. Otherwise, the model has to be complemented with special, non-virtual elements providing the precise, condensed, and easily retrievable information that consumers seem to want.

Our assessments provide an in-depth understanding of the current virtual consumer-buying behavior. Under the present conditions consumers mainly shop for well-known, uncomplicated products and services on the Internet. The present medium seems to be incapable of providing enough information, security, familiarity, and trust to enable consumers to make more advanced buying decisions online.

These findings have several managerial implications. Many information and communication technologies are still in an infant stage. Seen from the consumer's perspective, simplicity in all dimensions of the offering is of utmost importance. Simple representations of content (what is offered), context (how the interface is designed), and infrastructure (how the transactions and the delivery of the offering are arranged) are required in virtual environments (Rayport and Sviokla 1994, 1995; Yakhlef 2000). Simplicity in content requires that the offering be easy to assess without prior physical inspection. Under today's conditions, this limits Internet shopping to well-known items or to items with very little complexity. Simplicity in context encompasses the computer software as well as the design of the Web site. Since the virtual context has the potential to cause confusion in the mind of the consumer, the message has to be simple in order to be decoded in the way intended by the marketer. Finally, simplicity in infrastructure points to a need for improvements in the transaction procedure. There is a need for more convenient methods of payment, better delivery services, reliable confirmation of orders, and continuous feedback regarding how the consumer experiences the offering.

Current e-shoppers are mainly innovators, that is, people most attracted to, stimulated by, and motivated by the new technology. When e-commerce is extended to early adopters and the early majority, the need for simplicity will most certainly increase. If these improvements are not implemented, a backlash may occur.

RECENT FINDINGS

Our research on e-shopping is ongoing, and more complex and interesting implications continue to emerge. To illustrate the most recent developments of e-shopping in Sweden, we use examples from two different areas: a service domain (banking) and a product domain (grocery shopping).

Banking

The number of registered users of Internet banking services in Sweden has significantly increased since such Net-based banking started in 1996. In the spring of 2000 all Swedish banks offered some form of Internet banking service. The issue is, however, the proportion of bank users who are active users of Internet banking. We are observing that some consumers are defecting from Internet banking services, while others move on to more advanced services such as stock trading. Also, day trading is becoming increasingly popular.

The number of available transactions at e-banking sites has increased. The number of available services has increased and the nature of these services has changed. The first Internet banks offered only very simple services such as paying bills, checking the balance in an account, and so on. Currently, however, some banks offer, among other things, the possibility to apply for loans, invest in funds, and trade stocks. Such increase in transactional options has paradoxical effects. It spurs some consumers to adopt more services, while it pushes others to revert to older ways of doing business. Our research shows that some consumers find it easier to pay bills the traditional way by using giro (interbank transfer) than paying them online. They find the online solution time-consuming, arduous, and complex. These users deliberately "dis-adopt" these Internet services. Other consumers find it attractive to apply for loans (an occasional activity) or trade stocks (a frequent activity) online. One tentative conclusion that we draw from this is that a shift or divide is occurring regarding how the Internet is being used for personal financial management. Banks may have to come up with creative ways of reengaging those consumers who are getting turned off by offering more complex and engaging online options.

Grocery Shopping

At present virtual grocery shopping in Sweden remains a marginal activity. However, we have noticed some signs of defecting from virtual grocery shopping to conventional, brick-and-mortar shopping. Some consumers who have been buying most of their groceries online are now changing their shopping behavior. They tend to limit their shopping on the Web to staples and basic products and shop less frequently. Consumers seem to turn increasingly to local grocery stores and specialty stores for their perishables. However, consumers use more of the services offered online. Initially, most of the consumers went to the store to pick up the selected items. Now, they increasingly use the whole service package of selecting, picking, and receiving the delivery of goods. Also, online shopping has spread to a wider group of buyers. While the urban, dual-income households with children initially dominated the online grocery-buying population, the group has now been extended to include dual-income households without children. Small businesses such as offices, day-care centers, and service centers for the elderly are also appearing as new groups of online grocery buyers.

During the three years that virtual grocery shopping has been around in Sweden, the number of online grocers has grown significantly. In the spring of 2000, approximately 50 Swedish grocery stores offered virtual grocery shopping. Their Web sites are improving, though a majority of the Web sites are still text-based. Pictures, however, are becoming more common. It is easier now to acquire information aimed at special consumer interests. For instance, allergic consumers can search for products that are free of lactose or gluten. Moreover, some of the more advanced Web sites have started to collect information about the consumers in order to be able to build personal profiles.

Shopping on the Internet is still in an early stage of development, and our understanding of its conditions is limited. Hence, much more research is needed. Next, we point to some of the more urgent issues that need to be investigated.

ISSUES FOR FURTHER RESEARCH

One of the most urgent research questions is how attitudes and behaviors regarding e-shopping develop over time. What happens to these concepts when the e-shopping evolves from attracting innovators to attracting early adopters followed by the early majority? To answer these concerns, more process studies and more longitudinal studies are needed. Such studies should follow consumers' reactions and responses to e-commerce developments and changes over time. Another important issue is to learn more about e-shopping in an everyday life context. What kind of shopping and how much of the shopping do different segments of consumers and households conduct via the Internet? How is this way of shopping and information acquisition changing people's everyday lives? Conversely, which types of consumers resist the e-shopping format? For what reasons do they resist? Further, what are the characteristics of the heavy users, light users, and nonusers of e-shopping services? Is it possible to discern any patterns of users and nonusers over time? Finally, in our recent research, we have identified consumers who purposefully defect from, and abstain from, e-shopping. This reaction seems to share similarities with the way some people purposefully disconnect from electronic communications by getting rid of e-mail and cell phones. Could this be an emerging trend? If so, how is this trend to be understood?

QUESTIONS FOR DISCUSSION

1. Discuss for which product categories the mirror model appears more suited and for which the synergy model holds more promise. Provide a list of products that fall under each of the two models.

2. The chapter seems to suggest that, in order to make sense of the virtual environment, online consumers still rely on perceptual maps that replicate the structures of the physical environment.

3. What are the consequences of such a consumer strategy for marketing practice?

4. Do you expect this consumer strategy to persist in the future?

5. Assuming that, in the future, brick-and-mortar retailing will face increasing pressure from online retailers, what could the brick-and-mortar retailers do to successfully compete against the online assault?

6. What do you see as the major obstacles that online retailers have to overcome to succeed in the long run?

12

Advertising on the Net:
What Works and Why

Ruby Roy Dholakia and David R. Fortin

INTRODUCTION

Over decades, advertisers have learned to use a variety of media to reach specific target markets. With the advent of each new medium, advertisers have created messages that exploit the medium's physical capabilities such as color, audio, and moving images (video). While early Web sites were mostly text-based, technological developments now allow for a variety of features that combine the advantages of print and electronic media in order to provide customized information as well as more vivid forms of communication (motion, audio and video files, etc.).

• Is the Web simply another advertising medium along with other media such as television, radio, print and, so on?
• As a new conduit for advertising, how do/can advertisers use the capabilities of the new media to achieve their communication objectives?

In order to answer these questions, we need to understand the distinctive characteristics of the new media and how these features contribute to advertising effectiveness.

THE NEW MEDIA

Some researchers believe that the Web's *interactive* nature, (i.e., the ability of the user to receive and transmit messages) creates a totally new communication environment. Instead of the traditional model of one-to-many communication, the Web is a "many-to-many" channel of communication (Hoffman and Novak 1996; Rust and Oliver 1994; Venkatesh, Dholakia, and Dholakia 1995). Interactivity is the key characteristic of the new media that is expected to transform not only the way that advertising is designed and implemented but also the manner in which it affects consumers' opinions and attitudes.

Despite the "hype" about interactivity in the popular press, the term is used rather loosely and means many things to many people. Williams, Rice, and Rogers' (1988) definition of interactivity includes three dimensions-control, exchange of roles, and mutual discourse. Bezjian-Avery, Calder, and Iacobucci (1998) emphasize user control in their definition of interactivity. Hoffman and Novak (1996) distinguish two levels of interactivity: person interactivity, which occurs between humans through a medium, and machine interactivity, which occurs between humans and machines to access hypermedia content. Based on a review of the literature (Fortin 1998), we propose the following definition of interactivity, which encapsulates the specific features of an interactive medium: Interactivity is defined as the degree to which a communication system can allow one or more end users to communicate alternatively as senders or receivers with one or many other users or communication devices, either in real time (as in video teleconferencing) or on a store-and-forward basis (as with electronic mail), or to seek and gain access to information on an on-demand basis where the content, timing, and sequence of the communication are under control of the end user, as opposed to a broadcast basis.

The Interactivity Continuum

Based on the preceding definition, interactivity is not just a matter of "either you have it or you don't" (Heeter 1989). Interactivity is a quality of a communication setting that can *vary* within the same medium (Rafaeli 1990). A Web site, for example, could simply be a page of text without any links, feedback options, or search engine. Such a site would score very low on the interactivity continuum, even though it is part of a *potentially* highly interactive medium. Conversely, some television broadcasts such as infomercials and shopping channels that allow for immediate response through the use of toll-free telephone numbers or on-the-air live interaction with the show's hosts would score much higher on the interactivity continuum. This example also illustrates the use of multiple media to achieve interactivity in a communication setting.

In a survey of 101 Web sites, Ghose and Dou (1998) found several different interactive features such as keyword searches, dealer locator, software downloads, comments, and so on. As technology evolves, we will probably see an increase in the interactive capabilities of the new media approximating the level reached by face-to-face interactions. Rafaeli (1990) has also argued that once-passive audiences even within traditional mass media are now more active with letters to the editor, on-the-air talk shows, infomercials, and so on. Both trends--technology changes and audience behaviors--are likely to fuel increased use of interactive features in the future.

The Digital Continuum

The interactive features of the Web are embedded in its digital properties, and not all marketers can fully utilize these features of the new media.

Figure 12.1
The Digitization Continuum

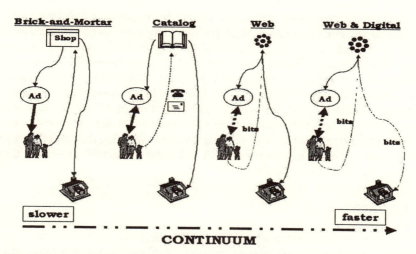

Traditional marketers relying on brick-and-mortar facilities face-to-face interactions for product inspections, order placement, and order fulfillment, are limited to using the new media as a vehicle for advertising and relationship building only. This is depicted in Figure 12.1 with solid lines showing physical transfer of information or goods and with dotted lines showing digital transfers. Interactive features of the new media can be used to create two-way communications, to build a community of interest, and to learn consumer preferences but not to actually deliver the goods over the digital channels. Examples include Macys.com or Walmart.com, which must still ship the goods to the customers.

Catalog marketers can more readily benefit from the new media since their customers are already familiar with nonphysical inspection of goods, and their order placement and fulfillment processes are already in place to meet customer demand. Digital catalogs are cost-effective alternatives to print catalogs; Web-based ordering also has many advantages over traditional mail or phone ordering systems. To the extent that catalog marketers offer goods and services that need physical transfers such as clothing, flowers, and jewelry, they are hampered in completing the entire transaction digitally. Ross-Simons.com, a major catalog house, for example, can make the search for products much easier for jewelry and gift items but must still rely on physical delivery of the ordered merchandise to the consumer. Even "pure-play" marketers such as Living.com or Virtual Vineyards cannot complete the entire transaction digitally and must rely on physical transfer of the ordered goods and services. Only marketers of digital products and services, such as software, financial services, photo finishing, travel packages, books, video, and music, can expect to digitally complete the total interactions with the consumer.

Because of the differences in the nature of their business, the "time interval" for customer interactions varies greatly. Currently, only airlines, software, photo finishing, and financial services can exploit the total features of the new media and complete the interaction in real time. Other products–such as books, music, and video, which are potentially digital–are still being sold in analog form. For most other companies, including pure-play Internet companies such as Amazon.com, eToys, and eBay, the biggest challenge is to reduce the time between order placement and order fulfillment–the interval between when the customer orders the merchandise and the time when the customer receives it. In this respect, even the brick-and-click companies (such as Barnesandnoble.com, Victoriasecret.com) can attempt to match their online competitors. It is not surprising, therefore, that most of the commercial interest in the new, interactive media is directed toward advertising and target marketing in order to stimulate information search and order placement rather than digital delivery of ordered merchandise.

INTERACTIVE ADVERTISING

It is not surprising that interactive advertising is one of the fastest-growing aspects of the advertising industry. Originally, it was available only on the Internet with a personal computer, but now interactive advertising is expanding rapidly into various new technologies such as DVD-video players, automated teller machines, vending machines, kiosks, and WAP phones. For purposes of this chapter, our focus is limited to interactive advertising on personal computers and the Internet.

Interactive advertising puts the user in charge of the medium. It allows users to personalize and customize their experience by being able to choose what they see and hear, when they see and hear it, and how and when they respond to it. When an ad pops up on a Web page, the user can choose to click on it and find out more about the product or service. Interactivity is also beneficial for the advertiser because it can give the advertiser an immediate response on how many people are interested in an advertisement. By learning user preferences via their demographics and clicking histories, content providers can tailor the messages to the user's interests (Ansari and Mela 2000).

Over the past three years, online advertising has exploded. While still a small portion of total advertising expenditures (less than 1 percent of total advertising in 1999), its growth rate far exceeds that for traditional media (Coen 2000). In 1999, Internet advertising grew 85 percent over 1998 after seeing triple-digit expansions in earlier years (see Table 12.1). Forecasters estimate Web advertising revenue to reach $3.8 to $5.8 billion by 2001 (NUA Analysis 2000).

Table 12.1
Growth in Online Advertising

Advertising Media	1999 Volume (millions of dollars)	% Total Advertising	% Change from 1998
Internet	$1.94	0.9	84.7
Newspapers	$46.65	21.7	5.3
Magazines	$11.43	5.3	8.7
Broadcast TV	$40.01	18.6	2.1
Cable TV	$10.43	4.8	22.0
Radio	$17.22	8.0	14.2
Yellow Pages	$12.65	5.9	5.5
Direct Mail	$41.40	19.2	4.5
Business Papers	$4.27	2.0	1.0
Billboards	$1.73	0.8	9.5
Miscellaneous	$27.57	12.8	7.3
Grand Total	$215.30	100	6.8

Source: Advertising Age.

- computers and software: $464.8 million
- financial services: $92.8 million
- direct-response companies (catalog and e-commerce vendors): $74.3 million
- local services and amusements: $52.3 million
- media and advertising: $51.6 million
- automotive industry: $47.9 million

Even traditional advertisers have joined the Internet advertising bandwagon. The top national advertisers–General Motors and Procter and Gamble–increased their Internet advertising, while their total advertising declined or stayed constant. They joined a diverse group of advertisers who use the interactive medium to reach an ever-growing population of Internet users (see Table 12.2).

FORMS OF INTERACTIVE ADVERTISING

There are various forms of online interactive advertising. A survey by the Internet Advertising Bureau (2000) found that banner ads constituted 55 percent of total online spending; sponsorships, 30 percent; interstitials, 5 percent; e-mail 1 percent; and other, 8 percent. A survey of advertising agencies also supported a similar pattern of Web advertisements (Arbitron 2000). Despite difficulties in accounting for ad spending, the consensus supports the banner ads as the dominant form of interactive advertisements on the Web.

Table 12.2
Top Internet Advertisers in 1998

Top 5 Advertisers	Advertising Volume	Top 6-10 Advertisers	Advertising Volume
Microsoft	$34.8 million	Infoseek	$9.3 million
IBM Corporation	$28.5 million	AT&T	$9.2 million
Compaq Computer	$16.1 million	Hewlett-Packard	$8.0 million
General Motors	$12.7 million	Barnes & Noble	$7.6 million
Excite	$12.3 million	Datek Securities	$7.6 million

Source: InterMedia Advertising Solutions (1999).

Banner Advertising

Banner ads constitute the bulk of online interactive advertising and are used by almost all advertising agencies involved in interactive advertising. A banner ad is a rectangular-shaped image typically located at the top of a Web page. Despite declining click-through rates–from an average of 2.5 percent in 1995 to 0.34 percent in March 2000 (Nielsen Net/Ratings) banner ads are still highly popular. The top banner ads indicate many uses of animation and other interactive features in order to increase clicking behaviors. The attempts now are to change both the size and location of banner ads in order to increase their effectiveness.

Sponsorship Advertising

Following the models of event marketing such as the Virginia Slims tennis tournament, sponsorship advertising involves an advertiser's paying for a particular Web page or section of a content. Without competing ads, sponsorship allows the advertiser to dominate the ad space.

Interstitial Advertising

Interstitial means "in between," and interstitial ads are a way of placing full-page messages between the Web pages. Using the television advertising model, interstitial advertising–in the form of a full-screen or partial-screen ad–is an attempt to force exposure to the ad by interrupting the viewer. This form of ad is more intrusive and requires the user to often "close" the message window in order to return to the original Web content.

Other

Included in this category is a host of practices such as keyword search, classifieds, and referrals. Keyword searches are frequently linked with "affiliate programs" pioneered by companies such as Amazon.com and CDNow. For instance, a search for a book title or an author on Yahoo! can lead to a link to

Table 12.3
Internet Advertising Objectives

	Short Term	Long Term
Increase awareness	30%	7%
Establish new channels	5%	14%
Increase revenue and sales	24%	44%
Increase market share	4%	12%

Source: "People Design Technology"

Amazon.com to purchase that book; a search for an album or musician can lead to a link for CDNow.

A second practice, called Web ring, is an extension of the linking principle that connects a network of sites related to the same subject or theme. The Web ring link can usually be found as an icon at the bottom of web pages. For example, PalmPilot achieved a significant boost in sales as a result of a Web ring approach. The Web ring included links to such sites as fan clubs and retailers. *Business Week* reported that PalmPilot is connected to no fewer than 200 sites via four rings.

Advertisers are also employing opt-in advertising, where consumers enter into explicit agreements to receive e-mails or banner ads related to their interests. Opt-in advertising can be seen as reducing clutter for the consumer, lowering search costs, and increasing the targeting precision of marketers (Krishnamurthy 2000).

No matter which particular form or forms of online interactive advertising are used, the advertising objectives are to get the consumer/user to:

- click on the ad and visit the advertiser's Web site and
- keep the consumer at the Web site as long as possible and increase the amount of time spent (stickiness).

These visits to an advertiser's site are expected to increase company/product awareness, establish new channels, increase revenue and sales, and increase market share. In a survey of advertising and marketing managers, the short-and long-term objectives of Internet advertising emphasize the importance of increased revenues and sales (Table 12.3).

Advertisers use two strategies to achieve their objectives–external communication to encourage traffic to the Web site and internal communication to retain visitors at the site. External strategies include banner advertising, link exchanges, and e-mails using the Internet/Web. Advertisers attempt to place these ads in high-traffic sites such as Yahoo! as well as targeted sites. Special offers, contests, and other incentives are frequently included to increase the appeal of these ads. According to various surveys, consumers like to look at ads that offer discounts, contests, and free offers (Business Week 1999).

The popularity of the Internet as an advertising medium has also meant a rapid increase in advertising clutter. Advertisers, therefore, use traditional media–such as television, billboards, and radio–to attract traffic to their sites in addition to interactive Web advertising. E-Trade, for instance, increased its ad spending by 424.5 percent between 1998 and 1999. Like other heavy dot-com advertisers, it used network television heavily *(Business 2.0*, March 2000). Victoria's Secret advertised during Superbowl 1999 to attract traffic to its own site. Millions of visitors tried to click on the Victoria's Secret site to view the fashion show, but the unprecedented traffic brought down the site instead. In later online fashion shows, Victoria's Secret made sure that it had enough server capacity to cater to millions of visitors simultaneously.

A FRAMEWORK FOR UNDERSTANDING INTERACTIVE ADVERTISING

Given the growing use of the Internet/Web as an advertising medium, it is useful to develop a framework for understanding interactive advertising. Figure 12.2 offers our framework for understanding interactive advertising.

There are two main aspects that advertisers manipulate in their advertising design–interactivity and vividness. Because of the interactivity continuum, advertisers implement interactivity in many different ways. Vividness is the second construct and relates to the breadth of the message–the number of sensory dimensions, cues and senses presented (colors, graphics, animation, etc.), and depth–the quality and resolution of the presentation (bandwidth) as defined by Steuer (1992). It is also referred to as "media richness" (Daft and Lengel 1986).

Vividness is often mistaken for interactivity (Rafaeli 1988; Steuer 1992). It differs, however, on the capacity for two-way communication; in fact, certain pieces of communication can be highly vivid but noninteractive (e.g., television, magazine). Similarly, certain forms of communication can be highly interactive but low in vividness. E-mail, for instance, is primarily text-based and can be highly interactive but low in vividness. Rich media are now being tried in e-mails to increase vividness.

The use of these two features–interactivity and vividness–is aimed to generate social presence, involvement, and arousal in the consumer (see Figure 12.2).

Social Presence

Social presence represents the degree to which a medium conveys the perceived presence of communicating participants in the two-way exchange (Short, Williams, and Christie 1976). By enhancing the interactive features of a medium, this could lead to an enhanced sense of warmth and personalness emanating from the medium itself. Social presence was used quite extensively in the 1970s as a construct to understand and enhance the effectiveness of print and broadcast media. This is also termed "telepresence" in Hoffman and Novak's (1996) model of network navigation. Interactivity is likely to create feelings of social presence for the user through the availability of open channels allowing for two-way communication.

Figure 12.2
Creating Involvement, Social Presence, and Arousal

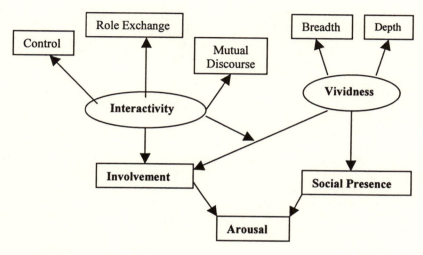

Involvement

Because interactivity can increase control of the content appearing in the ad and offer the opportunity to communicate with the advertiser and/or other consumers, it is likely to enhance the viewer's sense of "involvement." The effect may not necessarily be with the product category (or enduring involvement), but mostly with the ad directly (or situational involvement), as suggested by Zaichkowsky (1994).

Arousal

Arousal is a psychobiological trait of human behavior. Also called phasic activation, it is a short-term reaction of enhanced energy that increases the overall cortical processing of information (Kroeber-Riel 1979). Arousal can be generated by an increase in motor activity or muscular responses (Zajonc and Markus 1982; Wells and Petty 1981)–required by the increased interactivity of the ad–or it can also be the result of cognitive or affective reactions to a stimulus (Holbrook and Batra 1987). Because interactive features of an advertisement are usually quickly identifiable within the ad, there is a possibility that the mere availability of these features might increase arousal directly without the need for involvement.

EFFECTIVENESS OF INTERACTIVE ADVERTISING

Is interactivity effective? Earlier studies of the pre-Web era reported disappointing consumer interest in using available interactive technology (Lee

Table 12.4
Top Sites in Terms of Reach and Stickiness

Web Property	Reach *	Stickiness **	Web Property	Reach *	Stickiness **
eBay	7.5	1:48:41	AOL sites	40.4	22:43
Yahoo	36.8	57:18	Blue Mtn. Arts	9.3	15.42
Microsoft Network	24.8	40:30	iVillage	4.4	15:17
Excite@Home	12.0	28:56	Lycos	23.8	14:03
Go Network	17.0	23:47	ZDNet	5.6	14:01

Source: Nielsen/NetRatings 1999 (October 1999 data).
* Reach = Unique audience in millions;   ** Stickiness = Time per person hr:min:sec.

and Lee 1995; Neuman 1991).   Research evidence shows that enhanced vividness of the medium does not translate into increased persuasion or recall (Taylor and Thompson 1982; Walther 1996).

Is interactive advertising effective? As the focus shifts to the use of interactivity in an advertising context, some researchers have started to compare the effectiveness of the new media to that of traditional media (e.g., Bandopadhyay 1999; Bezjian-Avery, Calder, and Iacobucci 1998); others have focused on measurement standards for the new media themselves (e.g., Dreze and Zufryden 1998). Two common measures of advertising effectiveness are reach (traffic) and stickiness (Anders 1999; Hanson 2000). Reach refers to the number of unique visitors whom the site attracts, while stickiness refers to the site's efficacy in retaining visitors long enough for them to fulfill the intended purpose of the site (Bucklin and Sismeiro 2000).   Studies of advertising effectiveness show wide dispersion in these two key statistics.

As evident from Table 12.4, the effectiveness depends on the nature of the site. For e-commerce sites, the goal is a transaction favored by higher stickiness; eBay and Blue Mountain Arts have smaller reach but high stickiness. For news, data, and portal sites such as Yahoo! and Microsoft Network and AOL, the goal is exposure to the content, including advertising; they succeed by maximizing reach.

Are reach and stickiness the best measures of interactive advertising effectiveness? This can be expressed in terms of two main concerns:

- How can behavioral responses be used to measure and interpret effectiveness of interactive advertising?
- How can traditional (and nonbehavioral) measures of advertising effectiveness be applied to the new medium?

Figure 12.3, an expanded version of Figure 12.2, explores each of these issues.

Figure 12.3
From Arousal to Attitudes, Intentions, and Behaviors

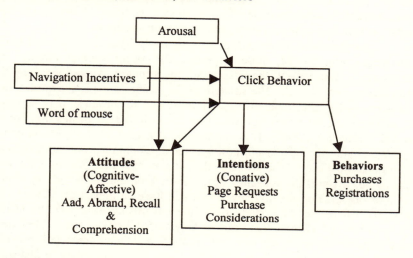

Behavioral Measures

The most distinctive feature of an interactive medium is the ability of the user/viewer to provide signals back to the advertiser. As we described, in the digital continuum, the expected time gap between advertising exposure and a behavioral response–a click–is minimal. Measures of these behavioral responses include "click-through" rates from banner advertisements to the advertiser's site, "page requests" for additional information from within a site, and "page views" of the requested information. The objective of most advertising for Internet sites is to stimulate one or more of these behavioral responses. "Click rates" have, therefore, become the standard measure for interactive advertising effectiveness.

Our framework implies that as the social presence, involvement, and arousal are enhanced with interactive and vivid advertisements, click rates should also increase. By "clicking" on the desired link (through banner advertisements, keyword search, e-mail, etc.), advertisers get an opportunity to present more information to the user and develop better understanding of the user's preferences and behaviors.

Nonbehavioral Measures

Several researchers feel that the emphasis on click-through is not a valid way to measure the effectiveness of online advertising. Briggs and Hollis (1997) claim that Internet ads have an attitudinal effect that occurs without clicking on the banner. Dreze and Hussherr (1999:12) argue that "click-through rates will not capture the full extent of an ad's effectiveness since pre-attentive processing does not lead to immediate action." In other words, advertisers that emphasize only click rates ignore the effects of effects that occur before or after clicking

(Chtourou and Chandon 2000). Attention has therefore shifted to measures that can capture ad effectiveness in terms of pre- and post behaviors such as attitudes (e.g., toward the advertisement [Aad], or toward the brand [Abrand], advertising recall, advertising comprehension, and behavioral intentions.

The nonbehavioral responses (see Figure 12.3) occur as a result of direct interaction with the ad; these responses also occur *without* direct clicking behaviors.   We expect the effects to be stronger when there are direct interactions with the ad. The strength of the relationships is shown in terms of thickness of the directional arrows. A consumer, for instance, may be exposed to a banner ad by Bonzi Software (the most-viewed ad banner for the week ended February 13, 2000). If the consumer chooses to click on the ad and visit the Bonzi site, the effects on attitudes, recall, comprehension, and behavioral intentions are likely to be stronger than if the consumer did not click on the banner ad. Even if the consumer does not click on the banner ad, the exposure (at a preattentive or attentive level) will still have an impact on attitude, recall, comprehension, etc. In a study of online advertising effectiveness, Millward Brown observed 17,000 Web users as they surfed 12 Web sites. They tracked their exposure to online ads and click-throughs and then intercepted them online to measure their response to the 12 advertisements. According to this specific study, 97 percent of the increase in sales came from exposure to the ad, not click-throughs.

Examined directly within an advertising context, the evidence supports the effectiveness of interactivity. Fortin and Dholakia (2000) found interactivity to increase involvement and social presence. Bandopadhyay (1999) found that recall, likability, and purchase intent levels were higher for Internet-based ads than for similar print ads. Venkat and Sobey (1999) measured click-through rate, recall, and attitude (Aad) and found significant effects of consumer involvement and ad size on effectiveness. Ghose and Dou (1998) found a positive effect of interactivity on Web site attractiveness/quality.

Not all forms of interactive ads are equally effective. As we can see in the comparison of interstitial and banner advertising, (Table 12.5) effectiveness measured in terms of behavioral and nonbehavioral responses differs between different forms of interactive advertising. In this particular study by MarketAdvisor (1999), interstitial ads performed better on all measures than banner ads.

INCREASING ADVERTISING EFFECTIVENESS

While there are some stories of great success, the general evidence seems to suggest that the actual traffic to an advertiser's Web site falls far short of the potential, particularly for banner ads. Generally, click-through rates on banner ads have decreased from 2.5 percent in the mid-1990s to 0.36 percent during March 2000 (Nielsen/NetRatings 1999). There have been several responses to address this lackluster performance by interactive advertising. This has been attempted through various efforts described in the following paragraphs.

Table 12.5
Interstitial/Banner Effectiveness Comparison

Effectiveness Measure	Interstitial Ad	Banner Ad
Branding:		
Ad recall increase	64-76%	30-51%
Brand awareness increase (indexed)	107-200%	100%
Reader got ad's main message	33%	16%
Noticeability:		
Look at "often"	36%	9%
Look at "never"	8%	48%
Click rates:		
Average click rate	5%	1%

Source: MarketAdvisor (1999).

Stimulating Traffic to the Web Site

This remains a critical challenge and matters more than ever.

Improving Interactivity

Since "advertising will be an important means of corralling customers and influencing the click" (Colony 1999), emphasis is being put on increasing clicking responses. Efforts include changing location of banner ads (Dreze and Hussherr 1999). A study conducted with Infoseek demonstrates the importance of ad location in the site (main page, thematic page, search page). ABC Net Marketing concluded that a banner placed at the bottom of the page generates 35 percent additional click-throughs than a banner at the top of the page. The "CLICK HERE" mention enhances the click rate by 44 percent (Marx 1996).

Other efforts are aimed at increasing the vividness of interactive advertisements through the use of rich media or variations of banners that are "enriched" with Java, audio, video, or more elaborate animations (i.e., Macromedia Flash). Jupiter Communications believes that these forms of banner advertisements will make up as much as 60 percent of online ad spending by 2002, equivalent to a $5.3 billion share of the estimated $8.8 billion. According to vendors of such rich media, this may increase the effectiveness of interactive advertising by boosting the time spent interacting with advertising. A Unicast study found that 55 percent of respondents who viewed their Superstitial interacted with the ad for up to 30 seconds. Response rates are higher, too. MBInteractive reports that an animated Comet cursor combined with a banner boosted ad awareness 222 percent versus banners alone. Rich media e-mail, in particular, is receiving a lot of attention because its interactive, graphically pleasing advertisement generates brand awareness and stickiness among its audience (Iconocast 2000).

Some advertisers are increasing use of other forms of advertising, particularly e-mail and online link exchanges to target specific consumer profiles. We cited the example of PalmPilot's boosting its sales due to its connections with no fewer than 200 sites via four rings. In an analysis of 101

Web sites, keyword search was found to be the most frequently used interactive feature (64 percent) (Ghose and Dou 1998). Amazon.com, for instance, uses keyword search on AOL to attract visitors to its site.

Use of Additional Incentives

In addition to the design and location of interactive ads, incentives such as contests, sweepstakes, special offers, and discounts are increasingly being provided to build traffic and stickiness. Iwon.com, for instance, gives away $10,000 a day to attract traffic. It attempts to direct traffic to its various pages within its site by offering a different number of points and advertises this heavily on CBS network shows. Launched in October 1999, it became the 28th most visited Web site, with more than 8.2 million unique users (Fortune 2000). Ghose and Dou (1998) found the use of sweepstakes/prizes to be one of top seven interactive features in a survey of 101 Web sites.

Use of Chat Lines, Discussion Forums, Online Communities

Allowing postings by users, such as on Amazon.com or Epinions.com, not only provides new and fresh content for the Web site but also stimulates "word-of-mouse" behaviors that can have a positive impact on site traffic. "Surfer postings" were also one of the top interactive functions in the Ghose and Dou survey (1998).

Stimulating Stickiness and Purchase Transactions

Some advertisers believe that the ultimate effects of clicking behaviors should be behavioral responses other than click-through rates–including time spent viewing an ad, depth, or number of pages accessed at the target site. Others emphasize purchase orders, particularly for e-commerce sites.

In terms of stickiness, eBay has been very successful, with over 60 minutes per visit. Iwon.com, ranked 28th in terms of traffic, does much better in terms of stickiness (Nielsen/NetRatings 1999). In examining purchase order sizes, Ernst & Young ranked the top five sites according to the amount of money that people spent at them. The ranks were as follows: Best Buy (US$233), Egghead.com (U.S.$217), 1800flowers.com (U.S.$173), Disney (U.S.$172) and Wal-Mart (U.S.$167). In terms of traffic, however, Amazon and eBay were the top sites.

Attention to purchase orders from exposure to online advertising is only recent, and the evidence is still quite new and tentative. Some suggest that online advertising generate-greater purchase orders, even if it does not generate overwhelmingly high click-through rates. A recent survey by Bizrate found that only 6 percent of online purchases were inspired by television ads, but 37 percent were through referred Web sites and 13 percent through e-mail marketing. Some have even argued in favor of offline sales as a result of online advertising. A study from Cyber Dialogue found that that in over 50 percent of cases, an online shopping experience generated offline sales and directly affected television shopping, direct mail purchases, and store traffic.

SUMMARY AND CONCLUSIONS

The popularity of the Internet and the Web as an advertising medium will persist as the number of consumers connected to the Net increases not only in the United States, but globally. All kinds of marketers–those with only brick-and-mortar presence as well as Internet e-commerce sites offering purely digital products–can take advantage of the interactive features of the new media to attract visitors to their site and achieve their communication and marketing objectives. As the chapter suggested, while behavioral response (clicking behavior) is one of the primary distinguishing characteristics of the new media, advertisers cannot measure effectiveness of interactive advertising purely on the basis of click-through rates. Attitudes, brand comprehension, and intentions are also important effects that are influenced by advertising and not captured by click-through rates.

Advertisers have to distinguish and use two elements–interactivity and vividness–in order to increase effectiveness of online advertising. Enhancing vividness by means of color, graphics, and animation is likely to favorably impact advertising effectiveness. The optimal mix would appear to be high levels of vividness and moderate levels of interactivity. Navigational links and e-mail exchanges are likely to be more effective ways of implementing interactivity in an ad that retains user control of the viewing process.

As we look ahead, we know that the medium will continue to evolve and that both advertisers and consumers will find new ways of enhancing interactivity and vividness of the medium. Our understanding of the process by which interactive and vivid advertisements can enhance social presence and involvement can only serve to increase the effectiveness of the new media. It is much too early to tell what shape interactive advertising will take and how it will shape consumer attitudes and behaviors in the future.

QUESTIONS FOR DISCUSSION

1. How can different forms of interactive ads be used in an online advertising campaign?

2. Why do increases in interactivity of online ads help/hurt advertising effectiveness?

3. How are vivid online ads changing audience responses?

4. What specific features of interactive ads contribute to reach and stickiness of an advertised Web site?

Part IV

Special Problems and Opportunities of Online Marketing

13

Acceptance-Oriented Design of Web Sites

Andreas Mevenkamp and Martin Kerner

The World Wide Web is nearly omnipresent. Almost every advertisement in traditional media features a reference to the company's Web site. Even in the credits of the German television news one finds the line www.tagesschau.de. There are predictions of exponential growth, a gigantic marketplace, and even a new world order. This drives more and more companies to rush into setting up a Web site.

These companies fail to consider that the acceptance of a Web site is influenced by a multitude of different factors and that the design requires completely new approaches. Successful communication strategies used in traditional media are often applied with only minor changes. They meet a highly involved and very sensitive audience.

An ill-conceived appearance has severe consequences. They range from the rejection of the Web site to severe damage to the image of the company. Because the Web is still on its way to becoming a mass medium, the current users belong to the group of early adopters. These multiplicators influence a large number of persons. This amplifies the effect on a Web site–positively or negatively.

So far there are only a few findings of how a Web site should be designed for widespread acceptance. This chapter should help to bridge this gap.

We introduce the acceptance process for Web sites. In the following we describe a method-package for analyzing the acceptance of a Web site. This package has been developed to examine the Web site of Siemens Nixdorf Informationssysteme AG (SNI, now Siemens Information and Communication). The findings are the basis for the design recommendations, which are given in the last section.

THE ACCEPTANCE PROCESS FOR WEB SITES

In classical acceptance theory (Kollmann and Weiber 1996: 57) the user's decision to take an offer is seen equivalent to his or her acceptance of that offer. In contrast, Web sites require also the consideration of the following usage of a site. Kollman and Weiber have formulated a corresponding definition:

Figure 13.1
The Acceptance Process for Web Sites

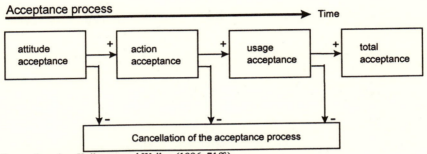

Source: based on Kollmann and Weiber (1996, 71ff.).

Acceptance–in regard to the sociocultural environment (value/objective layer)–is the actual realization of the rational willingness (attitude layer) in the acceptance of a technological innovation (action layer) and its continuous usage in a concrete application situation (usage layer) (Kollmann and Weiber 1996: 68).

The acceptance process for a Web site is thus divided in three phases: attitude acceptance, action acceptance, and usage acceptance (Figure 13.1).

Due to its process character the total acceptance of a Web site by the user is reached only if the individual preconditions for acceptance of all three sublayers are fulfilled. Barriers between the different phases have to be overcome to ensure a continuous use.

Attitude acceptance is reached if the potential user is convinced that the Web site satisfies his or her information needs. For this the user has to be made aware of the site, and his or her interest in it has to be aroused. Furthermore, the advantages of visiting the site have to be communicated. If this isn't fulfilled, the user is not step to the next phase. The site will not accepted.

Action acceptance follows the trial visit of a Web site. If the site meets the expectations of the user, the second acceptance barrier is overcome. The consequence is the adoption of the offer. If the test is not successful, the site is not accepted and will not be visited again. The opinion leaders have an important role in this stage because they communicate their experiences. This has an effect on the attitude acceptance of a large group of other potential users.

Usage acceptance is finally reached if the Web site is seen as positive in its continuous, problem-oriented usage. If this last acceptance barrier is overcome, the user has accepted the site.

Marketing has to take the usage conditions into consideration when defining the communication strategy. The marketing efforts cannot end with the provision of the information, like publishing an advertisement in print media or a television spot. The conception of a Web site also has to take the usage process into account. This is the only way to an acceptance-oriented and therefore successful design of a Web site.

ACCEPTANCE ANALYSIS METHOD FOR WEB SITES

The extended acceptance process of Web sites requires methods to allow efficient obtaining of statements to all acceptance layers. The methods used in the traditional acceptance research—like interviews, observations, or usage tests—result in an effort that can be justified only for the initial development or a fundamental design change. In parallel, many possibilities of this new medium are not used.

Hence, a special methodological package was developed for the analysis of the Web site of Siemens Nixdorf Informationssysteme AG (Mevenkamp 1997: 24ff.). It consists of methods for data collection and analysis designed to fit the requirements of the medium. Part of these methods is known from the traditional acceptance research and media analysis. They have been enhanced and supplemented by further methods.

Data Collection

The data needed for the acceptance analysis are collected using three different methods. Data reflecting the values/objectives layer is gathered with interviews. Data about the action layer and the usage layer can be derived from the Web Server Log Files. To determine what information is used and how the structure of the Web site influences the usage, the server-structure-analysis is used. All collected data are stored in a database, making a comprehensive analysis possible.

Interviews

Findings pertinent to the values/objectives layer and to the attitude layer can be collected only by interviewing the users of the Web site. An online interview meets the need for an efficient and low-cost procedure best. The questionnaire is integrated into the Web site. The user can access it at any time, complete it, and send it back.

During design and testing of the online questionnaire for the SNI study we found that a simple online questionnaire could not fulfill the complex requirements of the study.[11] This led to the development of an enhanced procedure for online interviews that are fully utilizes the possibilities of the Web: the interactive interview.

The interactive interview

In contrast to an online questionnaire the interactive interview consists of several modules. The questions are grouped by subject on a number of different pages. This is due to a number of reasons: Tests have shown that users do not accept questionnaires larger than one screen. They have a longer transmission time, and scrolling is necessary. If the user cancels the interview in the middle of the questionnaire all data entered by then are lost because the questionnaire has not been sent back. The division into smaller segments increases the response rate. The requisition of the next question automatically sends the answers back. This enables the analysis of partly completed questionnaires.

The main difference is the possibility to pose questions based on the answers given. The interactivity offers the opportunity to enter a dialogue with the interviewed person, comparable to the "less structured interview" known from the traditional interview techniques. The questions and their order are predetermined, but they orientate on the situation. Software on the Web Server analyzes the answers and selects the next questions.

Design of the questionnaire

For the design of the questionnaire all instruments known from the traditional interview techniques can be used. The tests during the design of the questionnaire for the SNI-study have shown some particularities: Questions that can be answered by a mouse click are more acceptable than questions that require text input with the keyboard. The HTML-Standard offers a number of design elements like check boxes (☒) or selection lists that make text entries unnecessary in most cases.

The questions have to be short and precise. Web surfers are not willing to read long texts. A large number of questions is accepted, though, as long as the design of the pages is inviting and the number of questions left to answer is shown.

To make the most of the interactive interview it is important to optimize the dramaturgy of the interview. The better that the questions match, the better the results derived from the collected answers. The sequence of the questions is important. The significant questions should be posed at the beginning in case the user cancels the interview.

If the Web site targets an international audience questionnaires in different languages should be available. Normally, an English questionnaire is sufficient. To target specific audiences further language options could be an advantage.

Experience from earlier studies has shown that the response rate is similar to the quote of written questionnaires (Sieber 1995: 282). Therefore measures should be taken to target an audience as large as possible. A contest is an effective method.

At the SNI Web study all users who sent back a fully completed questionnaire and left their e-mail address had the opportunity to win a fully equipped SNI personal computer. The link to the interview was placed on the home page of SNI featuring the prize. This resulted in a response rate of 84 percent (based on the estimated net reach of the Web site during the interview period).

Analysis of the Web Server Log Files

The Web Server logs all accesses in a log file. It is automatically compiled by the Server software. The following data can be used for the analysis of the user behavior:

- URL of the requested page
- Date and time of the request
- Internet address of the requesting computer
- Status code
- The page has been transmitted
- The page is available in the browser cache
- The page cannot be found on the Server
- The requesting computer is not authorized to access this page[12]

The status code is of special interest for acceptance analysis as well as for the discovery of design flaws. If a page is available in the browser cache the user frequently requests it. Attempts to access pages that cannot be found show ill-formed links within the internal, but also the external, referring pages.

The Log File is a text file. To set its data in relationship with other collected information the data have to be loaded into the database. For this special conversion software is used.

Server-Structure-Analysis

The server structure analysis detects which pages the users have visited and can help determine the effect of content structure on usage patterns.

A program recursively scans the directory tree of the server. Its structure and administrative information[13] of the documents are stored in the database. If HTML documents contain reference to further documents this information will be stored in the database as well. Unused documents–there is no other document referring to them–can be detected as well as blind links. The use of graphics can also be analyzed since graphics are integrated into HTML documents by reference.

Data Analysis

High data volume and multiple relationships characterize the data collected with the three methods introduced. The methods for the analysis of Web sites available till now offer only a very limited analysis because they use only a subset of the data collected.[14] The demand to show and analyze the complex relationships between the single data elements led to a new concept of visualization based on the concepts of the semantic data modeling. For the rating of the data, classifications known from the traditional media analysis are used.

Figure 13.2
Excerpt from the Data Model

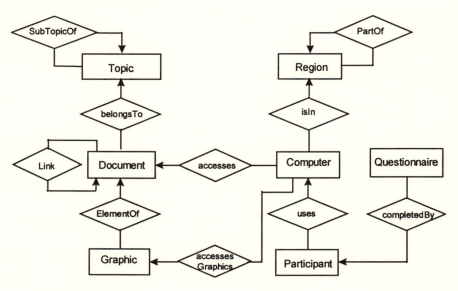

The Data Model

To model the complex relationship between the collected data a semantic data model is used (Elmasri and Navathe 1996; Goble and Bechhofer et al. 1995). Figure 13.2 shows the main object and their relationships. The extended entity relationship (EER) scheme used can be understood easily by referring to the following description (an in-depth discussion of the EER modeling concept can be found in Elmasri and Navathe 1996).

The single documents[15] and Graphics are modeled as objects. In HTML the graphics are integrated in the documents as references to the corresponding files (ElementOf). The references between the documents are modeled by the relationship Link.

Every document is assigned to a topic (belongsTo). The Topic themselves are grouped in a hierarchical order (SubTopicOf).

Page and graphics access are modeled by the relationship accesses and accessesGraphic. The computer is situated in a Region that can be part of a larger Area (PartOf). The Participant in an interview uses a computer to complete a Questionnaire (completedBy).

Classification of Web Contents and User Accesses

Due to high access, frequency analysis of single documents makes sense only in a very limited number of cases.[16] In the following sections we introduce several classifications for viewing data from different interesting perspectives.

Figure 13.3
Contents Classification of the SNI Web Site

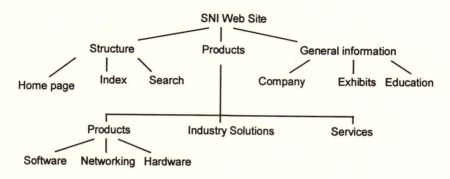

Classification of the Content Categories

To derive data about user interest in information the documents should be classified according to their contents, based on the structure of the Web site. A document can belong to more than one category.

A second important criterion is the functions offered on the Web site, like indexes, search, or help functions. In single cases an analysis of an outstanding page, like the home page of a Web site, is advisable.

Figure 13.3 shows a section of the classification used for the analysis of the SNI Web site.

Another important classification is the differentiation of the pages in layers. The layer number describes how many links a user has to follow to get from the home page to the document. From the distribution of the accesses among the pages of the different layers it can be concluded how many links the users are willing to follow.

Classification of User Accesses

The Internet domain of the computer addresses stored in the log file allows a distinction of the user accesses by region. This can be a geographic region as well as a speech area or an economic area.

As described earlier, the server status codes allow conclusions on the user behavior. So the user accesses are also classified by status code.

Figure 13.4 shows exemplary a section of the object hierarchy used in the SNI study. For reasons of simplicity only hierarchical relationships are shown. Nevertheless there are relationships between all object categories. For instance the Domain de belongs to the European Community (EC), to the German area of speech, and to Western Europe. From there the Web site is accessed by Employees and by external users. The access is documented by a Server Status Code.

Figure 13.4
Classification of the Accesses on the SNI Web Site

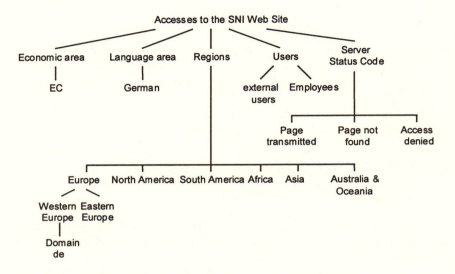

Measurement Methods to Analyze Accesses to Web Sites

In contrast to traditional media the methods to measure the accesses to Web sites are under rapid development. There is a growing interest in standardizing the measurement methods, especially the measurement of the effectiveness of online advertisements. The drivers of such development are mainly the companies using the Web for advertising.

Fantapié and Hoffmann propose the parameters of contact duration, gross-reach and net-reach known from the traditional media analysis. They define the following calculation methods (Fantapié and Hoffmann 1996a: 128ff.)

The *gross-reach* of a Web site is defined as the number of accesses to the home page. Because a user can access a home page more than once, the *net reach* is calculated by the different users accessing it. Because only the computer address is known, a computer is considered to be equal to a user. Is has to be neglected that more than one person can use a computer.

The *contact duration* states how much time a user spends viewing a certain page. It is calculated from the time span between the access to the viewed page and the access to the page requested afterward. For the last page a user accesses the contact duration can though not be calculated.

To determine the effectiveness of online ads two standard measurements are used in Germany: Page Impressions and Visits. A *Visit* is a successful access to the Web site from an external Web address. It defines the contact of the user with the advertising medium. *Page Impressions* define the number of access to a page by any user. This is a measurement for the usage of a single page.

The criteria introduced are a basis for the proposed methods for the measurement of the usage of Web sites. They have been enhanced and extended to allow a comprehensive and differentiated view on all data available.

Reach Calculation

To define the gross-reach by accesses to the home page necessarily leads to wrong figures. Not all users who do not access the Web site by the home page are registered. On the other hand the home page is the central page of a Web site. A large number of users access the home page several times to orien thenselves and to visit other sections of the site. To count every access to the home page during a user's visit leads to highly overstated figures, so the concept of a session–comparable to the visit concept described earlier–is introduced.

All the user's page accesses during a continuous visit are consolidated into a *session*. An access is considered part of a session if the time span between this and the last access to the Web site is not longer than 10 minutes. This value has been derived from experiences during the test and carrying out the SNI study. Other studies use other definitions for this period, e.g. 15 minutes for the visit concept (also Jaspersen 1996: 66; Rengelshausen 1997: 137; Bruhn 1997: 116).

The number of sessions defines the *gross-reach* of a Web site. The gross-reach of sections can be calculated as well by examining only the respective subset of pages using the classifications introduced earlier. The net-reach can be calculated analogous from the number of computers accessing this segment.

Besides the calculation of the reach of a Web site, calculating the reach of single pages, like the home page or the index, can lead to interesting findings. The examination of accesses to single frames and objects (Peters and Karck 1998: 243-47) is reasonable only for the advertisement effectiveness measurement.

Contact Duration Calculation

For determining the contact duration we need to consider that images are stored as references in a Web page. The browser requests the referenced images after loading and interpreting the page. Therefore between the loading of the page and its final rendering there can be a substantial transmission time. This cannot be derived directly from the log files because they track only the time when the request was received.

To analyze this transmission time, the *loading time* is defined as the time span between the request of the page and the request of the last referenced image. The transmission of the last image also takes some time. As the log file only states the time the image has been requested this has to be neglected. The loading time therefore is a little shorter than the actual transmission time.
Loading time is less critical for *text-based* pages, while it can have considerable impact on *image-based* pages, especially if the receiver uses a slow modem connection – long transmission times occur.

Observing the Actually Transmitted Information

Due to the strong increase of image-based Web pages and the parallel increase in the number of users, the amount of data transferred on the Internet is dramatically increasing. Therefore the transmission times increase tremendously–especially for image-based pages–in heavy traffic hours. This leads to users' canceling the loading of pages. Part of the information is not received.

Especially for image-based Web sites, the findings on the acceptance of specific design elements can be substantially distorted. Therefore it is necessary to check how often the loading of a page has been canceled and which information has reached the user until then.

On the basis of the actually transmitted information, statements about the acceptance of the Web site can be made. The loading time accepted by the user can be derived from the loading time of the page up to the cancellation.

Further Measurements

Measurement of a Web site cannot be based on its reach alone. Users accessing only the home page–possibly accidentally while searching for other information–are rated as high as users visiting the site intensely. Therefore also the number of page accesses during a session should be taken into account.

From the sequence of the pages requested the user's path through the Web site could be reconstructed. Web-Tracking allows discovering design deficiencies. Interesting questions concern out of which context the search function is accessed, how intensely it has been used, and in which context it has branched afterward.

From Web-Tracking another figure can be derived: Clicks show how often a link on a page has been used. This indicates attractiveness of a feature, like banners or icons.

Distortion of Result by the Use of Proxy Servers

Many companies, research institutes and Internet service providers use proxy servers to reduce the network load. Also the Web-browser can cache pages automatically. In both cases the calculation of the actual number of users is difficult. The use of proxy servers affects the log files in different ways.

If a proxy server is used, all accesses to the Web are directed via this computer. If a user requests a page that is stored in the cache of the proxy server this page is returned. The Web-server of the information provider is not accessed. Therefore this request cannot be found in the log file.

If the requested page is not available from the proxy server's cache, the server requests it and forwards it to the user's computer. The log file shows the address only of the proxy server and not of the user's computer.

Due to this, problems arise during the analysis of the log files:

- Not all page requests can be found in the log file.
- The requests of a proxy server cannot be counted toward a user's computer.
- Many users simultaneously use a proxy server. Because requests are originated by the proxy server, single sessions appear as one long, continuous session.
- The values for the contact duration are distorted. The next request from the proxy server is not similar to the next request of the user.
- Web-Tracking is not possible, because single users cannot be viewed in isolation.

The browser cache is not as severe a problem, because during every session the browser requests the page at least once.[17] Based on the server structure analysis, the path used by these users can also be reconstructed because the path to a specific page is known.

Methods for Error Reduction

Several methods for reducing these measurement errors are available. All of them have specific problems. They can be grouped into technical methods and methods to estimate the actual reach.

Technical Methods for Error Reduction

Technical methods for error reduction use different means of registering every access to a Web site.

A very restrictive measure is the assignment of user identifications and passwords. Normally, this fails due to the user's need for anonymity. In addition, administrative efforts are necessary. The method can be used only for specific sites with a limited user community and a high usage frequency, as in business-to-business marketing.

Use of cookies is problematic, as well. They are small information units stored on the local hard disk and are activated by the server during each request of a page. Many users disable this browser option due to their desire for anonymity.

The most secure method to register all user access is a design of the pages in a way that all access necessarily requires a data exchange with the server. Specific statistical software is used to log and evaluate the accesses.

For this reference to a program on the server, a CGI-script is placed in the page. While loading the page, the browser requests the server to start this program and transmit the results. Because this program can be run only on the server of the information provider, the proxy server forwards every request to the server. There the program is started. It has two tasks: First, it logs the user's access, and second, it transfers a tiny image– 1×1 point large, showing the background color of the page. The user does not notice this, and as the image bears no information, the user can view the page without being disturbed by the transmission time of that image.[18]

This reference has to be included in every page. Especially for Web sites of large companies that consist of some 10,000 pages, a subsequent introduction of this method is very costly. A way out could be the limitation to a number of selected main pages.

Methods to Estimate the Actual Reach

The measurement error generated by the use of proxy servers can be minimized without using technical methods. The use of the estimation method is especially useful for the ex-post analysis of log files.

Due to the aggregation of page requests by a proxy server, the reach calculated from the log files is below the actual reach. An estimation of the actual reach can be done with the following calculation methods.

The requests stored in the log file are divided into two categories: direct requests and requests over a proxy server. All log file entries of computers, which address or access frequency points to a proxy-server, are marked.[19]

For all computers that have not been identified as proxy servers the average number of page accesses and the average number of sessions is calculated. The number of page accesses by proxy servers is multiplied by the ratio of these two values. From this calculation the estimated figures for the reach of accesses by proxy servers can be derived:

$$PPage \times \frac{DSession}{DPage} = PSession$$

$$PPage \times \frac{DComputer}{DPage} = PComputer$$

PPage:	Number of pages accessed by proxy servers
DPag:	Number of pages accessed by directly connected computers
DComputer:	Number of directly connected computers
DSession:	Number of sessions by directly connected computers
PComputer:	Estimated number of computers accessing by proxy server
PSession :	Estimated number of sessions of computers accessing by proxy server

The reach of a Web site can be calculated by adding the values for the directly connected computers and the computers accessing by a proxy server:

$$PSession + DSession \ = \frac{PPage}{DPage} \times DSession + DSession \ = \text{estimated gross - reach}$$

$$PComputer + DComputer \ = \frac{PPage}{DPage} \times DComputer + DComputer \ = \text{estimated net - reach}$$

A basic assumption for this method is that user behavior of both classes is nearly equal. A precondition for this method is a sufficient number of users accessing the Web site directly. Otherwise concluding from this group to the total number of users is not possible.

An example: the pages of a company's Web site have been accessed 250,000 times. The log file shows that 35,000 computers have accessed the site, 1,000; are identified as proxy servers. The number of page accesses from these computers adds up to 50,000. All requests can be bundled to 65,000 sessions; 55,000 sessions were held on computers directly accessing. For the accesses by the proxy servers the following figures can be calculated:

$$PPage = 50,000 \qquad\qquad DComputer = 34,000$$
$$DPage = 200,000 \qquad\qquad DSession = 55,000$$

$$\frac{50,000}{200,000} \times 55,000 + 55,000 = 68,750 = estimated\ gross\text{-}reach$$

$$\frac{50,000}{200,000} \times 34,000 + 34,000 = 42,500 = estimated\ net\text{-}reach$$

The estimated gross-reach of the Web site, therefore, is 68,750; the net-reach is 42,500.

The figures for the estimated reach are still below the actual, because the number of pages requested by the proxy servers does not include the pages stored in the servers' caches and has been sent to the requesting computers directly.

DESIGN OF WEB SITES

A Web site is primarily a communication medium. As it is used in different areas it cannot be assigned to one single instrument of the marketing mix. It is more a new communication instrument that stands outside the traditional instruments influencing each marketing area.

Therefore, the design of a Web site demands detailed planning. The advantages of a communication appearance in the Web can be transferred into a strategic success factor only if the Web is integrated into the marketing strategy of the company.

The following design recommendations for a company's Web site are based on an analysis of the Web site of Siemens Nixdorf Informationssysteme AG (SNI). In addition selected findings from studies from the areas of online media, communication design and software ergonomics are integrated.

Integration of the Web into the Communication Strategy

Using the Web demands substantial changes of the marketing communication. Because of the interactivity, there is a change from one-directional communication, to a dialogue with the company's environment. This requires adaptation of the communication strategy.

The users browse through the Web site of a company searching for information relevant to them. Hence all information about the company and its products that could be of interest to the user has to be processed accordingly and published on the Web site. Because the Web covers all areas of the marketing communication, a careful coordination of single communication processes is necessary.

To create awareness for the company and its products the traditional media fit best due to their high reach and accessibility for everybody. In traditional advertisements a reference to the company's Web site can be integrated. By coupling traditional media and the Web, (e.g; a prize draw that can be watched at the companies Web site), awareness for the site can be created.

A poll among the users of the SNI Web site has shown that only 8 percent of the participants accessed the Web site after they had seen a reference in traditional media. Hence, in the World Wide Web (WWW) awareness for a Web site has to be created, e.g. by placing banners at frequently visited Web sites. *Web portals* gain increasing importance according to this matter. These highly frequented Web sites are used by a large number of surfers as a starting point and for orientation. Among the important portals in Germany are Yahoo!, Netscape and AOL. Especially in international marketing it is important to be present on the portal since a global advertising campaign in traditional media is hard to realize.

Parallel to the creation of awareness for the Web site, awareness has to be created for the advantages of the Web among nonusers. Only after all reservations and fears against the new medium have been overcome can there be a broad acceptance for the Internet as an information medium. This, in turn, is the basis for the broad usage of a company's Web site. Special events, like a demonstration on trade shows or the sponsoring of Internet computers for schools, are especially useful to communicate the advantages.

After the first acceptance barrier has been overcome, the Web site has to meet the user's requirements. If the Web site is unprofessional or incomplete the user's first visit would also be his or her last. Therefore the site has to be well designed, comprehensive and actual right from the start. The network capacity has to be sufficient as well. Otherwise, users will be deterred by long waiting times.

A good Web design not only leads to a greater loyalty of the users but, through multipliers, reaches users who do not know the Web site. The popular e-zine Hotwired publishes a daily updated list of interesting sites (http://www.hotwired.com/surf/). Being listed there leads to hundreds of new, potential users.

To encourage frequent repeat visits, the Web site has to be maintained, updated, and enlarged on an ongoing basis. If in January one still finds the actual price list of July of the previous year the user is not likely to accept this site.

A number of factors determine the total acceptance of a Web site. A detailed planning of the site and the accompanying actions in traditional media is mandatory. The Web site does not resemble the traditional communication channels. Used in parallel to traditional advertising, it serves to amplify and extend the present communication instruments.

A Web site can be successful in the long term only when it is adopted to the user's needs permanently. This requires a new way of marketing communication: from single actions toward an integrated communication process.

Web Site Design

A Web site is accepted only if the user experiences a subjective benefit from visiting it. For the design of a Web site the user's needs have to be the top priority. This is true for the contents as well as the usage.

There have been some studies on the design of Web sites. In all cases the target was to classify the sites and their users and to identify successful content components (Fantapié Altobelli and Hoffmann 1996a; 1996b). The findings of these studies can be used only as a rough guideline for designing a Web site.

The findings for the SNI study have shown that the participants of those studies and their expectations for a Web site match only slightly those of the users of a specific Web site and their statements.[20] If the design of all Web sites followed the same principles the overload effects of the traditional media would soon be experienced here as well. Using Web sites should circumvent this effect.

Therefore every company should design its Web site individually. In the following we will show which factors must be taken into account.

Content Factors

To make a lasting impression on Web users a Web site has to differ from other Web sites (Förster and Zwernemann 1993: 87). A unique design based on the company's corporate identity is the foundation for this. The Web site has to be consistent and has to be adjusted to all other communication instruments following an integrated strategy.

One outstanding characteristic of Web sites is that users look for the information needed themselves. Concentrating on specific topics can mean, at the same time, neglecting the information needs of potential communication partners. The information offered must also be viewable from different perspectives. This regards the information itself–the information needs of an inexperienced consumer have to be covered as well as those of experts from a buying center: primary users of the Web have to be addressed as well as longtime Web surfers.

To address as broad a user spectrum as possible, country-specific sections in the respective language for important sales regions should supplement international Web sites. Buettner and Mann describe it as region-specific "micro-marketing" (see Buettner and Mann 1995: 306). Multilingual index and search pages help also to profile the Web site. Language consistence has to be maintained carefully.

Single creation of the Web site is not sufficient for longtime user loyalty. The information has to be updated and actualized continuously. In addition a user acceptance analysis has to be conducted regularly in order to identify further user needs. These have to be realized within an evolutionary improvement process (Glomb 1995: 124, 136; Kuhlmannand, Brünne, and Sowarka 1992: 106).

The following summarize the guidelines for Web site content design:

- Unique, individual design
- Match the corporate identity
- Consistent presentation of all information offered
- Consistency with all other communication channels
- All information available is published on the Web site
- Region-specific information
- Multilingual
- Support of different information perception perspectives
- Continuous maintenance and updating
- Evolutionary adoption to users' needs

Navigation Aids

Structuring the Web Site

Users will accept the Web site only if regular use is seen as easy and advantageous. The basis for this is a good and clearly understandable structure of the Web site. The organizational structure of the company should not be used as a basis for this. The structure has to be built according to the user's information needs, for instance a diversion into "about the company", "product information," and so on. Here, commonly known terms should be used.

The site index should be diverted into several layers, according to the user's capacity/capability to process information.[21] In addition overviews on specific topics should be offered, e.g., a list of the products shown at the last trade fair or a list of solutions realized with the company's products.

Compiling pages to thematically structured, hierarchically ordered collections of documents is another aid to the user.[22] For this the use of special server software is necessary. This software allows assigning pages to one or more subjects.[23] Information about a new product can be assigned to the category of fair news, a specific product class, and a specific problem solution.

Pages of completely different sections of the Web site can be set in an associative relation without the authors having to link it (like a "superhypertext" imposed over the actual hypertext). With an extended navigation system, the user is able to get an overview on all information available to a specific topic and the hierarchical relationships. By stating the subjects interesting to him or her, the user can be offered all documents fitting his or her information needs. Also he or she can be shown a collection of related information.

Figure 13.5
Navigation System of the SNI Web Site

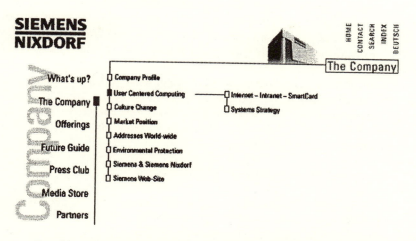

By this system-generated list of relevant information, based on each user's individual needs, a more precise addressing of the user is possible. The information is adapted to the user's perception perspective to a level that would not be possible with a manual structuring of the Web site.

Due to this, the user experiences a substantial improvement in usage. Users can find exactly the information they need. In parallel, if an interesting document has been found while browsing the Web site, all related information that is available can be displayed. So users can find information that they would not have found if they had used conventional search and index pages.

Visualizing the Site Structure

The user has to have an orientation aid available all the time. Therefore a quickly understandable visualization of where on the Web site the page viewed is located and which selections are possible is necessary. The navigation system of the SNI Web site is shown in Figure 13.5. It has been derived from the menu techniques of graphical user interfaces.

An important orientation aid is the precise description of the links; if the information does not fulfill the user's expectations repeatedly, the user will become frustrated and surf to another site. Therefore it has to be clear in advance what is behind a link (Förster and Zwernemann 1993: 94). The opportunity to show information about the links in the browser's status line should be used here.

Additional Navigation Aids

Another very important aid is a search engine. It can be used by users who could not locate the information needed in the index. This applies also to users who have a specific question and do not want to look it up in an index. The queries, in turn, show which information should be offered additionally and where the index pages can be improved.

To enable effortless usage, the structure and functions of the Web site have to be self-explaining. There should be a help-function accessible from every page. Especially functions outside the HTML standard elements, like navigation systems or associative document collections, should be explained here.

Furthermore the user has to have the opportunity to send feedback. By stating the e-mail addresses of the contact persons for the product segments questions can be answered, and criticism and hints can be accepted. This serves to improve the Web site and increases acceptance. Another possibility is to offer short questionnaires about current subjects.

Locating the Web Site within the WWW

Beside the effortless orientation within the company's Web site the easy location of the Web site on the WWW is of outstanding importance.[24] Therefore a URL should be used that can be clearly associated with the company, e.g., www.ibm.com or www.deutsche-bank.de. Additionally special URLs can be used for well-known products, e.g., www.coke.com or www.smart.de.

As important as an illustrative Web address is the listing of the company in national and international Web directories. Because these directories have detailed industry and product categories, the company must be listed in all relevant categories.

Some Web search engines classify and reference the pages of a Web site by the contents of the Meta-Tag within the HTML code, so a list of keywords in this tag is mandatory.

Summarized View on the Navigation Aids

In the following we summarize the recommendations for designing the navigation aids:

- Comprehensive and clear structuring of the contents
- Structuring according to the user's information needs
- Dividing the index into several layers
- Additional, subject-oriented indexes
- Associative compilation of pages in subject-oriented, hierarchical collections
- Visualization of the page's position on the site
- Clear denotation of links
- Search engine
- Help function
- Possibility to give feedback
- URL associated with the company or a product
- Listing in Web directories
- Keywords within the HTML Meta-Tag

Access Times

Transfer and loading times are important factors determining the acceptance of a Web site (Hünerberg and Heise 1995: 7; Jarzina 1995: 48; Fantapié and Hoffmann 1996b: 71; Bless and Matzen 1995: 306; Förster and Zwernemann 1993: 97; Kuhlmann, Brünne, and Sowarka 1992: 50; Hirschberger-Vogel 1988, 83f.). Long access times lead to the rejection of a Web site, that in all other areas has been rated as good (Bless and Matzen 1995: 309). Therefore hardware and network should be planned to guarantee short access times also during heavy traffic hours. The transfer rate of the user's Internet access also has a significant impact on transfer times. Because this cannot be changed, the pages have to be designed accordingly.

Page Design

The human ability to process textual or verbal information is limited. Approximately seven different simultaneously offered informal units–so called chunks–can be processed in parallel in short-time memory. According to knowledge and personal abilities this amount can differ by up to two units (Shiffrin 1976: 177f.).

Visual information does not have this limitation. Due to different processing (Fritz and Thiess 1986), information overload is not likely to happen. The use of pictures and graphics eases the information perception of Web users. The demand for more graphics on Web pages faces capacity boundaries of today's infrastructure. Too many images lead to long transmission times, which will not be accepted by users.

As a compromise we propose the use of graphics in proportion to information depth: for constantly used elements, like navigation buttons, graphic symbols should be used. The amount of graphics used should increase with the information depth of the pages. Pages used to access the information, therefore, have short transmission times. Information-bearing pages could have a high amount of graphics. The user at the end of his or her search will accept a longer transmission time if the information is easier to understand.

In the following we give design recommendations based on these findings.

Layout

No elements distracting the user's attention should be used. Therefore all pages should have a unique layout and color concept. This should take the company's corporate identity to allow an easy association to present knowledge into account. Ornamental backgrounds or images could lead to possible distraction of the users.

The same icons should be used on all pages. Their number should be kept small. Besides ease of use, this also shortens the transmission times. The icons are available from the browser's cache and do not have to be loaded every time a new page is accessed.[25]

Icons should be self-explanatory. They should be derived from the standard icons known from graphical user interfaces. Their position on all pages should be the same in order to allow fast orientation and easy association with the main topic of the page.

Design of the information units

The number of information units should be limited to seven Chunks per page; at least for the home page and the overview pages. All pages should bear a navigation aid to allow an easy orientation on the Web site. This is especially important for comprehensive documents on lower hierarchical levels.

The basic page layout and the position of the navigational aids determine the orientation of the elements. It should be observed that connected information should be presented on one screen. Otherwise interrelations would not be seen due to lacking an overview.

Usability tests during the SNI study have shown that users dislike scrolling between different screens. If it cannot be avoided that a page consists of more than one screen, an overview at the top of the page should be offered. Navigational elements within the pages allow quick orientation and movement.

Complex matters are easier to understand if they are explained with images, animation, or video sequences.[26] They should always be used in context with the other information on the pages. To activate highly involved Web users, graphics are utilizable only to a very low degree.[27] In order to support the user's information perception, the information depth has to be adapted to the message intended.

Images within HTML pages are loaded after the page has been loaded. If graphics are used for important elements describing the contents of the page–like the headline–the user can determine only after the complete loading of the page. Pages used to access the information therefore have short transmission times.[28] The information-bearing pages could have a high amount of graphics. The user is at the end of his or her search and will accept a longer transmission time if the information is easier to understand.

In the following we give design recommendations based on these findings.

Layout

No elements that detract from the user's attention should be used. Therefore all pages should have a unique layout and color concept. This should take the company's on of a Web site. Users without such resources should not be excluded from using a site. They should be offered a version with less graphical elements to lower the transmission times.[29]

For detailed descriptions there should be an option to choose between hypertext and the traditional sequential text. Users who prefer traditional presentation of information are addressed, as well as those who favor a targeted information selection.[30]

Ornamental graphics text should be used sparsely. The key messages must be identifiable at once. Long text passages are contradictory to the idea of fast and easy information selection. They will not be read at all, or only partially.[31]

Summary of page design recommendations

In the following we summarize the recommendations given in the previous sections:

- Avoid information overload
- Use a unique layout and color concept based on the corporate identity
- No or little use of ornamental backgrounds or graphics
- The same position for navigational aids on every page
- Continuous use of a minimized number of self-explaining icons
- Limitation of the pages to one screen
- Short, terse text
- Explanation of complex subjects supported by graphics, animations or video sequences
- Information depth of pictures fitting the intended message
- No graphics for context defining page elements
- Text not displayed by graphics
- No animated intros
- Choice of display mode options
- Choice between hypertext and linear text for detailed descriptions

SUMMARY AND CONCLUSIONS

The World Wide Web is one way to escape the dilemma of lack of information in the face of information overload. In an interactive dialogue users can choose the information relevant to them. Companies have the opportunity to communicate the advantages of their products more intensely and more interactively. They can be present internationally without time limitations.

The complex acceptance process demands a detailed planning and steering of the Web presence. Ill-considered actions can harm a company more than they can help. Web users are still innovators. Appearing incompetent to these multipliers can have severe consequences: the target group will not use the Web site, and the image of the company is damaged (MGM 1995: 13).

To gain acceptance from the first visit on, a large amount of optimally adopted information has to be available. The coupling of the Marketing Information System and the Web site eases this and bears a high synergy potential. If the Web site is designed according to the proposed design guidelines many factors hindering acceptance can be eliminated. The success of a Web site ultimately depends on the information offered and the subjective needs of the users.

The Web site can lose user acceptance during every visit. Therefore the site has to be updated and adapted to user needs in an evolutionary improvement process. The proposed method package for acceptance measurement permits efficient and inexpensive information gathering.

In order to overcome the dilemma of the lack of information in the overflow of data, the Web has to be turned from an insider to a mass medium. Internet access and the usage of the programs have to be simplified and the network bandwidth enlarged. Also all communication channels should be used to create not only awareness of the company's Web site but also interest. A broad interest in the Internet as a communication medium has to be generated through comprehensive, well-designed Web sites that offer the users a significant advantage compared to the information available in traditional media.

QUESTIONS FOR DISCUSSION

1. What are the relative advantages of classical media and the Web-based "new media" for a company's marketing strategy?

2. How can a company combine traditional and online media in its marketing strategy?

3. Choose three Web sites and analyze them based on the criteria established in this chapter?

4. Select an industry and compare a German and a U.S. Web site in this industry. What content should an effective corporate Web site feature, and how should it be structured?

14

Internet-Based Surveys: A Suitable Data Collection Method for Empirical Research?

Wolfgang Bandilla and Peter Hauptmanns

INTRODUCTION

In the past few years, Internet-based surveys have rapidly gained in popularity. Such surveys have already been used in discussions on numerous questions of sociological as well as applied issues (for an overview, see Batinic 1997a). It is undisputed that the Internet can be employed for conducting experiments, for instance, when studying cognitive psychology theories (see Reips 1997, 1999) or conducting exploratory studies, and also as an aid for testing new instruments (Gräf 1997, 1999).

If these techniques are also to be used for commercial surveys, how can the possibilities of the Internet be evaluated? The prospects of commercial, Internet-based surveys are highly attractive. Surveys based on extremely high case numbers can be conducted within short periods and with comparatively small financial expenditure. Then again, nobody would argue that in the near future it would be possible, for instance, to conduct general representative population surveys on the Internet. Even if the Internet is currently experiencing a veritable boom, the small proportion of the population with access to the Internet or online services already speaks against this argument. In the spring of 1998, the ARD/ZDF Online Survey estimated the number of online users in Germany at over 6.6 million people, over 10 percent of the population (van Eimeren, Oehmichen, and Schroter 1998: 423). According to findings of the third wave of the Society for Consumption, Market and Marketing Research's GfK Online Monitor, already 8.4 million people[32] were online by the winter of 1998/1999. Both studies, conducted as computer-assisted telephone interviews on the basis of representative samples, concurrently calculated rates of growth of over 50 percent within the previous 12 months.

In this chapter, we point out which characteristics must be considered when conducting online surveys and, in particular, how the problem of self-selection affects results. For this purpose, we present different survey techniques in the first part and later discuss partial results of a survey conducted exclusively online. We then present results of a 1997 survey on online use conducted in

Germany via telephone. To conclude, in the form of an outlook, we present our views of future developments–some already evident–in order to point out the opportunities of these new Internet-based survey techniques.

TECHNIQUES FOR INTERNET-BASED DATA COLLECTION AND THEIR LIMITATIONS

In principle, Internet services are no different from other communication infrastructures. The use of these services is therefore comparable to written or telephone communication. In this sense, Internet services are applicable to a field of surveys. Particularly common (cf., among others, Batinic and Bosnjak 1997: 221ff.) are e-mail surveys, newsgroup surveys, and surveys on the World Wide Web, which we discuss in the following section.

The simplest variation of a survey using the Internet is the *e-mail survey*. It takes advantage of the special advantages of e-mail, such as speed, asynchronicity and economical handling (Bosnjak 1997: 21).   Similarly to a mail survey, a questionnaire is sent to select e-mail addresses. It is then completed by the recipient and subsequently e-mailed back. A modification of this procedure consists of first dispatching a short mail to announce the survey, calling for participation. Only on the express agreement of the participant will the questionnaire be dispatched.

In the case of e-mail surveys, it must be noted that the willingness to read an e-mail in the first place depends on the degree of acquaintance with the sender and on interest in the topic or the subject matter. Recipients use the "reference" header in an e-mail and the topic specified in the subject line as cues regarding whether to open or trash an e-mail message (see Tuten 1997). In many countries outside the United States, e-mail use is associated with incremental costs: telephone charges, provider fees dependent on time or transmission volume, mailbox size limits, and so on. In such cases, a lot of unwanted e-mail or nonimportant mail cannot be dispatched. The real concerns have less to do with the actual magnitude of these costs (which are frequently insignificant) than with the principal condition that a survey should not generate material costs (in whatever manner) for the participants. A postal survey dispatched with the note "fee to be paid by recipient" is probably unthinkable for any survey researcher. For most U.S. e-mail users, incremental usage cost is not an issue.

Alternatives to e-mail are *surveys in newsgroups* ("electronic discussion forums"; see Turoff and Hiltz 1988), on Usenet, or publishing questionnaires, which are then to be returned via e-mail. Both in German- and English-language Usenet, special newsgroups concerned with surveys have been established (de.alt.umfragen or alt.surveys). Any Usenet user may subscribe to these groups. Subscribers can therefore implicitly expect to encounter surveys in these groups. In practice, however, this method is also hardly applicable, since only a relatively small portion of Usenet users subscribe to these groups. Even a superficial analysis of the contributions (postings) in these groups demonstrates very quickly that only a particular clientele refers to these groups (or articulates itself in these groups), namely, those who themselves conduct surveys and deal with this subject matter. Applied to a larger share of surveys, this target group might be too selective by far.

The third remaining variant is the World Wide Web. At present, most surveys conducted with the help of the Internet are actually on the Web.

At present, the technical possibilities for conducting *surveys on the Web* are already very good. Forms with selectable response defaults, Java or JavaScript commands (see Schuster 1997), image, or sound support facilitate a questionnaire design better and easier for the participant to manage than a printed questionnaire (e.g., via automatic filter guidance, concealment of irrelevant questions, etc.). In this context, the increasing appeal of Web surveys comes as no surprise. Yet, even in the case of this type of survey, the same problems as those already mentioned crop up on the side of the potential survey participant. The survey has to be found on the Web, and answering the catalog of questions is usually connected with costs.

According to the results of an Academic Data Survey in Germany (presented later in more detail), 31 percent of respondents estimated the *cost* of Internet access as "expensive" or "very expensive." In addition to the provider fees, fees for the telephone connection are a significant factor (in particular in the case of local area calls, which are metered), especially when considering the relatively high fees in Germany. Some services still charge for online time as well. To participate in an Internet survey, the participants should already show substantial interest in participating and be willing to bear these costs. Exceptions are those for whom access is free, e.g., at their place of work or education. Both these lead to biased sample distributions of an already reduced population ("Web users" vs. the general population).

Of even greater importance for sample distortions is the question of probability for a Web user to actually be included in the survey sample. A particular survey is no more than one of several million addresses (URLs) on the World Wide Web (WWW). The chances of accessing a survey URL by pure coincidence are minimal. The existence of such surveys therefore needs to be publicized.[33] Announcements in Usenet newsgroups, links to the survey from as many sites as possible, placing ad banners on frequently visited Web sites (in particular, search engines), and other similar activities can increase awareness of a survey.

However, there are limitations: ad banners are frequently costly for the marketer. Links are typically included in other sites only if there is a topical connection to the site of origin. As mentioned earlier, announcements in newsgroups or mailing lists are often aimed at a very limited population of online users.

There is doubt, therefore, as to whether these methods are sufficiently successful. In the "offline" world, this sort of procedure would be comparable to a telephone survey advertised on billboards or in telephone announcement services: "We would like to interview you; please call us under the following number." It would be relatively unlikely to lead to a representative sample.

On the Web, this is different: many Web surveys claim representativeness without justification. Representativeness is a self-imposed "seal of quality" necessary for selling surveys.   Given the present adoption rate and characteristics[34] of technology diffusion, it is obvious that representativeness for the total population of Germany, the United States, or any other part of the world cannot be claimed.[35]

What remains, then, is the question of representativeness of the population of Internet users or, to be more precise, Web users. This also cannot be obtained *a priori*, as described in the following section.   Normally, a Web sample is not random but is nearly always self-selected.   This leads to the question whether systematic differences exist between the participants of a survey and the nonparticipants.

Usually, this problem is addressed by subsequently comparing certain known population parameters and distributions with the appropriate parameters and distributions in the obtained sample (see Hauptmanns 1996). While this procedure is already problematic (see, e.g., Schnell 1993, 1997), it is not at all applicable to surveys conducted using the Internet, since next to nothing is known about the population. Furthermore, many surveys are based on varying definitions of Internet users, which are the result of different usage patterns (e-mail, Internet banking, information searches on the Web, etc.).   For example, can a T-Online (a German ISP) user who employs this service almost exclusively for bank transactions and hardly switches into the broader Internet be considered an Internet user? With regard to determining the population, how are people to be counted who almost exclusively use e-mail and none of the other Internet applications? Further examples can easily be listed with regard to the problem of definition (Hoffman et al. 1996).

Some surveys now rely on comparing their results with those of other Internet surveys. If the results correspond to those of one or two other surveys, then the survey's representativeness or validity is assumed. However, this failure to consider a systematic bias that either excludes certain parts of the population from participation or implies the general nonparticipation of certain parts of the population in such surveys might be equally inherent in all studies. In other words, one biased Internet survey cannot be a way to validate another biased Internet survey.

The decision whether or not to follow a link to a survey is influenced by various reasons of a general nature such as time, costs, expenditure, interest, and concerns about data privacy.[36] A rational Internet user must take into account the specific (material and nonmaterial) costs when participating in a survey.

Intermediate Summary

Surveys using Internet services can (at least at present) arrive at conclusions only on definable subsets of the population of Internet users. Examples would be defined populations such as "all members of an organization" (provided everyone has access to the Internet or Intranet), "all visitors of a specific Web site in a specific period," "all participants in a mailing list," and the like. At present, general use of the "online survey" method is not feasible for representative surveys applicable to the entire population of a country or region. The main problems are:

- Due to varied access to Internet services, the Internet user population is difficult to define. There is no generally valid definition.
- Compiling a genuine random sample (which allows generalization to the population and can thus be referred to as "representative") is impossible, particularly in the case of Web surveys that require self-selection by respondents.
- Typically, the sample is self-selecting. An active sample compilation does not take place. Systematic failure mechanisms are to be expected. No information is available on nonrespondents.

Despite these methodological problems, the number of surveys conducted using the Internet is on the increase. Based on data from one of the best-known Web surveys, the GVU's WWW User Surveys, we will discuss the distortions that must be taken into account when using such survey techniques. Subsequently, the results of a representative telephone survey on computer use in private households by the research firm Academic Data are described. The results of this study show the characteristics on which the group of "Internet users" differs from the non Internet-using population in Germany.

THE GVU'S WWW USER SURVEYS

The Web surveys conducted by the Graphics, Visualization, and Usability (GVU) Center at the Georgia Institute of Technology since early 1994[37] are renowned for their large numbers of participants: usually between 10,000 and 20,000 and sometimes even more than 20,000 participants.[38] The results of these surveys tend to attract special attention in the popular computer press, in particular, when pointing out changes in the audience composition of Internet users.

A characteristic of these and any other similarly conceived surveys[39] is that anybody with access to the Internet and the usual browser software can participate in the survey without any further restrictions. Since 1995, the surveys have been conducted every six months on fixed dates, in April/May and October/November of each year. The field periods amount to four weeks. The surveys are essentially announced by appropriate references in newsgroups and mailing lists and via advertising banners on the large search engines or on other frequently visited sites. Besides detailed documentation, which also refers to the reduced authenticity of the data, due to sample and self-selection problems, the GVU Survey, in contrast to other Web surveys, is characterized by still another feature. Not only are the results of individual surveys disclosed, but the data records (including the codebooks) are also available in ASCII format for further analyses. These can be requested online.

When reviewing the results of these semiannual surveys more closely with regard to the variables of "age" and "education," a very homogeneous picture emerges: the younger age groups are dominant in all surveys.

Figure 14.1
Growth in Number of Computers with Access to the Internet

Source: Network Wizards.

Compared to the general population, the participants evidently have higher level of education. Between October 1995 and April 1998, the portion of participating women rose from 29 percent to nearly 39 percent.

How can these results be rated? For this purpose, the GVU results are to be compared with the development of computers connected to the Internet. This comparison is based on the Internet Domain Survey conducted regularly by Mark Lottor since 1987. According to these findings, a superproportional increase in computers (hosts) has been registered since 1995 (see Figure 14.1).

Particular attention must be paid to the fact that Lottor had to employ a new measurement technique at the beginning of 1998. The new technique was needed because the previously used procedure, due to technical restrictions, had increasingly underestimated the number of Internet computers (cf. a detailed description of the different techniques under the URL: http://www.nw.com). In Figure 14.1 the lower graph, therefore, refers to the old procedure, and the upper graph, to the new procedure or to the values adjusted accordingly. Even if it is impossible to project the total number of participants on the Internet from the number of Internet hosts, since it is unknown how many people per computer have access to the Internet on average (Batinic and Bosnjak 1997: 233), we must assume that–regardless of its measurement procedure-the number of persons rose superproportionally between 1995 and 1999, similar to the development of hosts connected to the Internet.[40]

Applied to the GVU, the superproportional increase in computers would have to be depicted within this period, in particular with reference to the question of how long the survey's participants had already been using the Internet. Table 14.1 shows that, with the exception of the October 1997 survey, the portion of Internet beginners decreased among the participants ("less than 6 months' experience" on the Internet) from 28 percent in October 1995 to only 5 percent in October 1998.

If the percentage shares of the half-yearly newly added hosts are calculated from the absolute Internet Domain Survey host numbers, and if these

Table 14.1
"Internet Beginners" in Comparison to Host Increase

(all data in percent)	Oct 95	April 96	Oct 96	April 97	Oct 97	April 98	Oct 98
Less than 6 months on the Internet	28	24	18	12	18	8	5
Increase of host "old" procedure	37	43	36	25	21		
Increase of host "new" procedure	40	75	14	30	19	14	24

values are then compared with GVU surveys three months later, with regard to the development of the share of Internet beginners ("less than 6 months' experience"), some clear discrepancies become evident, both in the case of the old and new measurement procedures.

For example, while in the first half of 1995 the number of the computers (hosts) connected to the Internet increased to 37 percent, according to the "old" measurement procedure, the October 1995 GVU survey indicated that only 28 percent of the participants had accessed the Internet for the first time within the last six months (i.e., between April and October 1995). When the adjusted "new" measurement procedure is applied (40 percent), the deviation is even stronger; that is, in the fall 1995 GVU survey, fewer people with little experience of the Internet participated than should have been expected according to the trend for hosts in almost the same period. With the exception of the survey conducted in October 1997, in which the portion of Internet beginners (18 percent) was relatively close to the increase in computers in the first half of 1997 (21 percent or 19 percent), Internet beginners are clearly underrepresented in the GVU surveys. Moreover, such distortions cannot be completely excluded for the other variables that describe the survey participants (e.g., age, education, and gender). The main cause for these discrepancies might lie in the self-selection effects described earlier, which crop up especially in Web surveys.

For this reason, in order to gain valid data on the structure of Internet users, it would seem most sensible (at present, in any case) to refer to collection methods that facilitate sample selections according to a well-defined design. In the following sections, results of a telephone survey by the company Academic Data are therefore described. The focus of attention was on structural data and on patterns of use in the online field. The survey thus allows first conclusions on the present situation in Germany.

WHAT DOES THE AVERAGE INTERNET USER IN GERMANY LOOK LIKE?

Demographic data and usage patterns vary relatively strongly between the different online surveys. As a result, e.g., the portion of female users of Internet services varies between approximately 12 percent (W3B-survey, http://www. w3b.de/W3B-1997/Okt-Nov/Zusammenfassung.html) and approximately 15 percent (3-Country-Survey, http://www.psychol.uni giessen.de/~Batinic/survey/ drei_l.htm) up to approximately. 20 percent (University of Leipzig Survey, http://www.marketing.uni leipzig.de/Minternet.htm).

By comparison, offline studies reveal a higher proportion of females. The 1997 ARD Public Broadcasting Online Study (see Van Einerem, Oehmichen, and Schroter 1997) indicated a female proportion of 27 percent, and the Academic Data Survey[41] referred to here established a female portion of approximately 28 percent of home-based Internet users. If use at the workplace is included, then the total percentage of women among Internet users amounts to 32 percent. We assume that these differences are due to the fact that the group of "Internet users" is divided into various subgroups with different patterns of use. Hence, parts of the target population cannot be reached—either because their Internet use profile shows signs of insignificant Web use, because their means of using the Web makes finding Web surveys difficult, or because participation in surveys does not apply to their personal use profile (or they do not consider taking part in a survey as a contribution toward reaching their personal preferences, because of their patterns of use).

Let us first take a look at the Internet users in general. The three largest Internet user age groups lie between 20 and 50 years, peaking at 30-40 years. The mean age for private use only is 35.7 years.   If those people who exclusively have access to the Internet at their place of work are added, it rises to 36.8 years.   The predominant share of Internet users has a higher level of education. More than 20 percent are university graduates, and more than half have at least a college-bound high school degree ("Abitur"). Of course, this is also reflected in the participants' vocational status: 11 percent are students, and 43 percent are white-collar employees. In comparison, the group of blue-collar workers is only marginally represented at under 4 percent.

Use of Various Internet Applications

E-mail is still the most widespread application on the Internet. More than 40 percent of the participants indicated using this application very frequently or frequently. A further 36 percent use it at least sometimes or rarely. Nevertheless, nearly a quarter of the participants indicated never using e-mail. Therefore, this quarter is expected not to participate in e-mail surveys and Web surveys announced via e-mail.

With regard to the Web, a similar picture results. This application is perhaps the best known, yet even in this case, more than a quarter of the participants indicated not using it (or not even knowing what it is). As a result, this group is not accessible for Web surveys either.

The results regarding use of the Usenet (i.e., newsgroups) are even more dramatic. Over 60 percent of participants never use this application, 7 percent do not know what it is. Only 6 percent of the respondent Internet users are very frequent or frequent users of newsgroups, whereby no differentiation can be made between active participants and passive ones, those who only read contributions.

Figure 14.2
Use of Internet Applications

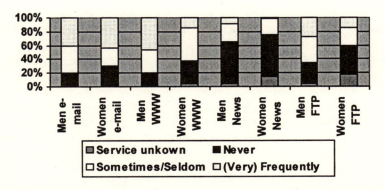

Significant proportions of Internet users do not use all applications and are thus unavailable for participation in surveys using the respective application. It seems as if there are certain preferences for particular applications, while others are neglected. In groups with a homogeneous composition with regard to their intensity of use, a majority of the participants must thus be found on the main diagonal of a simple cross-tabulation of two applications with each other (i.e., the same intensity of use indicated for both applications). With regard to e-mail and the Web, this applies only to a third of the cases; in the case of the Web and newsgroups, only 20 percent. The majority of Internet users, therefore, use the different applications–if at all–unevenly.

If we regard the intensity of use of the different applications differentiated according to the users' gender, there is a clear indication of the cause of differences between online and offline surveys. Due to their patterns of use, it is almost inevitable that the share of women is smaller in Web surveys than the actual share of Internet users. The Web is clearly male-dominated: nearly 46 percent of men indicated using the Web very frequently or frequently, as opposed to only 14 percent of women. In contrast, 34 percent of women never use the Web, compared to only 20 percent of men. If one were to presuppose that the relatively few women who use the Web frequently are not superproportionally motivated to spend their online time completing questionnaires, then the share of women in Web surveys must underestimate their actual share among Internet users. Perhaps the demography of Web surveys is actually, to some extent, a correct indication of Web users, but not of the demographic composition of Internet users in general.

Without being able to deal with it now in detail, the same can be applied to age distribution in an even more extreme form. The Web is incredibly popular among young Internet users, yet the intensity of use decreases with rising age. This also explains why, for example, older Internet users are underrepresented in Web surveys.

Men and women also differ clearly not only in their intensity of use of the Web but also in the way that they use this service. By far the greatest focus of attention for both groups is the search for information. In each case, around 90 percent indicated doing this on the Web. But only a minority intentionally looks for surveys to participate in. Web users stumble upon such surveys more or less coincidentally or via links on frequently visited sites such as search engines.

Coincidental finding probably occurs most when "surfing," or moving from one link to the next while looking for items of interest. Among men, nearly 70 percent indicate this type of Web use. In comparison, only 43 percent of women "surf," clearly a lesser proportion. Their chances of happening upon a survey are therefore smaller.

Similarly, the use of search engines, for men frequently seems to be the starting point for all Web activities: more than three-quarters of all male Internet users indicated using search engines, but again only 43 percent of all women.

If one tries to characterize this user behavior, then it can perhaps be stated that, for men, the Web is, to a greater extent, another kind of "toy" for "surfing." Women, on the other hand, use this medium less, but instead more intentionally or more seriously. On the other hand, they use the Web more frequently than men for requesting Television or print media information and also for online shopping. Maybe a strategic placement of links to surveys in this environment would be a method of including more female Web users in the survey.

Back to the differences between online and offline surveys. The presented results show clearly that women are underrepresented in surveys on the Internet. Women are probably more concerned that their e-mail address is passed on and that they might have to fear harassment as a result, despite the guarantee of anonymity. But the main reason for the discrepancy-and also for most other differences-is to be found in the different patterns of use for men and women or respondents and nonrespondents of a Web survey. It cannot, however, be attributed to women's larger "computer illiteracy" or a greater "fear of technology," as is frequently purported.

CONCLUSIONS AND OUTLOOK

At present, the main problem with online surveys consists in the fact that samples cannot be selected according to a well-defined design, as is the case with other data acquisition techniques in the field of empirical social research. Also, there is a lack of even moderately exact data on the Internet user population. With the ever-increasing spread of Web surveys, the problem of self-selection is particularly acute. One can assume that only certain groups of Internet users are willing to participate in these surveys and that the data obtained in this way are subject to strong bias. As a result, data obtained exclusively online are therefore not sufficient when, for example, collating information on the demography of Internet users and their behavior in the Net. In this context, it might also in the future be necessary to use collection techniques such as CATI or CAPI that are more cost-intensive, in comparison to Net surveys. Definitely of help in this context might be the ARD (van Eimeren, Oehmichen, and Schroter 1997, 1998) and GfK (Bronold 1999) representative telephone surveys on online use, both conducted on a regular basis since 1997.

The comparability of these and other surveys conducted "offline," suffers from the fact that the sample selection is based on differently defined populations ("14 to 59-year-old Germans" or "everybody over age 14") and that they are also based on different definitions of online use (see Wingert 1998: 212ff.).

What is still missing at present is a study that provides up-to-date, methodologically perfect and precise baseline data (see also Josse' 1998: 15). These data would permit empirically shedding light upon the, until today, unsettled problem of a proper definition of Internet use. In this manner, a representative online sample whose patterns of use could be traced over a longer period could be established for the first time.

Despite all of these methodological problems, there are fields where use of Internet-based data collection methods is perfectly justified. The following can be named as examples:

- Surveys in closed networks, for example, for pretesting newly developed instruments (Gräf 1997, 1999) or for conducting employee surveys in international corporations (e.g., Durstewitz 1997).

- Web site visitor questionnaires on their assessment of these sites. The online sampling tool "N Viz" (Hagenhoff and Pfleiderer 1998) has been in use in the field of market research for some time now. With the aid of this tool, the problem of self-selection is reduced by requesting each visitor of a site to participate in a survey.

- Experimentally conducted elementary studies that allow theoretically founded hypothesis testing (see, among others, Kranz, Ballard and Shear 1997; Reips 1997, 1998; Schmidt 1997). These so-called Web experiments (Reips 1995) represent the consistent extension of laboratory experiments onto desk computers. They not only are suitable for the replication of "classical" studies but can also supply answers to the question of the generalization ability of experimentally gained results, until now accountable only with difficulty. In many respects, the experiments are conducted in the same manner as if the test subject were seated in front of a computer in a laboratory—with the exception that the experimental material is transferred to the test subject's screen somewhere on the planet. Test subjects' reactions (e.g., navigation, response times, etc.) can be noted and incorporated in the statistical analysis.

- Exploratory surveys: studies such as the GVU survey can be counted in this category. Despite its methodological problems, such studies allow for a specification of the participants (e.g., two-dimensional distributions of demographic variables, as well as further relevant background variables) and can thus provide analyses of future survey results with valuable comparative information.

The last point is of particular relevance. Currently, we still have relatively little knowledge of the "Internet user" his or her actions, intentions, preferences, and so on. Each survey can contribute to expanding this knowledge, be it in the form of hypotheses and assumptions examined with other means or at a different time. Surveys for the formulation of a theory are already feasible today—yet not for the testing of theory.

Finally, it should not be forgotten that it is especially important for sociologists, social researchers, and market and public opinion analysts to quickly learn how to handle this medium, to test the opportunities and limits of its use, and to find ways of overcoming existing restrictions.   This will help avoid a future scenario when we could conduct methodologically refined and perfect studies on the Internet, but without the techniques that take optimal advantage of this possibility because of the lack of previous research within this field.

QUESTIONS FOR DISCUSSION

1.   What are the methodological limitations of conducting surveys on the Internet?

2.   What are some of the practical and methodologically sound applications of Internet-based surveys?

3.   How can researchers improve the validity and reliability of Internet-based surveys?

4.   Many authors and consultants use the GVU survey as an indication of Web trends. Is that legitimate? Should they caution the reader? How?

15

Virtual Communities as an Instrument of Internet Marketing

Stephan Bennemann and Jesko Schröder

This chapter deals with the role of Internet marketing in developing a virtual community. The concept of virtual communities developed by J. Hagel III and A. G. Armstrong is discussed. Furthermore, the prerequisites for developing a virtual community are presented based on an empirical study of a big United States truck company; this study, conducted in the United States, provides some guidelines for creating a virtual community from a client perspective.

INTRODUCTION

If one can believe the known numbers, including those presented in this book, most companies that are currently present on the Internet and the Web have not' earned much money from their Internet activities so far. Even "successful" companies like the online bookstore Amazon.com are no exception.

One important reason for the low profitability of Web activities is the lack of customer retention (e.g., Albers, Paul and Runte 1999: 956). Apparently, it has never been easier to search for the cheapest offer because it is always just a few mouse clicks away. Offers in cyberspace consequently break up preferences and significantly reduce switching cost and mobility barriers while diminishing the barriers of entry for competitors (see Chapter 3 in this book).

Quite a few companies regard this development as a threat to their existence. Bilstein of Simon, Kucher and Partner consultants called it the "horror vision of every firm" ("Streitgespräch" 1998: S. 48). An important goal for companies is therefore to (re)create customer retention. For that purpose, numerous ideas have been discussed, e.g., customer chats (see, for e.g., www.milka.de). Virtual communities are increasingly mentioned as a strategy of high customer retention in this context.

This chapter examines whether virtual communities can be used as instruments for Internet marketing and concentrates on the requirements for their success. For this purpose it is necessary to first illustrate the development of noncommercial virtual communities before evaluating the opportunities of commercial application. This is the basis of an empirical study in which we have examined the attitude of customers of Freightliner, a well-known United States truck company, and other manufacturers toward the creation of a virtual community formed by truckers.

THE EMERGENCE OF VIRTUAL COMMUNITIES

The term virtual community (VC) is closely intertwined with the development of the Internet. Until the early 1990s the Internet was accessible to only a few users, mostly scientists. Basically, these people accepted the "Netiquette"–informal guidelines that controlled communication in the Internet. Whoever infringed upon these rules, for example, by sending advertising via the Internet, was punished by a number of other users: the person's network access could be knocked out by sending thousands of protest e-mails, or e-mails of this origin were simply not forwarded by other servers anymore. The group of early Internet users can thus be regarded as a true "community," since it behaved like any other "real" community.

The technical platform of the Internet is the basis for different services. Beside popular services like e-mail and the World Wide Web, those are, among others, newsgroups, mailing lists, or bulletin board systems (BBS). The latter promote the users' discussion of various topics. There are different types of BBS: with/without moderation, bulletin board/mailing list, and so on. These forums, estimated at 60,000 in 1993, are mostly organized by voluntary operators (SysOp's). One common characteristic of all forums is their strictly noncommercial intention.

The WELL (Whole Earth 'Lectronic Link) is a BBS founded in 1984. In his book *The Virtual Community* Rheingold (1993) gave an in-depth description of "life," opportunities, and perspectives in this electronic community. At that point, the term VC had reached popularity to some degree.

From a marketing perspective, members of a VC represent a highly interesting group:

They have formed a relatively homogeneous group through self-selection (e.g., in a discussion forum of traveling or golf);

They are highly involved (Rheingold reported that he spent two hours each day in WELL);

They produce a large amount of interesting information and can, depending on the topic, be regarded as lead users or focus groups;

They are believed to be loyal to a certain VC over a long period of time, especially if they have to move or travel frequently.

THE CONCEPT OF A COMMERCIAL VIRTUAL COMMUNITY

Considering the characteristics of VCs just described above it seems obvious to use this potential for commercial interests. Companies could first collect information provided on other Web sites, as they do with other Internet services. For example, Stauss recommends continuously screening Internet customer communication in newsgroups and specific critics' Web sites in which the company and its products are the subject of interest (see Stauss 1998: 143).

Hagel and Armstrong go one step further and emphasize the opportunity to conquer the markets through virtual communities, as described in their book *Net Gain*, published in 1997. Both Rheingold and Hagel and Armstrong use WELL, but while the former describes life with WELL and derives perspectives for the future of VCs without deviating from the basic WELL concept, the latter significantly expand the VC concept: "Virtual communities will work as agents for their members and help them receive more information on both products and services as well as lower prices from suppliers while supplying a large amount of the need for interpersonal communication" (Hagel and Armstrong 1997: 23).

In addition to the social component that Hagel and Armstrong consider the most important task of VCs, a commercial component has far-reaching consequences: "As soon as a Virtual Community holds an important share of buying contracts within a commercial sector, the organizer of the community will probably have various opportunities to make decisive changes in the economic structures" (Hagel and Armstrong 1997: S. 88). Hagel and Armstrong also see the possibility of demanding commissions from suppliers (2–10 percent) and disintermediation of middlemen (Hagel and Armstrong 1997, S. 88).

The publication of the book promoted the popularity of the concept of Virtual communities, and a lot of other authors refer to Hagel and Armstrong (e.g., Albers, Paul, and Runte 1999; Seeger 1998).

The farthest-reaching concept of a commercial virtual community, however, is developed by Hagel and Armstrong themselves. Such a virtual community is determined by the following five characteristics:

A specific focus of interest to the members

The integration of content and communication

Focus on information provided by members

The choice between competing suppliers and offers

Commercially motivated organizers of virtual communities

"Virtual Communities" as defined by Hagel and Armstrong are distinctly different from electronic customer clubs (cf. Fritz 1999: 997) or cooperative Web offers of companies and associations (Schmidt 1998: 27), which do not fit any of the criteria just mentioned. The similarity of the basic structures of the commercial VCs, according to Hagel and Armstrong, and the classic VCs is so strong that the use of the term seems justified. In contrast to the already functioning classic VCs, however, the commercial VC's still need to prove that they work–something that Hagel and Armstrong admit: "Currently, there is definitely not one example of a virtual community that complies to all criteria" (Hagel and Armstrong 1997: 52).

THE PROBLEMS OF THE VIRTUAL COMMUNITY CONCEPT OF HAGEL AND ARMSTRONG

Without mentioning all aspects of communities in this chapter (see Höflich 1996: 260), it is evident that virtual communities have existed since the early years of the Internet and have functioned since then (e.g., the VC WELL, described in detail by Rheingold). However, Hagel and Armstrong have not demonstrated convincingly that a VC based on their concept is able to work. They state only that VCs will become the preferred shopping location for a major part of consumers (Hagel and Armstrong 1997: 49) or that the ties to the community will become stronger as the community promotes interpersonal relationships among its members (66).

A number of examples contradict the VC based on the concept of Hagel and Armstrong:

The German company Miniruf, which sells pagers under the name Quix has put great efforts in creating a Quix-Community as a subculture. In the terminology of Hagel III and Armstrong, Miniruf represented the community builder whereas the contents were supposed to be provided mainly by members. This attempt, which also included popular music groups, failed in the fall of 1998 (Rogler 1998; Klausing 1998). The whole company was sold to a successor, who intends to use Quix only in the operational segment.

Many specialized stores that are believed by many consumers to have a lot of competence have lost the competition with mail-order companies or specialized "megastores" because consumers have adopted a certain kind of behavior: get advice at the specialized store, and purchase at catalog dealers or specialist megastores. Except for the members' loyalty toward their community, Hagel and Armstrong offer no reason that VC members should behave in a different way. Analogously, a VC member could first get advice in the community and then turn directly to the supplier selected by the VC and share the margin (2–10 percent) that was originally earned by the VC organizer. Especially on the Internet, this saving opportunity would require no more than a few mouse clicks. In addition, the members' loyalty toward their community could be reduced because the commercial organizer claims the whole profit margin. Therefore members do not need to feel to withhold something from the community.

The Electronic Mall Bodensee (emb) has been on the Web since 1995. This virtual mall is sponsored by various research institutes and is largely financed by the European Union. Despite its clear focus on both small and medium-sized companies as well as the communication among its customers, it apparently did not succeed in creating a profitable community. This is even more surprising as emb's communication and contents are of such high quality that a private organization of VCs would have problems in finding opportunities for improvement.

The online bookstore Amazon.com is often described as best practice for the organization of a commercial VC (Lechner et al. 1998: 7; Schütz 1998: 31), however, not by Hagel and Armstrong. The company focuses on including its customers but does not concentrate on contents provided by customers. For example, Amazon tells its customers what book reviews should look like and to refrain from comments on other reviews. Interactivity between customers is, therefore, virtually impossible.

VCs are not needed anymore to find out the cheapest offer on the Internet. Price agencies like www.preiswaerter.de provide the information, requesting only small fees and taking care of the transaction details. Intelligent search engines, so-called shopbots, are available for free. Competitors would not have to overcome the barriers of entry created by the VC (Paul and Runte 1998: 161; Hagel and Armstrong 1997: 95), rather, emerging commercial VCs would first have to compete against already established players.

It seems doubtful that a VC, according to Hagel and Armstrong, would be able to work; at least it would not meet all five criteria. However, the question is whether a commercial VC could be created with less ambitious goals. This is the background for the conception of our own study, described in the following sections.

THE CREATION OF A VIRTUAL COMMUNITY BY FREIGHTLINER

Basic Conditions

Cost considerations kept us from founding our own commercial VC to study the opportunities of this instrument for Internet marketing. However, we took the opportunity to interview current and potential customers of the U.S. truck manufacturer Freightliner in December 1997. Freightliner, like many others, had already thought of establishing a VC. In contrast to the concept of Hagel and Armstrong this VC should not be run independently of suppliers (see later) but as an instrument of Freightliner's Internet marketing.

Due to this dependence on the supplier, two problems concerning customer retention emerge. It may be true that truckers would like to be active members of a future Freightliner VC but would buy their next truck from a competitor at the same time. Since a Freightliner VC should serve a commercial purpose but will not cover its own expenses, it is not enough just to create an association between the truckers and the Freightliner VC. The Freightliner VC should convert truckers from being members of the VC into customers for Freightliner trucks.

The trucker scene shows some special characteristics are be briefly discussed in a later section. The most important point, however, is that truckers have already been forming a VC for a long time by using CB radio as a means of communication. The nature of this community has been described many times, e.g., in country songs, movies, or soap operas on television. As to the creation of an Internet-based VC, this is a special characteristic fairly uncommon for most other markets.

GOALS OF THE STUDY

We begin with an evaluation of the technical and structural preconditions for the utilization of the Internet by truckers as well as the degree of utilization of other communication media. Consequently, the goal of the study was to answer the following questions:

What are the specific requirements for content of a trucker VC demanded by potential user groups, and which types of utilization can be expected?

Which user group is the primary target group, and which perspectives for enlargening the target group can be derived?

Which are the potential users' primary concerns and barriers to utilization?

RESEARCH DESIGN

The research goals just described aimed primarily at determining descriptive characteristics through exploring unknown structures and interdependencies. Therefore the study design had to be exploratory-descriptive (Nieschlag, Dichtl and Hörschgen 1997: 675, Fritz 1995: 60; Böhler 1992: 30). This study is supposed to give an overview of the dimensions and elements of the object of interest and thus can be characterized as a pilot study. The results of this pilot study can be taken as a basis for later studies of representative samples; however, the pilot study does not claim to be representative itself (Berekoven, Eckert, and Ellenrieder 1996: 95).

The empirical study started with expert interviews. These interviews were supposed to help gain a general overview of the subject. The interviews were not standardized or recorded. However, useful information and insights could be gained; this contributed to the organization of the empirical study and the theoretical framework. Subsequently, relevant secondary literature, such as trucking publications and Web sites, were analyzed to evaluate potential elements of contents for the creation of a trucker VC.

A framework for interviews with truckers was developed. The focus was on independent owner-operators, that is, truckers who own one or just a few trucks and drive at least one truck by themselves. This customer segment is very attractive for the Freightliner Corporation because of its high potential contribution margins. Limiting the study just to this trucker segment did not appear practical. Therefore two other groups of truckers were interviewed: dependent owner operators ("leased to a fleet"), who drive for other transport companies, as well as company/fleet drivers, who are employed by a transport company. The latter can be regarded at least as potential customers of the Freightliner Corporation.

The data collection method was determined not only by cost and time restraints but also by the fact that truckers, especially in long-distance trucking, are extremely difficult to reach because of their high mobility. For this reason we refrained from telephone interviews. Administration of mail questionnaires was possible, but response time could be estimated to be six to eight weeks due to the long absence of the operator-owner segment. Freightliner Corporation considered this too long (a later interview showed that 68 percent of the trips of owner-operators take longer than four weeks).

The only possible data collection method was the face-to-face personal interview (Berekoven, Eckert and Ellenrieder 1996: 104). Methodological disadvantages of the face-to-face interview that mostly concern the interviewer were offset by both a thorough questionnaire design and the use of standardized, fixed-alternative questions (Kotler and Bliemel 1995: 203 and Nieschlag, Dichtl and Hörschgen 1997: 738).

The content of the questionnaire was structured as follows:

Demographics of the respondents;

Access to, and utilization of, means of electronic communication;

Importance of different media and services within a trucker VC;

General interest in participating in a trucker VC and fundamental concerns against the utilization of trucking-related offers on the Internet.

The questionnaire design contained mostly fixed-alternative questions to make the collected data more reliable and easier to quantify and, consequently, to ensure a better comparability (Meffert 1992: 205). Furthermore, because of the complexity of the subject, the comprehensibility of the questions and their order were essential (Berekoven, Eckert and Ellenrieder 1996: 100). To avoid any misunderstanding concerning language and contents and to estimate the average time per interview, the questionnaire was pretested.

Due to time and cost constraints, the interviews had to be limited to a time frame and the Portland, Oregon, region where the corporate offices of the Freightliner Corporation are located. Besides, the difficulties in reaching the target group mentioned earlier played an important role in the determination of the interview locations; the only possible places were larger truck stops on freeways.

RESULTS

Response Behavior and Demographics

The overall number of truckers approached was n = 129, of whom 55 percent were willing to participate in the interview, 45 percent (n = 58) refused to participate. This refusal rate is acceptable for an exploratory design. When analyzing the study results, it has to be considered, however, that many refusals came from older truckers (50 years and above), who have a very low affinity toward modern information technology.

Not surprisingly, male truck drivers dominate the group surveyed. Concerning the age structure the 30 to 49-year-olds are prevalent (82 percent).

The group can be further divided into equal groups of independent owner-operators, dependent owner-operators, and company/fleet drivers. Ninety-six percent of all drivers belong to the interstate/long-haul segment. The relatively high share of the Freightliner brand can be explained by the selection of the interview locations.

The demographics of the truckers interviewed are as follows:

Gender:	Male	96 %
	Female	4 %
Age:	19-29 years	10 %
	30-39 years	44 %
	40-49 years	38 %
	50-59 years	5 %
	60 years and above	3 %
Brand of truck:	Freightliner	40 %
	Others	60 %
Driver segment:	Independent owner operator	35 %
	Dependent owner operator	31 %
	Company/fleet driver	34 %
Driving distances:	Interstate/long haul (over 400 miles)	96 %
	Intrastate/regional (under 400 miles)	1 %
	Local/metro	3 %

Access to, and Utilization of, Electronic Communication Media

Absence from Residence During one trip

Of the independent owner-operators, 68 percent are usually more than four weeks absent from their residence. This period of time is shorter for dependent owner-operators and company/fleet drivers. Nevertheless for 59 percent resp. 50 percent of these groups, a typical trip takes more than three weeks. The very high mobility of the respondents eventually results in a high dependence on electronic communication media like CB radio or telephones (see Fig. 15.1).

Share of Overnight Stays at Truck Stops and Motels During a Trip

The truckers interviewed spend the night mainly at truck stops and motels (83 percent of all respondents and even 96 percent of the independent owner-operators spend the night in 75 percent of all cases at truck stops and motels). Since company/fleet drivers have a higher share of short-distance trips (one to two days) on which they can spend the night at home, they stay less often at truck stops and motels.

It can be concluded that the majority of the respondents would have the opportunity to access the Internet at truck stops or motels at night (provided that there are sufficient lines/outlets/terminals).

Utilization of Electronic Communication Media during a Trip

Regarding the utilization of electronic communication media, basically all respondents use CB radio. In contrast, fleet companies employ satellite-based information and communication systems exclusively. Until today, this kind of satellite system did not possess gateways to the Web but mostly provided the opportunity to send and receive e-mails. Furthermore, there appeared to be a generally high dependence on calling cards. Of the respondents, 35 percent (44 percent of the independent owner-operators) additionally used a cellular phone. Laptops are not very common; the highest utilization rate was among the independent owner-operators (20 percent). An analysis of the different age groups in the independent owner segment shows that laptops are mainly used by the younger group (30 to 39 years). The share of laptop users in this group was 36 percent compared with 9 percent in the group of the 40 to 49-year-olds and 0 percent in the group 50 years and above.

Popularity of Internet Accounts

The diffusion of Internet accounts differs between driver segments. Currently, 48 percent of the independent owner-operators have access to the Internet, as well as 50 percent of the dependent owner-operators and 42 percent of the company/fleet drivers. Splitting up the independent owner operators into age groups shows that 82 percent of the age group 30 to 39 years have an Internet account, compared to only 27 percent of the age group 40 to 49 years and 0 percent of the group 50 years and above.

Of the respondents with Internet accounts, 94 percent access the Web from home, and 15 percent of them do it at truck stops. These are mainly independent owner-operators who possess a laptop of their own. In addition, there are some truck stops where the Internet can be accessed on public terminals.

Future Outlook of Internet Use

Of all truckers interviewed who do not have an Internet account, 71 percent intend to use the Internet in the future, among them 77 percent within the next 12 months. Among the independent owner-operators, their share is 69 percent, 77 percent within the next 12 months. A more detailed analysis of the different age groups shows that 100 percent of the 30 to 39-year-olds and 88 percent of the 40 to 49-year-olds plan to use the Internet in the future, but 0 percent of the group 50 years and older.

Figure 15.1
Utilization of Electronic Communication Media during a Trip

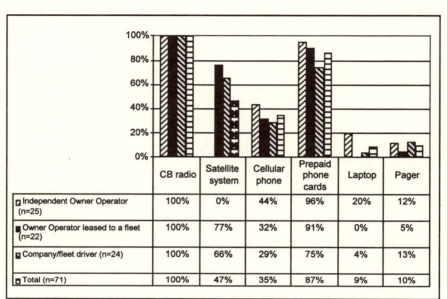

	CB radio	Satellite system	Cellular phone	Prepaid phone cards	Laptop	Pager
▫ Independent Owner Operator (n=25)	100%	0%	44%	96%	20%	12%
■ Owner Operator leased to a fleet (n=22)	100%	77%	32%	91%	0%	5%
▫ Company/fleet driver (n=24)	100%	66%	29%	75%	4%	13%
▫ Total (n=71)	100%	47%	35%	87%	9%	10%

Utilization of Trucking-Related Information and Services on the Internet

The degree of utilization of trucking-related information and services on the Internet is currently rather low among the truckers interviewed. Only 18 percent of all respondents have used trucking-related offers so far. Among the independent owner operators the share is 20 percent.

Requirements of a Trucker Virtual Community

Initially, the concept of a virtual community was explained verbally to the truckers. In the questionnaire the truckers were supposed to judge the importance of selected information and services in a trucker VC. The respondents were asked to rate the importance of each offer on a scale from 1 (= very low importance) to 5 (= very high importance); the arithmetic mean of the responses is shown in Figure 15.2. The summary (Figure 15.2) shows that "trucking-related news" (mean = 4.0), "weather forecast, road conditions" (mean = 4.0), and "map of truck stops, service stations, restaurant and motels" (mean = 3.9) are most important. In contrast, "entertainment, online games" (mean = 2.3) and "sales of gifts" and "sales of software products" (both mean = 2.7) are least relevant within a trucker VC.

From the independent owner-operator's perspective the services "applications for doing business" (especially electronic freight markets) (mean = 4.7), "buying or selling of used trucks" (mean = 4.4), and "sales of parts and accessories" (mean = 4.3) are regarded as most important. The services "entertainment, online games" (mean = 2.1) and "sales of gifts" (mean = 2.9) are of no importance to this group, either.

Additionally, older independent owner-operators (50 years and older) also attach high importance to "trucking-related news" (mean = 3.7). Generally, it can be observed that most services are more important to younger age groups than to older drivers (50 years and older).

Unlike the independent owner-operators, the dependent owner-operators attach not much importance to "applications for doing business" (mean = 2.9). For them, "trucking-related news" (mean = 4.0), "map of truck stops, service stations, restaurants, and motels" (mean = 3.9), and "weather forecast, road conditions" (mean = 3.7) play an important role. Less relevant, just as for the independent owner-operators, are "entertainment, online games" (mean = 2.2) and "sales of gifts" (mean = 2.5). As the dependent owner-operators, the company/fleet drivers consider "weather forecast, road conditions" (mean = 4.2), "map of truck stops, service stations, restaurants and motels" (mean = 4.0), and "trucking-related news" (mean = 3.8) most important, too, however, in reverse order. It is striking that this group attaches low importance to more services than the dependent and especially the independent owner-operators. The lowest ratings are given to "scheduled events" and "sales of software products" (both means = 2.5)

General Interest and Concerns in Participating in a Trucker Virtual Community

Figure 15.3 clearly shows that the independent owner-operators are the group with the greatest interest in a trucker VC. This is also reflected by the results of the previous section, which show that independent owner-operators generally attach more importance to the information and services provided by a trucker VC than dependent owner-operators and company/fleet drivers. Surprisingly, company/fleet drivers show a higher interest in a trucker VC than dependent owner-operators; the reason for this phenomenon, however, could not be found within the scope of this study.

Looking at the different age groups, it is striking that within the independent owner-operator segment, the general interest in a trucker VC seems to depend largely on the age of the truckers. While the interest of the age group 30 to 39 years can be considered very high (mean = 4.3) and still reaches mean = 3.8 in the age group 40 to 49 years, the interest of the over 49-year-old independent owner-operators is very low (mean = 2.3).

Finally, the truckers were asked which basic concerns they have with offers on the Internet that are directed specifically to them. From this information the following basic requirements for a trucker VC can be derived:

The cost of utilization has to be low (telephone and Internet service provider fees);

The utilization of the system has to be easy to learn (can be achieved by a self-explaining user interface);

Figure 15.2
Importance of Trucking-Related Information and Services in a Trucker Virtual Community

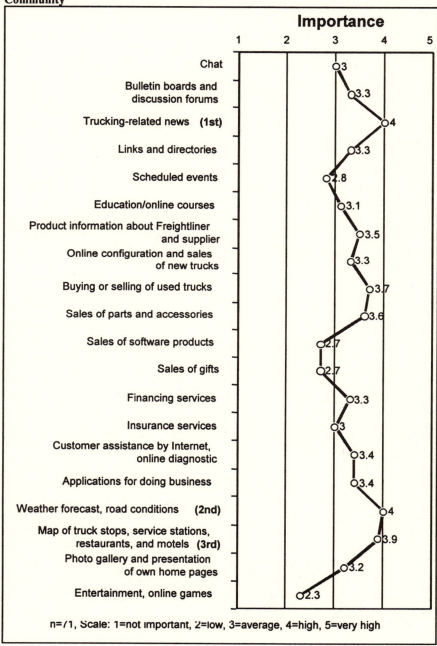

n=71, Scale: 1=not important, 2=low, 3=average, 4=high, 5=very high

Figure 15.3
General Interest in Participating in a Trucker Virtual Community

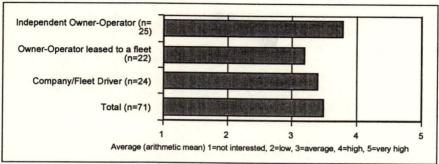

Offers that help the truckers directly in their job are very important (e.g., integrated freight procurement systems);

The security of transaction has to be guaranteed (especially with credit card numbers).

These aspects point out that truckers expect not entertainment from a virtual community but rather real benefits for their business.

DISCUSSION

The willingness to participate in a virtual community for truckers depends primarily on the availability of Internet or other online service access that can be used "on the road." "Onboard" solutions are hardly offered so far. Therefore, access at truck stops and trucker motels or by home computer may be a good alternative. Participation via home computer seems to be possible but not very promising since truckers most probably have other things to do when they return from the usual four-week trips than sitting in front of the personal computer (PC). This is something that they could have done already during the trip, for example, as front-seat passenger. At truck stops or trucker motels only modem lines appear to be realistic so that truckers would have to provide the laptop. Whereas today CB radio and cellular phones are frequently used by truckers, laptops are not very common. This is also true for independent owner-operators, although the younger age groups use laptops more frequently. For this reason, the first prerequisite for a trucker VC would be a stronger dispersion of laptops among the truckers.

An advantage for building up a trucker VC is the truckers' great willingness to use electronic communication media, which results from their high mobility. Also the relatively high popularity of Internet accounts is pleasing and will rise significantly in the near future–especially among younger truckers. Besides, a trucker VC would profit from the fact that trucking-related offers on the Internet are still relatively unimportant, so a trucker VC therefore, could become a pioneer.

The truckers consider the following services most important: "trucking-related news," "weather forecast, road conditions," "map of truck stops, service stations, restaurants, and motels," "links and directories," and "product information about Freightliner and supplier." The core contents of a future trucker VC would have to be service-related, which may include the utilization of chats as an instrument of customer service.

It became clear during the interviews that for independent owner-operators, a higher number of services are of great importance. The essential differences between the driver segments emerge from the evaluation of the services "applications for doing business" and "sales of parts and accessories." These services are of highest importance for independent owner-operators because they can be used directly for their business. For the other drivers, these services are provided by the fleet companies.

As a conclusion, especially younger owner operators can be regarded as a primary target group of a trucker VC. Besides, there definitely exists an interest also among dependent owner-operators and company/fleet drivers. Each group has its specific needs that request tailor-made services. It seems rather improbable that older truckers can be reached through a trucker VC because their affinity to modern information and communication technologies is too low. Concerning the growing popularity of the Internet, there is high potential, especially among independent owner-operators. This potential, however, depends largely on the improved opportunities of access to the Internet.

CONCLUSIONS

The creation of a virtual community is not an easy task for companies. This is shown by our discussion of the Hagel and Armstrong concept as well as our empirical trucker study. The conditions for building up virtual communities are favorable, especially among younger U.S. truckers, because they possess a high number of Internet accounts, a high affinity to electronic communication media, and a high interest in virtual communities. As the Internet is mostly used at home, the truckers' long absence is a hurdle for an Internet-based virtual community. In the short run, the technological development may lead to a higher dispersion of laptops, more Internet lines in motels, and high-performance onboard devices. But even under these conditions the creation of such a virtual community demands huge efforts from the community builder, because the truckers expect less entertainment but actual benefits for their business. A focus on contents that are provided community members is not very promising. The community builder would play the role of a supplier of (free) services, which, in contrast, is not included in the concept of Hagel and Armstrong.

QUESTIONS FOR DISCUSSION

1. Why did Freightliner establish a virtual community? Was their attempt successful? What were some limitations?

2. Besides those discussed in the chapter, what virtual communities do you know of? What business models do they use? How would you judge their success?

3. Compare virtual communities as a marketing tool with more traditional Web advertising, such as banners. What are the advantages and drawbacks?

4. Is the commercial use of a virtual community ethical?

16

Privacy Concerns in Electronic Markets: A Framework

Nikhilesh Dholakia and Detlev Zwick

In cyberspace, the identities of consumers and the Web sites of marketers can be regarded as digital representations. These digital representations are often different from how the consumers and marketers appear in the physical marketplace. The digital representations in cyberspace change the nature of *identity knowledge* (Marx 1999). Identity knowledge–in the sense of withholding or supplying information about oneself–is part of the consumers' strategy to control marketers' access to information about themselves. Marketers also employ a variety of strategies to profile, identify, verify, or disqualify consumers visiting their sites and to engineer the content accordingly. Such strategies allow consumers and marketers (Web sites) to choose between various degrees of identifiability and anonymity. In this chapter, we provide a framework to understand the identity-oriented strategies of consumers and marketers and suggest the appropriate stance that online marketers should take with respect to privacy in cyberspace.

CONSUMERS' PRIVACY OPTIONS IN CYBERSPACE

The Internet provides consumers the opportunity to practice anonymity or pseudonymity. Anonymity is the state of not being identifiable as a particular individual, allowing, for instance, for the assumption of a persona other than the one under which an individual normally functions (Nakamura 1995). Consumers can alter their age, sex, and any other qualities that they choose. This has been one of the appeals of Internet "chat rooms," where some people interact with others under the guise of being an entity other than who they are in real life (Turkle 1995).

Anonymity and its derivative, pseudonymity (an assumed name, but the true identity revealed to close associates), are attempts not only to protect the personal information that is somehow "in" oneself but to control what "leaves" one's self to enter commercial or other external territories. As Jones (1997) points out, at the core of identity protection is to control that which enters someone else's private space. Participation in an online, networked society may divest consumers of some control over the type and degree of personal information that is externalized and the transformation of such information in

Figure 16.1
Four Information Externalizing Strategies for Consumers

		Accuracy of Personal Information Externalized	
		High	**Low**
Amount of Personal Information Externalized	**High**	Identifiability	Anonymity/ Pseudonymity
	Low	Confidentiality	Secrecy

the commercial electronic space (Cavoukian and Tapscott 1997; Lyon and Zureik 1996).

Attempting to reclaim some control over their personal information in the networked society, most consumers engage in some forms of impression management. For instance, to participate in "restricted" forums or discussion groups or to increase chances for a loan application to be successful, consumers may present themselves in the "best possible light," sometimes even masquerading as someone else. Consumers adopt various strategies that allow them to control the amount and the accuracy of personal information that they externalize (see Goffman 1959: 141-66). Building on Gary Marx's (1999) conceptualization of "identity knowledge," we propose four different strategies that consumers apply to protect and manage their "virtual selves" (see Figure 16.1). Of course, consumers apply the same strategies in the "real" world as well, but because of the nature of the virtual space, these strategies seem much more prominent in cyberspace. The various types of identity knowledge–legal name, locatability, pseudonyms, pattern knowledge, social categorization, symbols of eligibility–are naturally based on assigning a measure of "reality" to concepts that are virtual.

FOUR CONSUMER STRATEGIES

The first strategy, identifiability, refers to the consumer's disposition to disclose all personal information with high accuracy. This allows marketers and others to acquire a high degree of identity knowledge about the consumer. Identifiability is therefore the least powerful strategy for protecting personal information. Indeed, it is a deliberate strategy to disclose one's identity. It creates transparency, allowing the world to see the identified consumer.

Confidentiality is the externalization of restricted, but highly accurate, information. Confidentiality then incorporates identifiability but restricts the information flow in terms of what is externalized and who gets to see it. It is based on trust. Brand equity, reputation of the marketer, favorable endorsements by an electronic community, and other elements may build such trust in the marketer.

Anonymity/pseudonymity are strategies that enable the consumer to externalize virtually infinite amounts of inaccurate personal information. We employ the term "virtually infinite" because pseudonymity allows for the continuous invention of new personae for which new personal information has to be imagined. When consumers use anonymity or pseudonymity, they are working on the assumption that they are deliberately avoiding identifiability and that trust is (willingly) suspended between parties.

Secrecy expresses a disposition toward the sharing of little and potentially inaccurate information. Identifiability and, to a degree, communication are avoided, and the relationship is characterized by distrust. Secrecy, of course, is the most extreme form of identity suppression that consumers can undertake in cyberspace.

Consumers' Choice of Cyberspace Self-Representation

Consumers choose to represent themselves according to how they perceive the trade-offs between:

- potential benefits of self-disclosure and
- potential risks from self disclosure.

Figure 16.2 outlines the various consumer self-disclosure strategies arising from these two considerations.

The default strategy is that of cautious confidentiality, represented by the central part of Figure 16.2. This is the arena in which risks as well as benefits are perceived to be moderate (or assumed to be moderate in the absence of any information to the contrary).

Consumers employ a strategy of identifiability when the risk of the cyberspace interaction is perceived to be low but its benefits are perceived to be high. An example of this exchange might be the shareware distributor who requires the customer to fill out at times detailed surveys. In return, the customer can download free software and be notified about upgrades.

Figure 16.2
Consumers' Self-Disclosure Strategies in Cyberspace

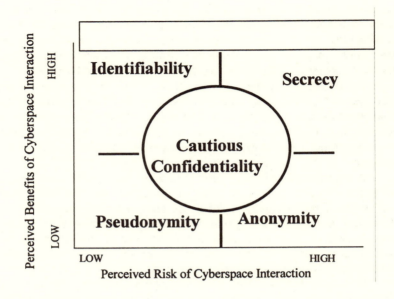

Pseudonymity is a strategy that is likely to be used in a situation of low perceived risk and low perceived benefit. The consumer is aware of the potential value of his or her identity information and is, despite low perceived risk, unwilling to share it with the marketer when the benefits are low. For example, when a consumer has to provide information such as mailing address or date of birth in order to get access to a desired MP3 file, he or she might simply use a pseudonym.

Anonymity becomes a useful strategy when the perceived risk of the interaction is high and the perceived benefits low. In erotic chat rooms, customers might perceive a high risk in disclosing their real identity for the benefits they receive in return (likely to be zero, as chat rooms are rarely set up to encourage people to meet in real life).

Secrecy emerges as a useful strategy when the perceived risk of the interaction is high, but the benefits are equally high so that some externalization of identity information is deemed necessary. Such a situation might arise when the consumer shops for a lower rate for health insurance. The provision of intimate personal information to additional sources can be perceived as risky but offset by the potential benefits of finding a lower rate. Similar concerns may arise when consumers visit some sex-oriented sites that they may find highly gratifying, but they are loath to disclose their identity to the site operator or fellow visitors.

INTERACTIVE SPACES ARISING OUT OF IDENTIFIABILITY CONDITIONS

Whether the consumer experience in the virtual realm is evaluated as positive or negative does not depend solely on the successful application of information protection strategies. Consumers in cyberspace are aware that they are engaged in some sort of interactive communication with a marketer. Therefore, consumers not only attempt to control their own strategies but expect marketers to pursue real-time strategies of their own. Thus, we argue that consumers hold beliefs about marketers' abilities to identify them in the virtual space and that these beliefs influence identity management and feelings of satisfaction.

Consumers' perceptions of how "identifiable" they are in cyberspace may not always match the reality of how identifiable they are to specific marketers. Through technologies such as profiling, collaborative filtering, and customer profile exchange, marketers have an increasing ability to identify consumers (Collett 1999; Pickering 2000). Consumers may not be aware that the content of a page that they are viewing is being dynamically generated based on profiling data.

The match (or mismatch) of consumers' self-perception of their identifiability and their actual identifiability can give rise to positive or negative consequences for the consumer. These situations are depicted in Figure 16.3. Potential consequences that are positive (from a consumer perspective) are identified by a plus sign while a minus sign, precedes consequences that are (or are perceived as) negative.

Perhaps the most common condition arises when the consumer perceives his or her identifiability to be low, but the marketer's actual ability to identify the consumer is high. The result of such a discrepancy between perception and reality can be positive or negative. If the marketer uses the knowledge in ways that cater directly and exclusively to the customer's needs, discreet delight might ensue. The delight may be closely linked to the fact that the consumer does not know about the marketer's abilities. Consumers' expectations are lower and thus easier to meet. However, this condition is also full of threats for the consumer. When consumers are unaware of their identity exposure, they may be much more willing to engage in risqué behaviors and in the process externalize sensitive personal information. The consumer is then skating on thin ice. Even when the consumer is not engaging in risqué behavior, an unscrupulous marketer may use profiling techniques to surreptitiously identify the consumer and engage in deceptive or high-pressure sales practices.

The second case in which consumer self-perception and marketing reality diverge is one where the consumer holds a strong belief that he or she is identifiable but is, in actuality, not or only slightly identifiable. This condition produces extreme behavioral schemes without putting the consumer at risk of predatory marketing. On the one end of the spectrum, the consumer engages in vanity surfing, which is characterized by frivolous and almost exhibitionist display of one's cyber identity. However, such a creative identity production has no consequences because the marketer's ability to notice the consumer's behavior is low. Assuming that they are identifiable and potentially subject to predatory practices, some consumers may engage in paranoid surfing. Afraid to externalize identity information, they avoid sites, do not use search engines, and refrain from lingering in one place for too long. Technically sophisticated consumers may employ identity masking or identity scrubbing techniques in excessive ways.

We can conceive of two conditions in which the consumer's self-perception and the marketer's actual ability to identify coincide. The first condition is characterized by low self-perception of the consumer to be identifiable and a low ability of the marketer to identify. As a result, the consumer enjoys a blissful anonymity in cyberspace. The consumer feels safe and tends to externalize information. Negative consequences, if any, are very mild–a benign neglect by marketers who are not ready to exploit this careless behavior.

Finally, we identify a condition in which the consumer's perception of identifiability is high, as is the marketer's ability. This condition is interesting because it can cause both a very positive and quite negative outcome. On the positive side, the consumer is correct to assume that he or she is identifiable. Externalization of information is then a planned and rational choice of the consumer. In turn, the consumer can receive customized services based on his or her known identity. Opposite this win-win situation, we find a potential for exploitation of the consumer's openness by unscrupulous or strategic-game-oriented marketers.

IMPLICATIONS FOR CONSUMER ORIENTED E-COMMERCE

The implications of new information and communication technologies for consumer behavior are dramatic. Consumers' activities in the commercial interaction space are governed by new concerns such as the externalization of identity data. These concerns arise due to an intricate interplay of a consumer's self-perceived identifiability in cyberspace and the marketer's actual ability to identify the consumer. A very thin line divides successful and disastrous consumer-marketer interactions.

Consider the case where the consumer perceives the marketer to know little or nothing about his or her identity, but in reality the marketer has developed a full customer profile. The marketer can choose between using and not using the profile to personalize the site's content and product offerings. Not using the information can mean that the customer does not find what he or she is looking for quickly enough and may defect from the site. Using the information for personalization can lead to customer delight, as the customer's effort to navigate the site is supported, but this reaction is not guaranteed. Equally likely, given consumers' concerns about privacy (Mchugh 2000; Reidenberg 1995), is the prospect of offending or shocking the consumer with information-based personalization. After all, the consumer is not expecting to be identifiable and thus to be identified. The sudden realization that he or she is identifiable may create an eerie feeling and spell the end of the marketer-customer relationship.

Similarly, when the consumer perceives himself or her self to be identifiable but in actuality is not, the marketer is likely to disappoint. Under such an interaction condition, consumers may choose vanity surfing, thereby challenging the marketer to cater to their personal needs. The marketer is then either forced to learn about the consumer's identity as much as possible in order to maintain the customer relationship or else lose the vain consumers to marketers who do more intensive profiling and data mining.

In sum, when injudiciously used, "identifier" technologies are a mixed blessing for marketers. To have the capabilities to generate accurate customer profiles does not mean that marketers should use them at all times. Not to have "identifier" technologies can be equally problematic. The common denominator is the consumer's self-perceived identifiability. Thus, the real marketing challenge–as interactive technologies advance–is not to offer personalization per se but what we call selective personalization.

SUMMARY AND CONCLUSIONS

Interactive, commercial cyberspace is more complex than its physical counterpart. Because of varying tendencies to disclose or withhold information, dialectical tensions exist between marketers and consumers. We do not wish to suggest that these tensions will disappear any time soon. It is, however, imperative to understand what creates these tensions and how they influence consumers' and marketers' behavior. Such understanding allows marketers and consumers to interact more meaningfully in the digital world and to create "better places" for themselves.

QUESTIONS FOR DISCUSSION

1. This chapter challenges marketers to use identifier technology judiciously. The authors argue that the objective for marketers should be to create a correspondence between the consumers' self-perceived degree of identifiability and the actual ability to be identified. How can marketers find out what the consumers' self-perception is about the site's ability to identify its customers?

2. Provide two instances when consumers are likely to choose secrecy as a self-disclosure strategy (see Figure 16.2). Do the same for the other three strategies.

3. Do you believe that privacy will continue to remain a concern for consumers in the future? If so, what solutions do you suggest to alleviate these concerns?

17

The Webs and the Web-Nots: Access Issues in the Age of Internet-Based Commerce

Nikhilesh Dholakia

With the dramatic growth of the World Wide Web (WWW), graphical and multimedia protocols on the Internet gained wide-ranging acceptance. Such protocols are the bases of new networked devices as well as a rapidly exploding range of new electronic commerce services. This chapter discusses the equipment, software, and infrastructure factors that affect the possibility and quality of users' access to the Web and of the growing Internet-based commercial offerings on the Web. Based on an understanding of these factors, it is possible to develop categories of access ranging from threshold access to premium access. The chapter offers a conceptual framework for understanding the technological aspects of access to the information superhighway and concludes with a discussion of the role of technological developments in affecting access.

WEBS AND WEB-NOTS

Those using cyberspace today are endowed with widely varying tools for accessing the fast-growing world of electronic information. Consider, for example, the situation of the following two people trying to access cyberspace in early 1999:

- Hari Rampal lives in Bangalore, India. He is a textile technologist by day and a cyberbuff by night. From his small apartment, he boots up his Pentium-clone computer and attempts to dial the Internet access number with his 28 Kbps modem. VSNL, the state-owned long-distance phone company, in collaboration with MCI International, is the main Internet access provider in India. VSNL's access phone numbers in Bangalore are usually quite busy. The modem redials every minute for about 15 minutes before Hari gets a connection to the Internet. He reviews the two e-mail messages that he has received from Australia and Mexico, quickly replies to one of them, and then attempts to download, in a batch mode, a videoclip of the latest *Star Wars* movie trailer. Hari estimates that the 4 MB file will take about 25 minutes to download, and so he goes to the kitchen to heat up his dinner. When he returns to his computer 10 minutes later, he finds that his connection got terminated because of poor line quality. Frustrated but not ready to give up, Hari fires up the modem again.

- Jane Kelly lives in Baltimore, Maryland. A systems programmer, Jane works with powerful workstations during the day. She likes to kick around in cyberspace in her spare time. She bought a 450-MHz Pentium III machine and connected it to the Internet with a cable modem service provided by Road Runner. Jane's cable modem service allows unlimited access, and, since it is based on the cable television infrastructure, it is always on–no dial-in protocols are required. One of Jane's favorite pastimes these days is to log on to a Web site called Amadeus. This site has high-fidelity digitized symphonies and concertos, which Jane plays through her 32-bit stereo sound card and speakers. The music is coupled with lovely scanned-in natural scenes that fill up Jane's .19 dot pitch 23-inch monitor. Jane has programmed her Netscape browser to skip to the next link after one piece of music is completely downloaded. "Come to think of it," muses Jane, "I have hardly used my TV or multi-disc CD player since I got hooked on Amadeus. And with the 16.7 million colors that my video card gives me, even *National Geographic* seems boring."

Although Hari Rampal appears to be much poorly endowed than Jane Kelly in terms of Internet access, even with his limited computing and telecommunications resources he is a part of a very privileged minority on a global scale (Sen 1995). After all, as advertisements from Lucent Technologies point out, over half the people in the world are yet to make their first telephone call.

Within the privileged world of cyberspace, however, these two cases illustrate that there are great differences in the speed, ease, and quality of access to electronic information among those connected to the Net. When we step outside the tiny fraction of the world's population that has computing and telecommunications resources available for potentially connecting to cyberspace, the disparities multiply manifold (see, e.g., Schwankert; 1996; Zgodzinski 1996). This is a larger issue that has global implications, and it is not addressed here (see Martinez 1994; Sun and Barnett 1994, for treatment of this larger issue). This chapter examines the main factors affecting a user's access to, and experience with, the World Wide Web, assuming that the minimal basic conditions for such access exist. Based on an understanding of these factors, a framework is presented to model the type of access that users have today and may have in the near future. Such a framework can be useful in developing and assessing strategies and policies at various levels-users, access providers, content providers, and regulators.

CYBERSPACE AS THE NEW MEDIUM

In his book *Being Digital* (1995), Nicholas Negroponte reported that the population of Internet users was growing in 1994 at the rate of 10 percent per month, a rate that would cover the entire world population if it were to continue till 2003. Other mid-1990s estimates pegged the Internet growth rate at around 15 percent per month (Vlahos 1995). As a medium for information provision and commercial transactions, the multimedia World Wide Web format has been growing at a phenomenal rate. For example, use of the Mosaic browser for

Table 17.1
Profile of World Wide Web Users–1995 and 1998

Demographic Variable	Profile of World Wide Web Users		Comments
	late-1995	late-1998	
Location	80.6% United States 9.8% Europe 5.8% Canada, Mexico	84.4% United States 5.8% Europe	User percentages located in Asia, South America, Oceania, and Africa are small but growing rapidly. There is clearly a greater tendency for U.S. users to respond to GVU surveys in 1998.
Gender	70.7% Male 29.3% Female	61.3% Male 38.7% Female	Europe continued to be more heavily male in terms of Web usage. By late 1998, just over 16% users were female.
Average Age	N/A	35.1 yrs. overall 35.5 yrs. Men 34.4 yrs. Women	European age profiles are younger than the U.S. profiles. In the first-time user group, women outnumber men.
Average Income	$69,000	$52,500	Significant nonresponse in income reporting.
Occupation	23.7% Education 31.4% Computer-related	26.2% Education 22.3% Computer-related	In Europe, users were more likely to be in computer-related fields.

Sources: Adapted from data from GVU 3rd and 9th WWW User Surveys, as reported in Kantor and Neubarth (1996) and on the GVU Web site. Also based on NUA Internet Surveys (1999) and RITIM research (1999). It should be noted that GVU survey respondents self-select themselves.

WWW increased at the rate of 11 percent *per week* from February to December 1993 (Negroponte 1995: 5).   Depending on who was estimating, World Wide Web traffic grew at an annual rate of 1,713 percent (Barol 1995: 29) to 2,300 percent (Taylor 1996: 132) in 1994. The Internet doubled in size from 6.6 million hosts to 12.8 million hosts in mid-1996, and the number of domains (such as bigcorp.com, state.edu, airforce.mil) quadrupled from 120,000 to 488,000 during this period (Kantor and Neubarth 1996: 46). Firms that track worldwide Internet growth–such as Nua Internet Surveys (http://www.nua.ie) –continue to report strong growth in Internet usage in all parts of the world. By March 2000, nearly 305 million people worldwide were estimated to be online. Of these, 137 million were in the United States and Canada, 83 million in

Table 17.2
Web Usage by Psychographic Segments

VALS 2 Psychographic	Profile of the Psychographic Category	Percentage of U.S. Population	Percentage of Web User Population	Comments
Actualizers	Active, discriminating, adventurous, in the prime of life Nearing the peak of occupational income. Read magazines like *Scientific American* and drive cars like Acura Travel a lot.	10%	50%	Heavily male-dominated (77% of users) 70% believe Web makes them more productive 70% also surf for fun 44% report conflict between work and fun surfing.
Strivers	Followers rather than leaders.	14%	13%	Spend more time than any other segment on the Web 70% report conflict between recreational Web-surfing and work probably use in college or right after it.
Experiences	Young, innovative, stimulation-seeking, fashionable	12%	18%	Use Web are cool toward it Easily bored by text-heavy and slow Web content.
Fulfillers	Older, practical, desiring order Read magazines like *Consumer Reports.*	11%	11%	Find the Web difficult to use in form and content Waiting for better navigation tools, contextual authority, and trusted brands on the Web.
Achievers	Stable, upscale, family-oriented segment Occupations like management and sales.	15%	6%	Heavy representation of women in this segment Time-pressured Not thrilled by male-oriented, disorganized Web Value personal relationships and find Web lacking.
Believers, Makers	Various profiles, usually associated with lower socioeconomic status	38%	2%	Lack of education, finances, occupational subsidies, as well as technophobia inhibit computer and Web use.

Sources: Adapted from "Exploring the World Wide Web Population's Other Half,"
http://future.sri.com/vals/vals-survey.results.html, accessed November 4, 1996; RITIM research
(1998-1999).

Europe, 69 million in the Asia/Pacific region, and 11 million in South America. Africa and the Middle East trailed significantly with less than 3 million users in each of these regions.

The rapid growth of graphical and multimedia formats such as WWW set the stage for cyberspace to become a major medium of communication and commerce. While the reach of the World Wide Web is still skewed toward high-income, young, U.S., male technophiles, survey evidence indicates that the Web is widening its reach and is gradually democratizing (see Table 17.2). Another survey by SRI International (1996), claimed to be more representative of the Web-using population than other surveys, correlates Web usage to SRI's well-known VALS 2 psychographic segments. Key results from this survey are shown in Table 2. By late 2000, the gender gap had nearly vanished: there were as many women as men on the Net. Also, by 2000, the number of Internet users whose mother tongue was not English crossed the number of users whose mother tongue was English.

Surveys such as these indicate that we can no longer view cyberspace as a specialized resource of the few but have to start treating it on a par with other widely available media and infrastructure resources such as newspapers, telephones, television, highways, railways, and airlines. This implies further that we must understand the factors that affect access to, and use of, cyberspace resources such as the World Wide Web.

TECHNOLOGY-RELATED FACTORS AFFECTING ACCESS

How well users can take advantage of emerging information, entertainment, and trading opportunities on the World Wide Web and similar Internet protocols depends on a number of factors. Included in these factors are the user's resources-whether owned by the user or available to the user as an employee. Also included are factors related to the electronic and telecommunications environment in which the user lives or works.

To illustrate the factors that affect the Web-browsing experience, we group them into three categories: equipment dimensions, software dimensions, and connectivity dimensions. These dimensions are evolving rapidly. It should be noted that the profiles of typical users on the three dimensions are reflective of a particular time–early 1999.

Equipment Dimensions

The type of computing equipment that the user has determines not only the type of access to the World Wide Web but the very possibility of Web access. Many of the low-powered or older computer configurations just do not allow Web browsing.

World Wide Web users are faced with some baseline processor requirements as well as memory and storage requirements in terms of RAM, and hard drive size. It is necessary to have a machine with a x486 or better processor, 66 MHz or more of clock speed, at least 8 MB of RAM and at least

500 MB of hard disk space. These are required because, to use today's popular browsers, an IBM-compatible machine must be able to run Microsoft Windows (preferably 95 or NT), and the specifications outlined are the minimum necessary for running Windows 95 and NT configurations. To view movie files in formats such as MPEG or Quicktime demands even larger processor capabilities. Therefore, to take full advantage of Web sites and their multimedia offerings, users need at least a Pentium processor operating at 75 MHz, a minimum of 16 MB of RAM, and a fairly large (500 MB or bigger) hard drive.

In addition to a computer with a powerful processor and adequate memory, users need good color and sound capabilities in their computer systems. Most creators of Web pages assume that the viewer has computers and monitors capable of displaying more than 256 colors. For very high-quality graphics, computer systems capable of 16.7 million shades are also available but are comparatively expensive. Similarly, if a Web site has a sound file, it is necessary to have at least a 16-bit stereo sound card and high-wattage speakers. On the Macintosh side of things, most newer models come with 256 colors and 16-bit stereo sound out of the box. An owner of an older Macintosh LCIII, for example, can upgrade to 32,000 colors for about U.S.$20-$30 by ordering more video memory. Just as with Windows machines, the full use of the Web requires a high-end PowerPC-based Macintosh computer. Multimedia capabilities suitable for the average user machines have been crystallized into industry standards for multimedia personal computers (PCs)-MPC and MPC-II. In a fast-changing technological environment, however, such standards become obsolete rather quickly.

Users who want to store, share, or reproduce information obtained from the Web have to think about additional equipment issues such as Zip drives, printers, and video recorders. Most users may be able to get good reproductions of Web images using a 360x360 color inkjet printer or equivalent. Those requiring high-resolution images-advertising agencies, graphic designers, and architects-may require a much more expensive, high-end color laser printer.

Software Dimensions

Software affects the Web experience in two ways. First is the programming language in which the Web pages are authored. While basic features of the Hypertext Markup Language (HTML) have become fairly standardized, the use of fancier textual, graphical, audio, and video features may affect users in cases where they do not have compatible browsers. Second are the type and version of browser that the user has. Not all browsers are capable of supporting all HTML, VRML (Virtual Reality Markup Language), or Java versions and features. As increasing amounts of multimedia content appear on (or are available through) the Web, it becomes not just desirable but necessary to have browsers with built-in capabilities to read, run, and display multimedia files.

Browsers have evolved at a breathtaking pace. From the early Netscape and Mosaic browsers that enabled the user to view text and graphics, today's browsers either come pre-equipped with, or are geared to provide downloads of, special applications to view specific multimedia formats. The browser along with its recommended suite of helper applications tends to be resource-intensive. In rare cases does the user pay a purchase price for the browser itself, but there is a cost in terms of the storage and memory requirements for the elaborate suite of applications. For example, the full-blown version of Netscape Communicator suite in early 1999 contained 475 files that required at least 40 MB of hard disk space and 32 MB or more of RAM for proper functioning.

While the older browsers are quickly disappearing in the advanced countries, they may continue to be employed to varying degrees in the rest of the world. Inadequate equipment configurations may hamper the deployment of newer (or any) browsers and Helper Applications in many situations in the developing world. It should be kept in mind that although computer prices do not vary greatly across the world, the ability of people to *upgrade* their computers does vary a lot. The very rapid upgrading cycles for computing equipment observable in the United States and Canada are unlikely to be found in most other countries, either because of limited economic resources or because the culture is not so technology-driven and upgrade-oriented.

As various methods of storing and delivering complex and executable content become widely available, users may not need the powerful hardware required today to download and display multimedia content. In fact, it is very likely that a lot of the intelligence for multimedia applications will reside in the network and be made available at the user's terminal on demand-a situation analogous to that of the television networks in the 1980s. This was the promise of the Network Computers (NCs) launched by Sun Microsystems, Oracle, Acorn, and others in 1996, although some observers remained skeptical as to whether these stripped-down machines can offer the kind of Web access that even reasonably powerful computers cannot (Vaughn-Nichols 1996).

Connectivity Dimensions

The type of connectivity that a user is able to get determines the speed and quality of data transmissions. For example, users may access Web sites using anything from a 1200 bps modem to a T3 line and soon perhaps an OC-12 line, which is equivalent to 12 T3 lines bundled together. Large multimedia files take a long time to download when the connection is slow. For example, a 4 MB video file containing a 30-second movie clip may take less than 10 minutes to download using a 56 Kbps modem but nearly an hour to download using a 14.4 Kbps modem. New browsers are "tuned" for a minimum transmission speed. For example, by mid-1999, Netscape and Internet Explorer browsers were tuned for a minimum transmission speed of 33 Kbps.

Even with a fast modem, the reliability and speed of transmission may be affected by the physical quality of telephone lines in the user's locality. For example, a 56 Kbps modem available on a home computer may yield a realized transmission speed not exceeding 33 Kbps because of the quality of the telecommunication line.

Table 17.3
Transmission Speeds over the Internet, circa 1999

Type of Connection or Link	Speed	Approximate time to transfer the contents of a 680 MB hard disk	Availability of such Connections or Link-type circa 1999
Standard Modem	56 Kbps	28 hours	Late model (typically post-1997) home and small business computers,
1-channel ISDN	64 Kbps	24 hours	Selected cities in the U.S. and other advanced nations.
2-channel ISDN	128 Kbps	12 hours	Selected cities in the U.S. and other advanced nations.
T1 or DS-1	1.544 Mbps	1 hour	Typical connection for mid- to large-sized organizations in advanced countries
T3 or DS-3	44.736 Mbps	2 minutes	Backbone between major U.S. cities; from U.S. hubs to Toronto, Ottawa, Mexico City, and South America; from U.S. East and West coast hubs to Europe and Asia
OC-3	155.52 Mbps	35 seconds	Between major connection points in the U.S. such as New York, Baltimore, Chicago, and San Francisco, and a few other U.S. cities
OC-12	622.08 Mbps	9 seconds	Major backbones such as those of MCI WorldCom. Availability mainly in North America but global expansion occurring through undersea fiber-optic cables such as FLAG.

Sources: Adapted from Susie Davis, Jim Ivers, and Scott Frommer, *U.S. Map of the Internet* (Westport, CT: Mecklermedia, 1996) RITIM research, (1999).

The hypertextual nature of Web content means that any particular file may travel from its original source to the ultimate user through a series of linked nodes. The slowest link on such an internodal path will determine the overall speed of data transfer. This is something over which the user has very little control. In some cases, deploying search engines may help in finding the fastest possible path to a desired content category. While the total number of Internet users in the "rest of the world" passed the number of users in the United States, the backbone of the Internet remains still largely in the United States. Table 17.3 shows that the U.S. backbone is in the process of being upgraded to an OC-

12 speed in some cases, but even T3 backbones are few and far between in the rest of the world, including advanced regions in Europe and Asia (Gregston 1996; Mesher 1996). This is likely to change because of massive efforts by governments and telecommunications companies to build high-speed Internet infrastructures in various parts of the world. For example, a joint venture of AT&T and Alcatel plans to ring the entire continent of Africa with a fiber-optic cable capable of transmission speeds up to 2.5 gigabits per second (Zgodzinski 1996).

At the content provider's end, the node capacity-in terms of number of users that can be simultaneously supported by that node-also affects the browsing experience of users. Users may not be able to access a certain node because of capacity constraints. This is particularly likely to happen in the case of Web sites that provide information related to popular topics or celebrities or event information about fast-breaking news stories such as sports events, mergers and acquisitions, terrorist attacks, natural disasters, or armed conflicts. In an organization with a Local Area Network, such constraints could also arise at the user's end if too many users are simultaneously trying to get on the Web.

To allow speedier access to popular Web sites, commercial online Internet access providers such as AOL as well as major Internet service providers (ISPs) have built "proxying" capabilities in their servers. When such a server detects that a particular Web site is popular and being accessed by multiple subscribers, it captures the information in its cache memory in its distributed network of localized servers. The Internet service provider thereby eliminates the need for subsequent users to establish a path to the source site. As the Internet content and usage continue to grow at explosive rates, fears of a breakdown of critical links in the Net are mounting (O' Flaherty 1996). This is likely to give rise to new and strategic approaches to the proxying of popular, specialized, or mission-critical sites. Such "mirroring" and "proxying" capabilities can multiply the availability of popular content; however, as intellectual property rights are strengthened in cyberspace, it remains to be seen to what extent such strategies will be permitted.

MAPPING ACCESS POSSIBILITIES: A FRAMEWORK

At a more general level, the type of access that a particular user has depends on three categories of resources: user's own resources, those made available to the user by service and content providers, and those available to the user in terms of the prevailing infrastructure. The interactions of these three categories of resources determine the quality of access.

User Resources

For any information technology, the access that users have to the technology and their experience with it depend, to some extent, on their resources. Four categories of resources are useful in understanding user behavior: money, time, space, and skills. In general, users who are endowed generously with these resources have the best possibilities of accessing new information technologies and of creating rewarding experiences. For most people, however, there are resource constraints. Access to, and experience with, new technological offerings, such as the World Wide Web, are shaped by the resource constraints and the way that users trade off their limited resources.

The resources of users affect all three categories of factors that influence access to the World Wide Web–equipment dimensions, software dimensions, and connectivity dimensions. Of the three, however, equipment-oriented factors depend almost entirely on the user's resource situation. Software dimensions depend somewhat on the user's resources, especially in terms of the type of software that the user can install on, or access from, the equipment available. Connectivity dimensions depend only minimally on user's resources. Connectivity depends more on the user's situation vis-à-vis telecommunications networks.

Resources Provided by Suppliers

As the trend toward the use of multimedia formats such as PDF and remote-residing applications written in languages such as Java gathers momentum, then the resource threshold at which users can access the Web will be lowered. The Network Computer strategy championed by companies such as Oracle and Sun Microsystems is clearly seeking to lower the equipment threshold for access to the Web. Similarly, powerful Internet access providers can install servers, switches, and backbones that can store, process, and transmit huge amounts of information. By moving the bulk of the information-processing tasks away from the users' terminals and into the network, access and content providers can make it easy for masses of users–through the use of Network Computers, Internet appliances, Information appliances, and other devices that can hook up to a television set–to access the World Wide Web and other multimedia protocols.

Such trends toward the migration of the intelligence from the terminal to the network merit careful watching (Gilder 1995). Depending on the directions and magnitudes of such changes, the landscape of the information business could alter in dramatic ways. Today's top firms or even sunshine industries could be eclipsed by new players capable of distributing intelligence across the network and enabling masses of users to access the information that they desire, on demand, through low-cost, user-friendly terminals that have a high display potency (see Schlender 1996). Acting against this NC-driven model of the Net are the ever more elaborate multimedia content creation at all types of locations and the desire of the users to store and process such content. Companies like Microsoft and Compaq are betting that these tendencies will continue to be strong and keep the demand for high-end PC-type products increasing for years to come.

Infrastructure Resources

Undergirding the whole issue of access to the Internet and the World Wide Web is the telecommunications infrastructure of a nation or region. Because it grew out of the U.S. Defense Department's Arpanet, the architecture of the Internet provides multiple paths to a site. These features make the Internet robust and survivable in case of natural disasters or armed conflicts. These same features, however, may make particular browsing experiences slow, unpredictable, and frustrating.

The local and regional telecommunications infrastructure of the user-server connections, local loop telecom lines, internodal connections, switching systems, and so on-can help the user overcome some of the frustrations of using the Web. Users fortunate enough to be located in new and high-bandwidth telecommunication regions can hope to enjoy a better quality of access than regions lacking such an infrastructure (see Table 17.2). The situation is analogous to electrical power quality and availability. Most regions of advanced countries enjoy uninterrupted power supply. This, however, is not the case in most developing regions where power outages are commonplace. Just as steady industrial progress cannot occur without reliable power supply, similarly steady Information Age progress cannot occur without a reliable telecommunications infrastructure. Most nations and regions are experimenting with a variety of strategies in the form of deregulation, privatization, and competition in the hope that telecom companies seeking business revenues will put a dense and reliable telecommunications infrastructure in place. Public and private policies needed to promote a high-level telecom infrastructure are complex and need systematic analysis (see, e.g., Dholakia and Dholakia 1994). As we mentioned earlier, in selected regions of the world, efforts to create high-bandwidth communication backbones are under way.

In the euphoric discussion about low-cost Web access devices and an expanding infrastructure to deliver Internet service, one issue is largely sidestepped: What will happen to the basic access charge for Internet service? Since dramatic growth in access will require huge investments in telecommunications and computing infrastructure, there is a distinct possibility that access charges could go up in the short to medium run before coming back to current levels in the longer run. This means that users could face a trade-off characterized by declining equipment and software costs but high monthly service charges.

A Framework for Categorizing Access

Based on the three categories of access dimensions, it is possible to divide the population of current and potential users into three categories-those having threshold access, those who fall in the "modal" access category, and those having premium access. Threshold access contains those users who have the bare minimum equipment, software, and connectivity configurations for Web access. These users can access the Web but may not be able to use its advanced features and usually have slow or no access to high-resolution images, fancy formatting, and movie clips. The modal access category contains the maximum number of current users. These users have adequate access to the Web under the prevailing state of technology. Most of the standard equipment and software as well as most of the content on the Web have been developed to be accessible and appealing to these users. The premium access category contains users who have access capabilities superior to the modal group. In terms of access quality, this group has the maximum variability-ranging from users with slightly premium access, to "power users" who may have an access quality that is on an order of magnitude beyond what is available to the modal user.

Frontier, Upgrading, and Enabling Technologies

It is interesting to examine the impact of technological change on the categories of access. Many technologies are geared toward improving the quality of access at the premium end of the user spectrum. We can call these "frontier" technologies. Examples are ISDN, cable modems, high-end processors and monitors, audio and video cards, and specialized browsers and multimedia software. Such technologies attempt to stretch the premium band and offer levels of superpremium access higher than what was possible before.

Other technologies are geared toward improving the quality of access of the average or the modal user. These can be termed "upgrading" technologies. Examples are upgraded versions of popular browsers and mass-market Helper Applications. Upgrading technologies improve the Web usage experience of the modal group but do not significantly enlarge this group. Finally, there is the category of technologies that help to expand the universe of Web users by enabling the nonusers to become users. We can call these "enabling" or "empowering" technologies. Such technologies tend to lower the threshold of access. For example, compression technologies such as HARK are attempting to retain very high fidelity in still images, movies, and sound, even at very high compression ratios. Similarly, PDF and Java formats enable the transmission of complex content to simple NC-type machines. A variety of products and services that bring at least some of the popular Web content to the television set is either in the market or in trial stages. Such technologies may make it possible for people with low-end computers and modems or even a television set with a cable connection to access Web features that are so far available only to high-end users.

The Politics of Access

In general, users tend to favor public policies and respond positively to corporate strategies that enhance the interests of the user category to which they belong. Thus, premium users would favor frontier technologies and do all that they can to promote and lay their hands on such technologies. Modal users would be especially interested in upgrading technologies, especially those upgrades and enhancements that can be acquired and deployed at little or no cost to the user. Threshold users and nonusers would be interested in enabling technologies. Advocacy groups that promote the interests of this last category of people would lobby for public and corporate policies that lower the threshold of access. Internet and Web access clearly emerged as major political issues in the 1996 U.S. presidential election and will continue to play a role for some years. By 2000, the politics of Internet access was an issue not just in the advanced Western nations but also in poorer countries such as Bangladesh and Uganda.

In a plural and diverse society such as the United States, we find all three groups, with varying degrees of political activity. Those developing and commercializing new Internet and Web technologies are also likely to take any or all of these three political positions because each political position corresponds to a particular business strategy. Thus, catering to the premium users with frontier technologies could lead to new business opportunities, perhaps spawn entirely new industries. Upgrading strategies help to maintain the loyalty of the modal group-the bulk of current users, the upper-middle-class in the advanced countries. Such technologies help to maintain and enhance the market positions of the key technology giants of today. Enabling technologies could lead to rapid market expansion by reaching out to masses of nonusers. Such strategies may prove to be wildly rewarding to those seen as the main providers of products and services that open up the mass market.

SUMMARY AND CONCLUSIONS

At any time–whether in the recent past or the foreseeable future–if we take a snapshot of the access to the Internet, the Web, and e-commerce options across the world, we are likely to find great disparities. Such disparities exist not just in terms of Web "haves" and "have-nots" but also–within the "haves" group–in terms of the available bandwidth, computing power, and cost of equipment and services. In this chapter we took a snapshot of such disparities at a point in the late 1990s. The situation, however, is essentially the same in the early years of the twenty-first century–only the terms of reference keep changing because of evolving technology and declining unit costs.

Such disparities have existed for all technologies in the past. The reason that the disparities of the Web era are raising major concerns is that the distribution of Internet access will define the economic, social, and political profile of the world for decades to come. Consider the case of the United States. Even though the United States has the largest base of Internet access of any nation on earth, the government has become very concerned about what it terms "the digital divide" (see http://www.digitaldivide.gov and http://www.digital dividenetwork.org). In the United States and other advanced nations, efforts are underway at various levels to provide a nearly universal level of Internet access to the population. Meanwhile, in the emerging world, the race is on to provide Web access under conditions that are much more challenging–many of these countries do not have even a rudimentary level of telephone access. In technological terms, wireless and television-based Web access methods are likely to be the way that emerging countries may be able to provide Web access to masses.

For online marketers, the Internet offers an opportunity to reach global markets that are unprecedented in terms of size and scope. There are, however, limits imposed on the scope and size of such markets by the availability of technology and the means to access the Web. If connectivity can be made as ubiquitously available as Coca-Cola, the world could enter a new era of global prosperity. Those marketers who will figure out ways of reaching the global markets–especially the markets in the poorer emerging nations–through not just physical but also electronic means will thrive in the digital future.

QUESTIONS FOR DISCUSSION

1. Why are advanced nations such as the United States–which leads the world in the field of the Internet–so concerned about the digital divide? What types of public and private policies can help to bridge the digital divide in the United States?

2. Suppose you were advising major wireless technology firms such as Nokia, Ericsson, and Motorola on ways of increasing Web access rapidly in the emerging world through wireless methods. What creative strategies can you recommend that will allow people in relatively poorly endowed countries to access the Web through wireless methods?

3. In some countries in Asia and Africa, a significant proportion of the population is illiterate. Suggest possible solutions to the problem of providing Internet access to illiterate people. What advice would you give to computer and electronics makers in terms of developing devices that even illiterate people could use to surf the Web?

Part V

Internet and the Transformation of Organizations

18

E-Business Strategies: American and German Approaches Compared

Detlev Zwick, Nikhilesh Dholakia, and Norbert Mundorf

The increasing strategic importance of electronic business for all companies is undeniable. Yet, much remains unclear about the dimensions of e-business. Furthermore, little is known about companies' actual performance in the new medium, the Internet. This study tackles both issues by (1) offering a framework for electronic business, (2) formulating a multitrajectory model of e-business readiness, and (3) assessing selected German and American companies' e-business performance according to our model.

A FRAMEWORK FOR E-BUSINESS STRATEGY: A THEORETICAL APPROACH

Introduction

Even though the Internet is viewed the world over as a key instrument of electronic commerce and, more generally, of "e-business," the Web presence of many major firms–particularly those outside the United States–leaves much to be desired (though this is improving; Griese and Sieber 1999). Although firms have invested in their Web sites, the results have been equivocal (Whinston, Stahl, and Choi 1997), often because of a limited understanding of the Internet as a marketing tool (Hutchinson 1998; Siebel and House 1999).

In this chapter, we propose a generalized framework for *e-business readiness*, as viewed from the perspective of a company's marketing-strategic disposition. The term "e-business" represents the entire range of Web-based external transactions available on a firm's Web site (Kauffels 1998). External transacting parties include customers in the wider sense [(Kotler 1996)]: individuals and households as well as manufacturers and retailers.

For a host of reasons a firm might decide to establish a more or less communicative, more or less selective, more or less transactional online presence. These reasons can be understood only from within the company (Rask 1999). Thus, short of full knowledge about these complexities, it proves very difficult for the researcher to *judge* a firm's e-business approach as adequate, lacking, or otherwise. What the researcher *can* do, however, is identify the different e-business strategies, or what we call *e-business trajectories*, theoretically available to the firm and analyze which one it has chosen to pursue in what way or to what degree. Knowledge of this kind (i.e., about the status quo of the firm's e-business approach) is valuable for at least two reasons: first, it can be used for an analysis of the strategy's utility given additional information such as the market that the company wants to target and the industry that it is in. Second, a description of the company's e-business strategy allows for a comparison against that of competitors.

Thus, in the first part of the chapter we formulate a model of e-business strategy, and in the second part we put the model to work by comparing American firms and their German competitors' e-business strategies.

Classifications

One of the earliest attempts to make sense of the Internet in commercial terms was undertaken by Hoffman, Novak, and Chatterjee [(Hoffman) 1995)]. They identified the emergence of six distinct functional categories of commercial Web pages that have become elements in the companies' integrated marketing program: (1) online storefront, (2) Internet presence, (3) content, (4) mall, (5) incentive site, and (6) search agents. These functional categories can be classified into a larger typology. The first three functions are part of what Hoffman, Novak, and Chatterjee (1995) call "destination sites," and the latter three are part of "web traffic control sites." Destination sites denote the ultimate destinations for consumer visits on the Web, while web traffic control sites function to direct consumers to the various destination sites.

Another classification has been offered by Quelch and Klein [(Quelch 1996)], who, unlike Hoffman et al., look beyond the U.S. market to suggest four types of Web sites, two including a global perspective: (1) communication and customer support sites, (2) service and transaction sites, (3) international communication and customer support sites, and (4) international service and transaction sites. Quelch and Klein's typology of Internet business models thus looks at the aspect of e-business at the firm level. Therefore, they don't recognize the distinction between traffic control sites and destination sites established by Hoffman et al. (1995). Instead, Quelch and Klein offer a useful functional typology of marketing-strategic applicability of the Internet for international businesses. A strength of their framework is the conception of different Web strategies as four "quadrants." Such an order is akin to a descriptive *mapping* of strategies and thus avoids their hierarchical ranking. This is appropriate, for in the absence of empirical data about the effect of different strategies on business performance segmented according to geography, industry, product category, and so forth, a hierarchical or credible normative conception seems currently impossible.

Set up along similar lines as Quelch and Klein is a third classificatory scheme that proves useful for our study. Rask (1999) offers a typology of commercial Web pages that is based on the company's "earnestness" with which it focuses on the new medium. Earnestness in his typology is based on the "interaction intensity" that the companies hope to achieve with their Web presence. In other words, the three interaction types, (brochure, manual, and shop) differ in interaction intensity because they all pursue different marketing "purposes." The brochure aims at informing potential customers about its or its products' strengths. With the manual the company tries to guide and support the customer who is using the company's products and services. The shop is used when the company aims to sell directly to the customers. Rask (1999) argues that the interaction intensity, in a sense a measure of the complexity of the Web site interaction between firm and customer, increases from brochure, to manual, and finally to shop. He then seems to suggest that companies aim to go through stages over time, moving from lower to higher interaction intensities. However, this is a problematic proposition, and his own longitudinal data show that in actuality such a procession through stages does not seem to take place on a consistent basis.

Rask does, however, state that not all companies are able to use the shop strategy or even the manual strategy. In fact, some firms in his study have actually reduced their interaction intensity over time. They began with a manual strategy but three years later changed to brochure strategies. Levi's Strauss is another famous example supporting the rejection of the proposition that a "natural" procession from a brochure or a manual to a shop strategy must take place. The company started off on the Internet with a shop strategy and reduced it to a brochure strategy after some time (Emert 1999). With Rask, we could argue that the shop, because of its high interaction intensity, requires an enormous commitment from the company to deal with arising complexities. If the complexities are not handled properly or if the return of investment is insufficient, the shop strategy can backfire as customers turn away from it dissatisfied, and the company loses money in the process. Thus, in the case of Levi's, it was strategically better to reduce its level of intensity from a shop to a brochure. Such a conception of Web strategies, while distinct in their interaction intensity, as ordered according to a relative and not an absolute goodness of fit, comes very close to Quelch and Klein's quadrant classification.

Also in other ways, the Quelch and Klein model and the Rask classification have a lot in common. They both distinguish between the communicational and transactional aspects of a firm's Web strategy. Moreover, both empirically identify several alternatives but refrain from normative statements as to which one is the best in all cases. For our study, we combine Quelch and Klein's quadrant classification and Rask's interaction intensity model into what we call on *e-business readiness map* (see also Mundorf et al. 1999). However, our theoretical view differs slightly from Rask's structure in that we see the types (e.g., brochure, manual, and shop) as *end points* of independent developmental *trajectories* whose *combination* results in multiple *intensity levels* that are *mapped out* in a three-dimensional space. Thus, while Rask's typology does not mention the possibility of hybrid Web strategies (in his view, a firm uses either one or the other), our model incorporates the possibility that a firm pursues multiple trajectories with differing emphases. Furthermore, our model departs from Quelch and Klein's four-quadrant structure by multiplying the number of quadrants, thus opening the model to a myriad of strategic possibilities. In sum, then, the *mult-trajectory mapping model* allows us more analytical power then does the existing classifications.

Not the endpoints in themselves are determinant of a firm's Web strategy (as implied in Rask) but the *combination of trajectories*. For example, a company that chiefly follows the communicative trajectory (brochure) but also has a shop orientation is on a different intensity level (and must be mapped differently) than a company that has not initiated a shop or manual trajectory or, conversely, offers all three. We must be able to account for these differences. Therefore, we diverge from the notion of a *unilinear* model (see Rask 1999; Zwick 1999), to a *multilinear* one (see Figures 18.1 and 18.2 for visual representations of this difference). With such a model at hand, we obtain a much more refined representation of the true Web strategies pursued by the researched companies. Consequently, we can offer a more valid comparison between Web strategies used by U.S. companies and their German competitors.

There are, then, three e-business trajectories that companies can choose in their effort to add value to their products and services: communicative, service and support, and transactional. These trajectories yield various *end points* that we call, following Rask (1999), brochure, manual, and shop (see Table 18.1). Companies can focus on just one or include two or all three trajectories into their e-business strategy. Thus, we formulate a *multitrajectory mapping model of e-business readiness* from a market-oriented perspective.

Stage Model versus Mapping Model

In an earlier paper (Zwick 1999), we aimed at engineering a universal stage model as a normative guide to describe and assess a firm's Web strategy. Most stage models develop unilinear descriptions of a particular phenomenon (such as child-to-adult development). However, for theoretical and empirical considerations, such a universal (or unilinear) stage model does not seem appropriate for exploring the complexities of commercial Web strategies. Not all firms necessarily seek the same end point (telos) of their e-business activities.

A stage model is based on two fundamental assumptions (cf. Inhelder 1969). First, there are distinct differences between the several stages marking an objectively discernible variation in the aspects to be observed. This contrasts to a mapping model where even minute variations can be represented. Second, the development is *teleological* and *linear*. In other words, the stages delineate a process along an ideal line toward a particular end point (or purpose) of development. The mapping model, on the other hand, does not prescribe a single ideal point. It is descriptive, not prescriptive.

A typology of Web marketing strategies needs to recognize that some companies might want to evolve into transactional e-tailers akin to Amazon.com, and others might prefer to use the Internet predominantly for a communicational or service and support function. Importantly, these three strategies are not "accumulative." That is, to be a shop, a firm does not necessarily have to incorporate all the features of firms pursuing a kiosk or

Table 18.1
Possible E-Business Orientations

Trajectory	End Point
Communicative	Brochure
Supportive/Service	Manual
Transactional	Shop

boutique format. Thus, we can find three distinct trajectories leading to three singular end points:

What is needed, then, is an e-business model allowing for *differentiated linear trajectories* leading to *various* ideal end points. However, despite the possibility of different e-business trajectories for different companies, recent research seems to suggest (Mundorf 1999) that a minimum degree of Web presence needs to be reached for any strategy to be effective regardless of the desired telos. Such a universal cutoff point determines what we call the *hygiene level* of e-business readiness. The hygiene level can be described as the fundamental platform that all companies must equally provide any differentiation of trajectories can be built upon it (see Figure 18.2).

To be sure, the proposed multitrajectory mapping model is *not* a normative model. In other words, we are not suggesting that a particular company or even all companies must aspire to the same end point. Thus, between the different trajectories and their functional end points there can be no hierarchical ranking or qualitative comparison. However, as Rask (1999) argues, there does exist an important quantitative difference between the orientations based on the interaction intensity of site and customer. Based on interaction intensity, a hierarchical comparison can take place. In sum, our objective is to develop an analytical tool that (1) allows us to locate the company's current position on the map of strategic possibilities, (2) indicates the interaction intensity level associated with the "geographic" location of the firm, and (3) and compares location and intensity level of German companies with those of American competitors (see Figure 18.3). Finally, the results of the study allow us to make an informed statement as to what a company would have to do if it chose to change its e-business orientation (location and intensity level).

Figure 18.1
Linear Model of Web Strategies

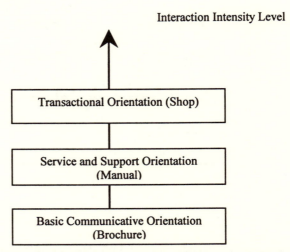

Finally, in order to avoid the theoretical difficulties that arise from the distinction between business-to-business and business-to-consumer approaches, we reject this differentiation for our study and suggest that all companies must take a *business-to-customer* approach. Following Kotler and Armstrong (1996: 66), customers can be found in consumer markets (individuals and households), business markets (manufacturers), and reseller markets (wholesalers and retailers). Thus, irrespective of their specific market (i.e., customer), *all companies potentially can adopt a total customer orientation* (Narver and Slater 1990). By taking this approach, we "bracket" or "control for" the difference among companies' product and service offers and put all firms on the same conceptual plane.

Trajectories and End Points

It should be clear that each trajectory pursuing a different end point has its unique dimensions and characteristics and must therefore be analyzed individually. In other words, a firm whose chosen trajectory is toward full transactional online presence (shop) has to excel on dimensions that are irrelevant for companies whose goal is to merely use the Internet as a communicational tool. Therefore, we need separate discussions regarding the nature of for the brochure, the manual, and the shop.

Brochure: Communicative Trajectory

The communicative trajectory has as its end point the brochure. The brochure aims at informing potential customers about the company's existence, strengths, and offers. Thus, the brochure is not much more than advertising online. The interaction intensity between customer and site is naturally very low

Figure 18.2
Multi-Linear Model of Web Strategies

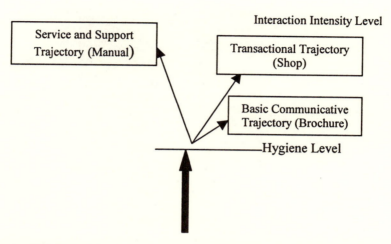

and is only slightly enriched via e-mail links. While the products are displayed and explained, selling does not take place online. Good examples of this type are the BMW Web site in Germany and the Kroger site in the United States.

Manual: Service and Support Trajectory

The service and support trajectory is pursued when the firm's goal is to offer a manual to its customers. This can include a Frequently Asked Questions (FAQ)section, software upgrades for existing hardware, a customer service e-mail link, and order tracking information. The manual is more complicated to operate for the company. Special software has to be installed to handle the interaction complexity and intensity. If successful, it can be very lucrative because it reduces customer support costs dramatically, even more so in the global context (Aspen 1998; Hoffman and Novak 1997). The manual strategy does not aim at offering the firm's products and services for sale online. A good example would be the IKEA Web strategy. The company's Web page allows for extensive searches of the product catalog. It also offers support for the assembly of its furniture, a FAQ list, and design tools for customers who want to be creative. However, no sales are made online.

Shop: Transactional Trajectory

The transactional trajectory aims at using the computer-mediated environment mainly to generate sales. The main purpose is to offer and sell the company's products and services. Brochure and manual orientations may or may not be used. Some shops, for example, Kingsbook.com, an online bookstore

Figure 18.3
Multitrajectory Mapping Model

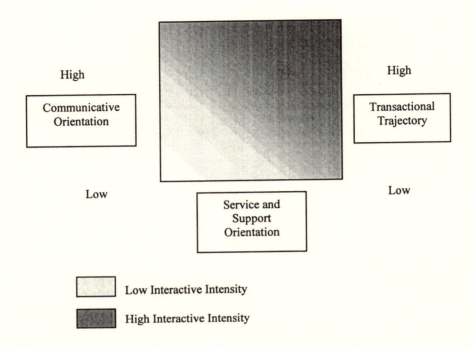

that focuses solely on the transactional trajectory, simply provide the basic information needed to finalize the sale. Others, such as Amazon.com, pursue not only the transactional trajectory but the service and support and communicative trajectory as well. Hewlett-Packard, for example, demonstrates with its Web site the full integration of all three trajectories, albeit with slightly different emphases. The site offers extensive information on its products, and a detailed service and support area, but only a relatively narrow product line.

Global Orientation

In our discussion about the various trajectories that firms can pursue and the different interaction intensities that they can choose, the aspects of internationalization and globalization have been overlooked. This neglect must be redressed because one of the chief reasons for the attractiveness of the Internet for the commercial sector is its internationalization of markets in the Information Age (Dholakia 1999, 34-35; Dholakia 1999, 304). For many companies a primary motivation to build and maintain a Web site is its ability to connect with an international audience (Aspen 1998; Stauss 1997). International customers add value but rarely costs. Thus, as Quelch and Klein (1996) have pointed out in their quadrant model, the internationalization aspect must be part

Table 18.2
German-American Competitor Pairs

German	American
Volkswagen (Volkswagen.de)	General Motors (gm.com)
Miele (Miele.de)	General Electric (ge.com)
Deutscher Paket Dienst (dpd.com)	United Parcel Service (ups.com)
Lufthansa (Lufthansa.com)	Delta (Delta-Airlines.com)
Deutsche Telekom AG (Telekom.de)	AT&T

of the evaluation of all trajectories. In other words, the communicative, support and service, and transactional trajectories must be evaluated *also* for their ability to interact with an international audience.

THE E-BUSINESS READINESS OF AMERICAN AND GERMAN COMPANIES: AN EMPIRICAL APPROACH

In the second part of the chapter we explore the Web strategies of selected American and German companies using our multitrajectory mapping model (see Figure 18.3). We have formed five pairs, each consisting of one American and one German company (see Table 18.2). The companies were chosen for their similarities in product offering and customer profile. In other words, they can be considered competitors in the global marketplace.

We want to know whether differences exist between the companies regarding their Web strategies. Therefore, each company's Web page is examined to identify its respective "trajectory mix," that is, its emphasis on reaching each of the three end points (brochure, manual, shop). In addition to the three trajectories and end points, we assess the company's international or global orientation (see Table 18.3). This information allows us to determine the interaction intensity that the firms have chosen, which, in a last step, is then represented visually in the multitrajectory map (see Figure 18.3). Thus, we first discuss each pair in detail. We then contrast them with each other and finally provide some conclusions.

Volkswagen and General Motors

Volkswagen (VW) and General Motors (GM) are two of the largest car manufacturers in the world. Both companies have performed successfully in recent years in local and global markets (Guilford 1999; Green 1999). However, in some respects their Web strategies seem to differ.

Volkswagen uses the Web mainly for communicative purposes. The company excels in presenting its product line in a computer-mediated environment, thus fulfilling the aspects of a brochure. It offers detailed information about its cars, minivans, and small trucks. In addition, customers can find information about leasing and financing, car insurance, and servicing. The site does not provide much of a service and support function for customers who already own a VW car. For instance, there is no FAQ or positing area where owners could ask questions and find answers to possible problems regarding their used cars. For VW direct bank customers who have been financing their car, the site offers no access to account information or transaction. Furthermore, the site offers a link to the VW Club, but to join online is not possible. VW does not emphasize the transactional trajectory at all. It offers no possibility to purchase a car online. Another possible function to benefit the customer, such as the online configuration of a VW car, does not exist, nor does the option to locate a car at a dealership. The only aspect set up to support the customer in his or her buying process is the "store locator" function. After providing some personal information, the search engine finds the nearest dealership and displays its address, phone, and fax number. VW makes an effort to cater to a global marketplace. Its Web site is offered as full-text, foreign-language version in 19 countries worldwide.

General Motors' Web presence is much more comprehensive than that of VW. Regarding the communicative trajectory, the Web site offers not only the usual sections concerning the company's products and services but also a virtual auto show and company tour. The interactive "GM Experience Live" show is an excellent way of representing the company and its products to the visitor. In addition to a full brochure strategy, GM aggressively pursues the service and support trajectory. For example, potential customers can explore financing opportunities online, calculate quotes and rates, and apply for a contract. Once GM customers, they can access their account online, choose and change payment options, refinance, and so forth. For visitors searching for a GM vehicle, the site offers a "Good Deal" section. If the visitor does not find the desired car, he or she can specify preferences and receive an e-mail notification as soon as an offer comes in. Finally, the GM site has a clear commitment to the transaction trajectory. In essence, the shop is realized on the GM Web page. A visitor can specify what car he or she is looking for and locate it online using the GM search engine. In addition, the site assists him or her in finding the best price among all GM dealerships and in contacting the dealer with the offer. In sum, the GM site is poised for high interaction intensity by equally strong emphasison the brochure, the manual, and the shop. The Web site also tries to cater to the global marketplace by offering links to 50 countries worldwide. However, GM does not offer full-text, foreign-language versions but offers predominantly English-language foreign sites with very little information.

Miele and General Electric (GE)

GE and Miele are large producers of kitchen and household appliances with global production and distribution systems. Both companies are successful actors in a competitive and increasingly global marketplace that need to understand the imperative of using the new information technologies to coordinate and expand their operations. GE, of course, has a much more extensive business portfolio providing services such as insurance, warranties, mortgages, and even investment services. For our discussion and in order to allow for a meaningful comparison with Miele, we limit the investigation to GE's appliance business.

Miele uses the Web extensively for communicative purposes. It has set up a comprehensive brochure covering in detail and visually adept the firm's product lines. In addition, the Web site offers other relevant information about the company that is of interest for investors, journalists, and other potential stakeholders. While Miele does emphasize the brochure function, the company offers only a crude manual format on the Web. One can find a FAQ section where the visitor can learn about how to preserve energy and protect the environment by using Miele products. Supporting its kitchen appliances, the Web site has a "recipe of the month" section, and, supporting its washing machine business, a section is provided where visitors can learn about cleaning and treating particular materials. The site does not offer any shop function. In fact, Miele does not even support a store locator search function. In addition, the Web site does not even inform the visitor which stores carry the company's products. In sum, Miele has mastered the Web as a communicative means but neglects its capabilities to fulfill service and support functions. However, while a marginal emphasis is put on the manual, no effort is made at all to integrate the shop into the firm's Web strategy. As a result, the overall interaction intensity is kept quite low. Efforts are made toward catering to an international, but not yet global, market. The Web site offers links to 10 European full-text foreign-language sites, and the United States, Asia, Africa, South America, and Australia are not represented.

General Electric has a strong brochure and manual orientation but only a medium emphasis on the shop. Products are well displayed and described in detail. A good example of how GE realizes the brochure format very effectively is its "product comparison" feature. This feature allows the consumer to contrast the performance of up to three products within the same product category (e.g., washing machines) online. The Web site displays the results of the comparison in a convenient table format, which enables the consumer to quickly survey the advantages and disadvantages of each item. The consumer can make a much more informed choice without spending extensive research time. The manual is realized only in the guise of FAQ and an answer center for customers who intend to buy, or have already bought, a GE product. The answer center allows for more specific questions not covered by the FAQ. Via e-mail, the visitor can post a question and receive an e-mail response with a customized solution. The transactional trajectory is developed but not yet fully realized. The visitor cannot actually buy appliances from the Web site but can, however, search for the desired product and locate the nearest physical store where the item might be found, though GE does not provide hyperlinks or any other "digital" way of contacting the retailer. It should be pointed out that the visitor can search a "What's Hot" section, where he or she finds several promotional offers. The visitor can then, for example, print out a coupon that entitles him or her to a price discount in the physical store. Finally, while the GE Web site does not support purchases of appliances, it does offer accessories and replacement parts. In sum, based on its emphasis on the communicative and service and support trajectory, the GE site displays relatively high interaction intensity. In addition, the transactional trajectory, while not yet fully developed, is emphasized by the company. The Web site's effort to address a global marketplace is quite poor. The Web site for Europe is written in English and consists of no more than some product descriptions. There is no store locator function, FAQ section, or e-mail contact. For a company operating globally, GE does not use the Web site sufficiently.

Deutscher Paket Dienst (DPD) and United Parcel Service (UPS)

DPD and UPS are two formidable players in the delivery business. Clearly, UPS is the larger company of the two with operations worldwide. DPD, however, is one of the largest delivery firms in Europe and has been growing aggressively over the last five years. However, while the difference in size is considerable, the nature of the business is very much the same. A meaningful comparison of the two companies' Web strategies is possible.

DPD's Web strategy emphasizes mainly the brochure and service and support format. The site lists and explains in detail the company's product line and the process of packaging, sending, and receiving DPD deliveries. The customer can find a manual explaining how to fill out the delivery slip and package label. In addition, the site allows the customer to track the order. The customer can also print package labels right off his or her computer but needs to contact the local DPD representative to find out how to actually do that! The site does not offer anything toward a transactional trajectory. Packages to be sent out have to be dropped off at the local DPD store, and the package material must be bought there, too. In sum, DPD pursues a Web strategy of low interaction intensity. The brochure is realized to a satisfactory degree, but the service and support trajectory is not as well developed as it probably could be. DPD does not emphasize the shop at all in its trajectory mix. Finally, as a European company, DPD offers three full-text, foreign-language Web sites (Italian, French, and English), thus doing a good job in communication to the international market.

UPS's trajectory mix demonstrates an impressive emphasis on all three end points. In addition, the site offers comprehensive coverage of the global markets that it serves. The company's Web site is replete with product displays, shipping directions, and little tools such as "Quick Cost" and "Transit Time" that allow the customer to calculate the cost and time requirements of the delivery. Also, UPS uses the Internet to communicate to the customer specific information pertaining to a particular delivery. The customer can thus ask for delivery confirmations or shipment notifications via e-mail. The site also supports the transactional trajectory in various ways. For example, the customer can schedule the pickup of his or her shipment online, order UPS-specific package supply, and download customer-specific software that facilitates the finalization of the transaction. In sum, UPS has developed a fully integrated and matured trajectory mix. The company makes a conscious effort to exploit the Internet to its fullest and does not seem to be concerned about the very high interaction intensity that ensues.

Lufthansa and Delta

Lufthansa and Delta are among the biggest air carriers in the world, competing in a fiercely competitive marketplace. During the 1960s and 1970s, the airline industry was among the first to aggressively build huge data networks (Schiller 1999). The Internet as the network of networks is therefore only a logical progression toward the total interconnectivity of company databases, strategic business units, and the global customer. Because of the nature of the product, airlines are prone to develop a comprehensive trajectory mix, emphasizing every end point.

After the privatization of Lufthansa, the airline enjoyed increasing popularity among travelers, because enhanced service orientation has led to heightened customer satisfaction (Field, 1998). The company's Web site provides, as expected, a comprehensive and balanced trajectory mix. The communicative trajectory is realized via detailed descriptions of the services that the company offers. In addition, the site dedicates one area to explain innovations designed to facilitate travel for the customer. The service and support trajectory is mainly characterized by the continuous, real-time updating of departure and arrival times of Lufthansa planes at airports across the world. The site offers another interactive feature with a flight planner that allows one to get a full overview of the connection between two cities. In addition, the visitor can check for availability on particular legs. Finally, frequent flier customers can check their account balance online. The transitional trajectory is realized in two distinct ways. Of course, the most obvious one is the possibility for the visitor to search airfares and purchase a ticket online. In addition, however, Lufthansa sells travel accessories in what could be called their online boutique. There, visitors can find products such as suitcases and travel apparel. In sum, Lufthansa has put together a comprehensive trajectory mix emphasizing equally the brochure, the manual, and the shop. However, despite the equally balanced trajectory mix, none of the three formats is highly interaction-intensive. On the other hand, the company's global coverage is tremendous. One can choose among larger regions such as Asia-Pacific and the Americas and then among individual countries within these zones. A full-text, foreign-language version of the Lufthansa Web page can be downloaded.

The Web strategy pursued by Delta Airlines is, in principle, similar to that of its competitor. However, we find a fuller realization of each trajectory. The site allows the visitor to get information on flights, availability, and airfares. Moreover, information regarding a variety of special product links is provided as well. There is, for example, a dining program, an e-mail center, on MCI sign-up sheet, and a Sky Mile Credit Card, to name but a few. The service trajectory is very well developed. Besides the possibility of finding and purchasing tickets online, the visitor can explore the "special" section for cheaper flights. Moreover, Delta entertains a virtual mall called the Skymall. Here, an amazing array of products can be purchased, ranging from computers, to mattresses, to personal care products, to pets. Surpassingly, Delta actually built a full-blown mall within its core business of selling air travel. In sum, Delta, like Lufthansa, has an equally balanced trajectory mix, yet on a higher overall interaction-intensity level. In comparison, there is much more visitors can learn, do, and buy on the Delta Web page. However, the Web site is missing any international or global orientation entirely. There are no links to regional or national Web pages. It thus seems that Delta's Web site neglects to address the international audience.

AT&T and Deutsche Telekom

Deutsche Telekom and AT&T are two formidable companies in the world telecommunication and information technology market. In an industry where mergers, acquisitions and strategic alliances have increased dramatically during the second half of the 1990s (Yang 1999), AT&T and Deutsche Telekom have forged large empires. However, increasing global competition forces both companies to develop consumer-oriented marketing strategies, be it for their traditional products such as telephone services or as Internet service providers (Morri 1998). Whatever the objective, the Internet is likely to play a major road in the companies' consumer marketing efforts.

Deutsche Telekom's Web strategy actively focuses on the delivery of products over the Internet. The trajectory mix illustrates the company's strong shop and service and support orientation. The visitor can order everything from the Web site directly: Internet service, phones, plug and play accessories for the PC, fax or phone devices, and calling plans. The products are explained in detail and visually displayed, even when the product is a calling plan. The manual is equally well developed. The customer can get online account information, and telephone numbers of service agents, visit the FAQ section, and send individual questions to the service center. The communicative trajectory is very well developed and does not need much description. It seems that there is almost nothing one cannot find on the company's Web page, if it is relevant for the firm, the customer, or the telecommunication industry. Telekom addresses the international audience selectively by offering its Web page in German, French, and English.

AT&T's Web strategy is very similar to that of Telekom. All available products are explained well and also visualized to some degree. The

Table 18.3
Trajectory and Interaction Intensity of German and American Companies

Company	Brochure	Manual	Shop	Globalization	Interaction Intensity
VW	++	+	0	++	Medium
GM	++	++	++	+	High
Miele	++	+	0	+	Low-Medium
GE	++	++	+	0	Medium-High
DPD	++	+	0	+	Low-Medium
UPS	++	++	++	++	Very High
Lufthansa	++	+	++	++	High
Delta	++	++	++	0	High
Telekom	++	++	++	+	High
AT&T	++	++	++	+	High

0   not emphasized
+   somewhat emphasized
++   strongly emphasized

organization of the Web page is more customer-oriented than that of Telekom. The various product and service options are easier to find. Similar to the Telekom shop, the company uses the Web site to sell a host of telecommunication services and products. The site's service and support section is also identical to that of Telekom. The visitor can ask for service numbers, send e-mails to the service center, and manage his or her AT&T account. In sum, the trajectory mix is well balanced and makes a strong attempt to realize all three end points. AT&T's specific effort to address international audiences is limited to Asian-Pacific customers, with full-text, foreign-language sites in Korean, Chinese, and Japanese.

Discussion

Within the multitrajectory model of e-business readiness proposed here, we find differences between the members of each pair. With the exception of Telekom, all German companies demonstrate a tendency to have Web sites with lower interaction intensities than those of their American competitors. While all of the German companies have fully realized the brochure format, only Telekom has done the same for the manual. However, all German companies do emphasize the service and support trajectory on their Web site somewhat, but maybe not enough. The Internet has been discovered by many customers as an interactive and fast avenue to get information, help, and advice on all possible topics. Thus, the least that they expect, from companies' Web sites is fast and accurate product-related information. The risk that firms take with an underemphasized service and support trajectory (perhaps due to the overwhelming interaction intensity [Rask 1999]) is high, especially considering the global impact of virtual word-of-mouth diffusion (Stauss 1998).

The transactional trajectory is the weakest of all parts of the trajectory mix. In other words, shops are even less emphasized in the Web strategies of German companies than the manual and the brochure. Only Lufthansa and Telekom have emphasized or realized the shop online against *all* American companies. Overall, we observe a clear bias among German companies to develop Web strategies that focus on communicative and service and support functions. While such a disposition toward low interaction intensity might be desired, we would argue, based on our results, that the German companies do not yet fully exploit the commercial potential of the Internet. After all, given that their American counterparts are using the Web more aggressively as shop, it seems obvious that there is no imperative *against* the transactional trajectory for any particular industry. Thus, German companies surveyed in this study might potentially log behind in using the Internet for marketing management purposes.

As Table 18.3 shows, in all cases but one (Telekom-AT&T) American companies have a higher interaction intensity than that of their German competitors. The difference emerges mainly due to the American firms' overall strong emphasis in the transactional trajectory. But also the manual strategy is realized with more force by the Americans than by their German competitors. This points to the stronger service orientation of American companies, which face higher customer expectations regarding service orientation and quality (Witkowski, 1996). Despite the overall breadth of their trajectory mix, American firms show a peculiar negligence of the global dimension of the Internet. Only UPS addresses the global audience broadly, while General Motors and AT&T attempt rather feebly to communicate with international markets. General Electric and Delta entirely ignore the global reach of the Internet.

Evidence suggests (Balikowa 1995; Hirschman 1988; Holbrook 1986) that global information technologies play a dominant role in the production of one of the most debated contradictions of the late twentieth century: the growth of a global consumer culture with homogeneous consumer tastes (Levitt 1983) and the simultaneous reinforcement of local differences (Wilk 1995). Our study shows that German companies demonstrate much more sensitivity concerning the intricacies of the global-local nexus. Offering full-text, foreign-language Web sites, all German companies try to *localize* their communication. No American company makes such an effort. Indeed, none even offered a Spanish version!

CONCLUSION

In the first part of the chapter we drafted a multitrajectory model of e-business readiness, which we put to use in the second part. Our multitrajectory model is based on the assumption that the companies can pursue three main trajectories on the Web: communicative, service and support, and transaction. Therefore, companies have to make a decision as to whether they want to emphasize one, two, or all three possible trajectories. Moreover, companies must make a conscious decision whether they wish to apply their trajectory mix to a local (national) or global audience. Any decision regarding the trajectory mix as

Figure 18.4
Companies' Position in the Multitrajectory Mapping Model

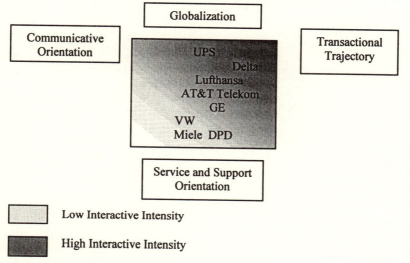

Low Interactive Intensity

High Interactive Intensity

well as the globalization aspect affects the *interaction intensity* to which a company is exposed to on the Internet. The degree of interaction intensity chosen by a company has a tremendous effect on almost all its operational units (Rask 1999). Therefore, the question about what constitutes an appropriate trajectory mix for a firm is a complex one and cannot be answered from the outside. With our multitrajectory model we can give an answer as to what particular interaction intensity a company has opted for *and* how its strategy compares to that of a competitor's (see Table 18.3).

Thus, in the second part of the chapter we put our model to use and investigated 10 companies, 5 American and 5 German, for their trajectory mix. Each American firm was compared with its German competitor to see whether we can find any differences in their respective Web strategies and approaches. Overall, we found that American firms are more willing to tolerate higher interaction intensities than their German counterparts (see Figure 18.4). In two cases, AT&T-Telekom and Delta-Lufthansa, there was no difference. However, on the globalization dimension, American companies do not do as well as their German competitors.

Of course, our study should not be mistaken as a comprehensive survey of German and American companies' Web strategies. Indeed, all we wanted to accomplish was to develop a useful framework for assessing a firm's Web approach and to suggest with some examples how such a framework could be used empirically. The managerial relevance of our model and its implications for strategic decision making should be obvious. Not only can a firm locate its position on the multitrajectory map with ease, but also in one glance the firm can compare its own position with that of its competitors. Armed with this knowledge, a company can make better decisions about future directions concerning its marketing mix in general and its Web trajectory mix in particular.

19

Virtual Classrooms in the New Economy: Global Education through the Internet

Norbert Mundorf, Wolfgang Fritz, Nikhilesh Dholakia, Chai Kim, and Martin Kerner

INTRODUCTION

Most chapters in this book have focused on the business dimensions of the Internet. One of the critical impacts that have emerged from the Internet is its potential to enhance education and training and to make educational efforts relatively independent of location. In the new economy, processing information is much more powerful and cost-effective than moving physical products. "Increasingly, the value of a company is found not in its tangible assets, but in intangibles: people, ideas, and the strategic aggregation of key information-driven assets." ("The 10 Driving Principles," *Business 2.0*, April 2000). In order to enhance the value of these intangible assets, they have to be state-of-the-art. In education this can be achieved by reaching people independently of where they happen to be at a certain time and when they happen to be available. For college students, exposure to new information technologies teaches them to optimally utilize these technologies and explore innovative communication strategies and helps them experience virtual global networks firsthand. This chapter gives a brief overview of trends in distance learning; it discusses one innovative experiment in global distance learning; and it provides an outlook of what might be ahead in virtual education.

GROWTH OF DISTANCE LEARNING

The Continuous Learning Economy

Because of the increasing competition in the global economy, continuing education is a growing concern. To remain competitive, employees have to improve their job skills. Increasingly, they have to acquire new sets of skills to change jobs or just to keep their existing jobs. Also, education is valued more highly than in the past. The cost of corporate training has skyrocketed (as has the cost of ignorance). Recruiting and retaining employees, especially in the high-technology sectors, requires investments in continuing education. The availability of continuous training is a significant recruitment and retention tool. The number of adult learners with complex schedules has risen dramatically (Martin, 1999). Finally, the cost of college education has escalated. Distance learning can help address these concerns.

Evolution of Distance Learning

The concept of distance learning has been in existence for more than a century in terms of correspondence courses and later through the use of radio, television, and the video cassette recorder (VCR). The widespread availability of computers in schools and homes and of satellite and videoconferencing technology has led to the prospect of interactive distance learning that is accessible to considerable parts of the population. Interactive evening or weekend courses can make it easier for employees to improve their skills without the inconvenience of additional travel. Schools in remote or resource-poor areas can receive quality and diversity of educational offerings similar to what is available in wealthy suburbs. Finally, distance learning can improve the quality of, and lower the costs of, college education by linking small colleges or remote branch campuses to the educational opportunities provided by research universities (Martin 1999). The role of the instructor changes considerably. From just a teacher, the instructor becomes a person who orchestrates a variety of learning resources. The instructor becomes the node for linking students to resources and providing support for self-directed learning (Patterson 1999).

The majority of four-year colleges and universities now offer distance learning. Several institutions currently offer degree programs entirely at a distance, by which students can earn their sheepskins without ever having to visit the campus—unless they want to show up on graduation day. These include Boise State University, New York Institute of Technology, Rochester Institute of Technology, and the University of Maryland (Goldberg 1998).

Information technologies can provide students with far greater involvement in the process of learning. These interactive technologies also offer students far greater control over that process than is possible in many traditional learning environments. There are two categories of distance education delivery systems, synchronous and asynchronous.

Synchronous and Asynchronous Systems of Learning

Synchronous instruction requires the simultaneous participation of all students and instructors. The advantage of synchronous instruction is that the interaction is done in "real time" and is thus more similar to conventional instruction. Using real-time, online discussion can recapture some of the immediacy of classroom instruction. It can capitalize on the popularity of chat and instant messenger functions among teenagers and college students. Chat is even possible internationally, as long as differences in time zones and schedules are taken into account. For instance, chat between Germany and the United States would be subject to a six-hour time difference (Germany being "ahead"), as well as a semester schedule that allows for only six to seven weeks of overlap in the fall and less in the spring. Recently, one of the authors utilized chat with small groups of American and German students interested in e-commerce, with German participants (voluntarily) online around midnight.

Asynchronous instruction does not require the simultaneous, real-time participation of all students and instructors and is thus more flexible than synchronous instruction. Students do not need to be gathered together in the same location at the same time. Moreover, with the use of e-mail and other forms of communications, asynchronous instruction allows and even may encourage community. A possible disadvantage to consider with e-mail-based interaction is the one-sided emphasis on written exchange. Also, for some types of courses, testing is problematic.

Distance Learning in Universities

Many universities offer a wide range of distance learning courses. Initially, they were mainly targeted to part-time students with full-time jobs. At the University of Rhode Island, for instance, Web-based courses during the summer attract considerable numbers of out-of-state, full-time students. Many students submit their assignments and comments from home.

Another format has been courses that rely on videoconferencing. At the University of Rhode Island, such courses are usually taught at the rural main campus and transmitted to the urban satellite campus. Highly specialized courses (e.g., nursing) are even transmitted to a network of regional universities. These courses currently use compressed video; however, desktop video is a feasible alternative given adequate transmission speeds.

Many colleges and universities are currently experimenting with degrees based on electronically delivered courses. Besides saving resources and increasing course offerings, electronic learning systems help colleges to project the image of a "high-tech" institution. Training of instructors and quality control are key concerns in such electronic course offerings. Rather than replacing the current educational system, in the foreseeable future distance learning is expected to complement it.

Distance Learning in Corporate Settings

Distance learning is equally significant for corporate training (Martin 1999). Especially those companies with widely distributed locations can save considerable resources in time and travel by utilizing Intranets and other communication technologies for training purposes. Some companies, such as General Electric (GE), also use their Extranet to collect supplier information, which is then used to train sales or service personnel.

STRENGTHS AND WEAKNESSES OF DISTANCE LEARNING

Facilitating and Inhibiting Factors

Farrell (1999) discusses factors facilitating and inhibiting the development of virtual classrooms. Among the factors spurring the growth of electronic distance education are:

- Increase of information technology (IT) available to educational applications and decrease in hardware cost
- Capacity of technology to "unbundle" functions that were traditionally all handled by one educational institution in one physical location
- The growth and increased obsolescence of knowledge, which coincide with the need for constant updating and demand for lifelong learning opportunities
- The realization that the "quality of the learning experience can be enhanced by applying information and communication technologies" (5)
- The demand for access by learners isolated due to physical location or reduced mobility
- Increased competition in postsecondary education
- Expectations of cost reductions

He also points to several factors that are inhibiting the growth of distance education:

- Limited access to networks in less developed parts of the world
- Lack of access for individuals in many target demographics (the information "haves" and "have-nots")
- Copyright restrictions that discourage interinstitutional or even international sharing
- High upfront costs of implementing systems and training
- Limited online learner support
- Reluctance of teachers and faculty to embrace the technology and give up control of the face-to-face classroom interaction
- Insufficient arrangements for the transfer of course credits
- Preference of younger, more visible constituencies for face-to-face learning environments

Effectiveness of Distance Learning

Mottl (2000) believes that online learning is destined to become standard operating procedure in the near future due to the simple fact that it can nearly halve the costs of conventional classroom instruction, even though the cost for course development and infrastructure can be considerable. Also, using the Web for training purposes decreases the restrictions of location, seat limitations, and travel costs. The shortage in able instructors is also a main reason for the predicted success of distance learning.

For distance learning to succeed, there must be an unprecedented level of trust between the instructor and the student (Decker, et al. 2000). The instructor must be proficient in the subject matter in order to field questions, and inquiries and to suggest approaches as problems occur. He or she must develop an effective syllabus and take time to improve teaching style. Last, students must be proficient in the prerequisite knowledge and must have a disciplined attitude and be able to learn independently. According to Decker et al. (2000), concerns about distance learning include the technical problems with speed and bandwidth, the decreased quality of education, and the issue of cheating.

Hecht and Klass (1999) examine the effectiveness of streamed Internet audio and video technology when used for primary instruction in off-campus research classes. Several groups of off-campus students enrolled in both a spring quantitative and a fall qualitative research class. Both classes (1) combined asynchronous, Web-based materials with synchronous audio and video transmission with real-time chat and discussion software and (2) transmitted the audio and video components of the live class from the instructor to the live students. The results indicated that it was possible to deliver even highly technical, research-oriented courses over the Internet. Both courses, however, also reported encountering problems such as a sense of disconnection and added time pressures for instructors.

Hodge-Hardin (1997) compared the math achievement of students when taught in the traditional classroom setting and when taught in an interactive television setting (ITV). Results show that ITV can be considered an adequate method of providing developmental algebra instruction beyond the confines of the campus. The effectiveness of the ITV courses was measured by using the student's final numerical grades as a dependent variable.

Even secondary schools now experiment with Web-based environments, both to enhance in-class learning and, in some cases, to accommodate students living in remote locations. While most studies focus on college-level experiences, Cavanaugh (1999) looked at the effectiveness of interactive distance education using video conferencing and telecommunications for K12 academic achievement. The study included 929 participants who were analyzed across sample characteristics, study methods, learning environment, learned attributes, and technological characteristics. Distance learning by itself showed only a small positive effect, while the group that received classroom instruction coupled with off-campus learning via various telecommunication methods boasted the highest positive effects. These results were congruent across subject matter and content areas with the exception of foreign languages, as it is difficult to mimic the sounds made by the human voice on a computer.

The conclusion for this study was that distance learning should enhance, complement, and expand education options, because it can be expected to result in achievement levels that are at least comparable to traditional instruction in most academic circumstances. However, at least for younger students, the face-to-face complement adds to the quality of the classroom experience.

Cohn (2000) is one of the skeptics who claim that although digital degrees are inevitable, they still do not provide a "real" education, since students never get the chance to become well-rounded and never truly experience diverse cultures and perspectives. Cohn believes that distance learning has merit in terms of its convenience, economy, and geographic freedom. Overall, however, he contends that distance learning cannot provide all the elements that should combine to give students a truly well-rounded education. Cohn's argument seems to revolve around the underlying theme that there is more to a college degree than simply the books.

CASE STUDY: GLOBAL E-MAIL DEBATE AND INTERCULTURAL DIALOGUE

As we have pointed out, distance learning can use many different technologies and formats. One format that has been used in transatlantic and transpacific distance learning courses is the "e-mail debate." The main idea behind this format was to increase the sensitivity of students to intercultural differences in a global environment.

Rationale for Globalization

While distance education plays a significant role in the U.S. educational system, other countries and organizations worldwide have also begun to adopt it. We are experiencing an ever-increasing level of economic, social, and political globalization (Garten 2000). Learning to deal with cultural differences has become critically important for successful business as well as political endeavors. National economies, the changing nature of work, and political necessities all call for increased globalization (Kim 1999). In many cases lack of intercultural understanding has hampered global business negotiations. Especially for U.S. companies the lack of intercultural competence has proven to be a significant impediment to successful placement of expatriates (Kim 1999). Consequently, intercultural training of future employees is pivotal for their success in the workplace and the long-term success of the companies employing them.

Global E-Mail Debate

For more than a decade we have successfully used the Internet as a training tool for intercultural awareness, sensitivity, and competence. Dr. Chai Kim (1999) pioneered the international e-mail debate in the late 1980s. Since then a large number of students and faculty in the United States, Europe, and Asia have been involved in such debates and variations thereof.

These applications of the Internet illustrate how IT can be used to prepare future employees for some of the challenges of the global workplace. Obviously the Internet is no substitute for the "real thing." American students, in particular, are reluctant to spend any significant time in foreign cultures, much less in foreign-language environments (Kim 1999). Through Internet-based approaches, they can not only collect information about the host country but also develop intercultural awareness (the ability to identify and explain cultural similarities and differences; Chen and Sarosta 1996), intercultural sensitivity (the ability to acknowledge, respect, tolerate, and accept cultural differences), and finally intercultural competence (the ability to negotiate their way across multiple cultures).

Description of E-Mail Debate

Students introduce themselves through the "Handshake in Cyberspace" (Kim 1999: 623), which now often includes an invitation to mutual Web sites. The debate is conducted by exchanging a series of documents called the constructive argument, the refutation, and the rebuttal. Students conduct research on an assigned debate resolution and exchange their initial position paper simultaneously. Rules are explained on a Web site available to the participants. They then exchange reactions to each other's arguments (refutation), and they go through another round of discussion in the rebuttal. At the end of the debate cycle, students exchange evaluative comments. Respective instructors in each participating country grade the team effort.

Research Findings

Responses to the e-mail debate were generally positive, and general improvements in writing and critical thinking skills were observed (Kim 1999). Due to the complex cross-cultural nature of e-mail debates and lack of appropriate methodologies, quantitative assessments of their impact on intercultural awareness and sensitivity have been difficult. While Chen (1998) initially failed to demonstrate significant effects for combined debates from different countries in pre- and posttests, later analyses of data from German students (Fritz, et al., 1999) did reveal significant differences on several of the items used in the questionnaire. The only item that produced significant change on perceptions of their own culture was disagreement with the statement: "German people tend to emphasize the spiritual life." While there was little influence on the view of their own culture, the respondents' view of the American culture showed some significant changes. As can be seen in Figure 19.1, greater agreement emerged on the items:

- "American people see themselves as individualists,"
- "American families move more often than do families in other countries,"
- "American people tend to emphasize change more than tradition," and
- "American people tend to emphasize the future more than the past."

Similar patterns were found regarding intercultural sensitivity. While overall differences were small, several individual items produced statistically significant before and after differences. Compared to a control group, German students participating in an e-mail debate disagreed more strongly with the views that:

- "It is difficult to communicate well with people from a different culture,"
- "To marry people from other cultures is acceptable,"
- "There is little we can do to improve intercultural understanding," and
- "Cultural differences exist in society, but we can never fully understand those differences."

Apparently, the e-mail debate removed some of the emotional impediments to communicating with members of another culture. However, it led to a slightly greater reluctance toward marrying persons from a different culture (in spite of a generally positive attitude toward cross-cultural marriage). One reason for this somewhat greater reluctance may be that the e-mail debate *increased* the perception of cultural differences and thus may counteract a somewhat naive set of expectations. These results are only partial. More research will be needed to assess how e-mail debates (and other IT-aided, cross-cultural learning methods) can influence intercultural awareness, sensitivity, and competence.

FUTURE PROSPECTS

The reservations and criticisms about Internet-based distance learning methods notwithstanding, it is clear that the favorable economics of distance learning and the ability to serve vast, dispersed groups of learners will continue to push university-based education as well as corporate training programs toward increasing adoption of distance learning methods. Research from various sources, including the case of the e-mail debate discussed here, shows that effectiveness of Internet-based methods can be increased when Internet-based techniques are combined with reflective, fact-to-face methods of learning.

In the future, multimedia interactivity may allow Internet-based communications to incorporate some elements of real-time "presence" of the real-world classroom. Some of the reflective discussions of the classroom that are lost in the current Internet-based methods can be brought back, without the need for everyone being in the same physical space at the same time. For this, the current technology of specialized videoconference rooms or screen-mounted video cameras is not adequate. Technology will have to evolve to the point where some of the real-time sessions will use a virtual reality interface that imparts the feeling of being in a classroom. A true test of this would be if students and instructors feel the need to dress in publicly presentable ways before "entering" such sessions. In the global context, a further challenge would be to overcome the disparities of time zones and the barriers of languages. In terms of time zones, we will likely see the evolution of workdays that divide the 24 hours into segments that maximize the opportunities for cross-global real-time contact. In terms of languages, the evolution of computerized translation systems would eventually ensure that real-time conversation could occur even when people are speaking different languages. Given the pace of technology development, these things are likely to happen sooner than many people expect.

SUMMARY AND CONCLUSIONS

This chapter has provided a glimpse of trends and opportunities in distance learning. We are currently experiencing a phase of trial and error in this area. Even though up-front costs are considerable, the economics are clearly favorable for distance education in the long run. Nevertheless, it is unlikely to lead to the demise of campus-based college education as we know it, not only because of the doubtless benefits of face-to-face interaction but also because of the unique dynamics of campus life. Also, assessment of teaching and learning effectiveness has not been resolved for distance learning.

However, utilizing information technology will supplement the conventional learning experience and provide students with tremendous opportunities. In particular, virtual classrooms can add to intercultural experiences international knowledge. The potential for corporate training is similarly staggering. Employees of global corporations will have access to up-to-date knowledge, and information from different countries will be made available instantly. This may also help train expatriates in intercultural awareness, sensitivity, and competence, thus reducing the cost of failure in this area. Also, the cost of corporate seminars that require travel and hotel accommodations can be trimmed considerably. Finally, training new employees will also be more efficient and standardized.

Like electronic commerce, virtual classrooms are still in their infancy. Both have tremendous potential, but considerable failures are to be expected. Just as electronic commerce will not replace the malls and shops, virtual classrooms will not replace their conventional counterparts. But, with any luck, they will help increase the vitality and diversity of our lives.

QUESTIONS FOR DISCUSSION

1. What are the advantages and disadvantages of asynchronous and synchronous communication in distance learning?

2. How can global corporations utilize the experiences with global classrooms for intercultural training of their employees?

3. What types of business models are likely to succeed in the for-profit and the nonprofit sectors of Internet-based delivery of education? Why?

4. How will the emergence of virtual classrooms change the conventional college experience and the economy of the higher education sector?

5. Will virtual global classrooms help bridge the gap or widen the gap between the technology "haves" and the "have-nots"?

Notes

1. Unless otherwise stated, the data items presented in bullet forms and in the text of this chapter are from three sources. The first is NUA Internet Surveys. URL: http://www.nua.ie/surveys/. NUA compiles its data from several sources worldwide. The second source is CyberAtlas, a subsidiary of internet.com, which also complies research data from multiple sites. URL: http://cyberatlas.internet.com/. The third data source is research conducted by RITIM, the Research Institute for Telecommunications and Information Marketing at the University of Rhode Island. URL: http://ritim.cba.uri.edu/.
2. The glossary at the end of this book provides simple defintions of many such terms.
3. The term "informationalization," referring to the thorough transformation of a product or process by the application of information technology, was used as a central concept by Stan Davis and Bill Davidson (1991).
4. The term "conversation" has been used to characterize electronic, interactive marketing by Professor John Deighton of Harvard Business School. The concept of a multilogue involving communities is discussed by Firat and Dholakia (1998).
5. See, for example, Andrew Tanzer (1997), in this article, Richmond Lo, manager in IBM's Greater China Croup, is quoted as saying: "People in the cities [in China] have a TV, stereo, fridge and washing machine. Now they want a PC. It's a symbol of modernity." Lo estimates that by the year 2000 China could be the number three market in the world for new PC sales, after the United States and Japan.
6. Creative efforts of social entrepreneurs may overcome some of the barriers of education and income. In Bangladesh, Mohammed Yunus, a social entrepreneur known for extending banking services to the poorest villagers, undertook the challenge of introducing mobile telephony to this segment. In the late 1990s, he started a mobile phone service where established women leaders in villages, selected for their integrity, were provided mobile phone that they rented out to villagers to make calls.
7. There are exceptions to this. In Japan, fax was adopted widely by households because the language is pictographic, and fax enabled households to exchange hand-calligraphed messages.
8. All quotations in the chapter are translated from Swedish.
9. A longitudinal study entails studying a sample of firms over time, while a cross-sectional study examines a range of firms at one time. With longitudinal studies, comparisons over time are possible, while cross-sectional studies allow comparisons across the sample of firms.

10. This case study and the empirical results reported in this chapter are from the ongoing research project on "Consuming in Cyberspace" at the Stockholm University School of Business. As a part of this project, 15 master's theses, two doctoral dissertations, and over 150 in-depth consumer interviews have been completed.

11. This also seems to be the reason that in most acceptance studies on interactive information systems personal interviews have been used.

12. This happens, for instance, if external users try to access pages that are restricted to internal use.

13. These are, for instance, size, type, and date of the last edit.

14. There are a huge number of programs for the statistical analysis of log files available (see Yahoo! 1997). On the other hand, there are a number of methods to analyze the data gathered in the interviews (see u.a. Huttner 1989).

15. These are also documents in a format different from HTML and also pages outside the SNI Web site that are referenced on a page within the site.

16. The more than 70,000 documents on the SNI World Wide Web Server have been accessed over 3.4 million times during the analysis phase.

17. It is possible to configure the browser in a way that it never again requests a page stored in the cache. As Web pages are continuously changing, a user will not use this option.

18. The browser just shows in the status line that data are transmitted.

19. These are computer names like proxy, cache, www, and continuous, nonsequential page requests with a distance below one second. A full distinction of both classes with this method is not possible.

20. Demographic structure and expectations of a Web site of the participants of SNI study, for instance, differ extremely from the findings of popular German online surveys.

21. In addition, usage tests during the SNI study have shown that users disapprove the Web site because of handling difficulties with long lists.

22. This method has been introduced with the methods for acceptance analysis.

23. An experimental system for the World Wide Web called Hyper-G has been developed at the Technical University, Graz, Austria; see Kappe and Andrews et al. (1995); Kappe and Pani (1995).

24. In the SNI interviews most of the participants stated that they found the Web site by entering the URL directly.

25. A prerequisite for this is that the same URL for similar icons is used on all pages.

26. Due to the transmission time and running time, the user should have influence on the display mode.

27. The analysis of the SNI Web site has shown that only 2 percent of the users followed a link behind a large advertisement image.

28. Only a minority of the users wait until the page has been loaded. In the case of the SNI home page, this was 11 percent.

29. Yamaha (http://www.yamaha.com), for instance, offers a text-based and two different graphical versions of its Web site.

30. In addition, this offers the opportunity to save the document for offline reading. Also here it is important not to display text with graphics. A standard browser saves only the HTML page and not the embedded graphics. Therefore, the graphics cannot be viewed later on. Another way to overcome this obstacle for the user is to use offline browsers, which save all elements.

31. This was confirmed by the usability tests during the SNI study. For optimal text designs, see Hagge (1994:172ff).

32. GfK Group, Press Release February 23, 1999.

33. In his survey Frequently Asked Questions (FAQ), Batinic illustrated at length how to proceed (http://www.psychol.unigiessen.de/~Batinic/survey/frag_faq.htm; cf. also Batinic 1997b).

34. A telephone survey conducted by the Academic Data market research institute in Essen (http://www.academic-data.de) in 1997 estimated that only 22 percent of German households owned a computer. Of these, only a fifth had access to the Internet (or 4.4 percent of all households). In 1998, the ARD Public Broadcasting Online Study determined a ratio of over 10 percent online users in the population, of these a third at their workplace and not at home (cf.van Eimeren, Oehmichen, and Schroter 1998).

35. It is open to question whether a development similar to the spread of telephones and their use for surveys can be estimated to the extent that in 10 years' time representative population samples can be surveyed with the help of the WWW, as Werner optimistically assumes (1997: 167).

36. Or just to obtain falsified results for the survey "for the fun of it": on the Borussia Dortmund soccer club's Web server, for example, visitors were asked to guess the club's position for the end of the current season,; 83 percent thought that Dortmund would be relegated from the first division. This was, in fact, the result of an automatic script used by a computer-savvy fan of a rival soccer club (Schalke 04) to deliberately distort the results.

37. To be found at the following URL: http://www.ccgatech.edu/gvu/user_surveys/.

38. The methodological procedure of these WWW surveys geared toward large numbers of participants is mildly remindful of the "Literary Digest Disaster" at the beginning of survey research, as cited in many textbooks on statistics Bryson 1976: 184-85).

39. The most renowned survey in German-language countries is the biannuually conducted Fittkau and Maaß W3B-Survey (http://www.w3b.de), which has recently been introduced in Europe in nine different language versions.

40. This comparison is based upon the fact that the "user per computer" value remains constant over time.

41. The results are based upon data culled in a survey by Academic data in Essen on Computer use in private households (cf. Esser and Hauptmanns 1998; executive summary under http://www.academic-data.de). The survey was conducted as a telephone study in households in Germany. The sample was selected randomly from a list (directory inquiries CD-ROM) and subsequently further randomized via a "random last digit" dialing procedure. 2,600 households were polled. The questionnaire time was between 5 and 9 p.m., and the person in the household who used the computer most was interviewed.

Glossary

The following is a glossary of Internet, e-commerce, and m-commerce acronyms and terms. It provides definitions in simple, user-friendly language. This glossary draws from CyberAtlas (http://cyberatlas.internet.com) May 2000, as well as from RITIM research (http://ritim.cba.uri.edu).

Ad Clicks	Number of times users click on an ad banner.
Ad Click Rate	Percentage of ad views that resulted in an ad click, also referred to as "click-through."
Ad Views (Impressions)	Number of times an ad banner is downloaded and presumably seen by visitors. Corresponds to net impressions in traditional media.
Applet	A Java program that can run on a Java-enabled browser.
ARPAnet	The scientific and defense research network established by the Advanced Research Project Agency of the U.S. Department of Defense. Generally regarded as the foundation network that eventually evolved into the Internet.
Authentication	Validation of the identity of a remote user or computer.
Backbone	A high-speed line or series of connections that forms a large pathway within a network.
Bandwidth	How much information (text, images, video, sound) can be sent through a connection. Usually measured in bits per second.
Banner	An ad on a Web page that is usually "hot-linked" to the advertiser's site.
Bitnet	Because It's Time Network–a large, wide-area network used extensively by universities, a precursor to the Internet.
Brand Inflection	Adaptation of a brand for the online environment.

Browser Caching	To speed surfing, browsers store recently used pages on a user's disk. If a site is revisited, browsers display pages from the disk instead of requesting them from the server. As a result, servers undercount the number of times that a page is viewed.
BTO	Build-to-Order: a method of building devices such as personal computers (PCs) with well-known, branded components (such as Kingston memory, Intel chips, Western Digital hard drives). Assembly of the device occurs after an order with a specific configuration has been received.
Cable Modem	A modem designed to operate over coaxial cable television lines, delivering much greater bandwidth (high-speed Net access) than telephone lines.
CGI	Common Gateway Interface: an interface-creation scripting program that allows Web pages to be made on the fly based on information from buttons, check boxes, text input, and so on.
CME	Computer-Mediated Environment: a network that allows interactive, computerized access to hyperlinked content and facilitates computer-based communications and transactions.
Cookies	A message given to a particular Web browser by a specific Web server and sent back to the server each time the browser requests a page from that server. Cookies are used to identify users and possibly prepare customized Web pages for them. Derived from the terms "magic cookies" used in Unix computing.
CPM	The cost per 1,000 impressions for a particular Web site, print ad, or television commercial.
Cyberspace	Coined by author William Gibson in his 1984 novel *Neuromancer*, cyberspace is now used to describe all of the information available through computer networks.
Digital Certificate	An electronic card or passport that establishes the holder's credentials when doing business or other transactions on the Web.
Digital Signature	An electronic signature that can be used to authenticate the identity of the sender of a message, the signer of a document, or the owner of a credit card.
Domain Name	The unique name of an Internet site. Of all the top-level domains, .com (commercial) is the most widely sought and used.
DSL	Digital Subscriber Lines: technologies that allow a large amount of data to be packed into ordinary twisted pair telephone wires, thus turning phone lines into high-bandwidth lines. Often referred to as last-mile technologies because they are used between a telephone switching station and a home or office. ADSL, HDSL, and SDSL are versions of DSL (or xDSL).

E-Commerce   Any business that is conducted online. Includes buying and selling as well as the delivery of commercial information and services. Older forms of e-commerce, such as Electronic Date Interchange (EDI), are being replaced by Internet-based e-commerce and by m-commerce.

EDI   Electronic Data Interchange: the network-based transfer of data between companies that do business with each other. EDI systems are rapidly converting from those based on proprietary networks to systems based on the Internet.

EFT   Electronic Funds Transfer: any electronic method of transferring funds from one party to another. Consortia of banks and financial institutions usually manage EFT systems.

Encryption   Transformation of data into a coded form that is practically impossible to read without the appropriate decoder (a cryptographic key).

Extranet   An Intranet that is partially accessible to authorized outsiders. Extranets provide varying levels of secure access and are becoming a popular means for business partners to exchange information.

Firewall   A system designed to prevent unauthorized access to or from a network, used to prevent unauthorized Internet users from accessing private networks such as Intranets and Extranets. Firewall techniques include packet filters, application gateways, circuit-level gateways, and proxy servers. For greater security, in addition to employing firewalls, data can be encrypted.

FTP   File Transfer Protocol: a protocol used for storing and sending files via the Internet.

Gopher   A server-based system that presents its contents as a hierarchically structured list of files. The system predates the World Wide Web. Today, most Gopher databases are being converted to Web sites, which are easier to search, catalog, and access.

Hit   Hits are generated for every element of a requested page (including graphics, text, and interactive items). Because page designs vary greatly, hits are a poor guide for traffic measurement.

Host   An Internet host used to be a single machine connected to the Internet (which meant it had a unique IP address). Now virtual hosting allows one physical host to act as several virtual hosts.

HTML   HyperText Markup Language: a coding language used to make hypertext documents for use on the Web. HTML allows text to be "linked" to another file on the Internet.

Hypertext   Any text that that can be chosen by a reader and that causes another document to be retrieved and displayed.

Internet   The collection of independent, interconnected networks that use the TCP/IP protocols and that evolved from ARPANet of the late 1960s and NSFNet of the early 1970s.

Interstitial   An advertisement that appears in a separate browser window while a user waits for a Web page to load. Interstitials often contain large graphics, streaming cotent, and applets. While more users may click on interstitials than on banner ads, an interstitial ad can be annoying if it slows access to the user's destination page.

Intranet   A network based on Internet protocols but controlled by an organization, usually a corporation, and accessible only to the authorized members of that organization. Intranets are insulated from the larger Internet by "firewalls," security systems that fend off unauthorized access.

IP address   Internet Protocol address. Every system connected to the Internet has a unique, numerical IP address in the format A.B.C.D where each of the four sections is a number from 0 to 255. Most people use Domain Names instead. The network and the Domain Name Servers handle the matching of Domain Names and IP addresses. With virtual hosting, a single machine can act like multiple machines (with multiple domain names and IP addresses).

IRC   Internet Relay Chat: a worldwide network of people talking to each other in real time.

ISDN   Integrated Services Digital Network: a digital network that achieves speeds of 128,000 bits per second over a regular phone line at nearly the same cost as a normal phone call.

ISP   Internet service provider. Some ISPs are affiliated with major telecom companies (such as Germany's T-Online). Also, some ISPs such as FreeServe in the United Kingdom provide free services to subscribers, deriving their revenue from advertisers.

Java   A high-level programming language developed by Sun Microsystems similar to, but simpler than, C++. Java is particularly well suited for the World Wide Web. Small Java applications–called Java applets–can run on the user's computer through Java-compatible Web browsers such as Netscape Navigator or Microsoft Internet Explorer.

Legacy System   A company's existing (often old) computer system.

Link   An electronic connection between two Web sites (also called "hot link" or hyperlink).

Listserv   The most widespread of mail lists. Listservs started on Bitnet and are now common on the Internet.

Loading Time   The time elapsed in copying a file from a network file server to a computer on the network. Slow Internet connections result in long loading times and agonizing waits for the users.

Marketspace   Introduced by Jeffrey Rayport and John Sviokla, the term refers to the virtual context in which buyers and sellers discover one another, and transact business.

M-Commerce   Any monetary transaction conducted via a mobile telecommunications network using handheld communication, information, and payment devices such as mobile phones or palmtop units (PDAs).

Meta Tag   A special HTML tag that provides information about a Web page. Unlike normal HTML tags, meta tags do not affect how the page is displayed. Instead, meta tags provide information such as who created the page, how often it is updated, what the page is about, and which keywords represent the page's content. Search engines use such information when building their indexes.

MIPS   Millions of Instructions per Second: a measure of computer processing speed.

Newsgroup   A discussion group on Usenet devoted to a specific topic.

NSFnet   Successor to ARPANet, NSFNet was a wide-area network sponsored by the U.S. National Science Foundation (NSF) to link universities and research facilities. After ARPANet, NSFNet is generally regarded as the next major network that led to the Internet. Dismantled in 1995, NSFNet was replaced by a commercial Internet backbone.

OBI   Open Buying on the Internet: an architecture for business-to-business procurement systems.

Page   Web sites are a collection of electronic "pages." Each Web page is a document formatted in HTML (Hypertext Markup Language) that contains text, images, or media objects such as RealAudio player files, QuickTime videos, or Java applets. The "home page" is typically a visitor's first point of entry and features a site index. Pages can be static or dynamically generated.

Page Views   Number of times user requests a page that may contain a particular ad. Indicative of the number of times an ad was potentially seen, or "gross impressions."

PDA   Personal Digital Assistant: the technical name for palmtop or pocket computing and communication devices.

PDF   Portable Document Format a file format developed by Adobe Systems for storing and sending formatted documents so they can be seen on a monitor or printed in the exact format as they were intended.

PKI   Public Key Infrastructure: a way of creating a secure network within the generally nonsecure Internet. PKI uses specialist authorities, digital certificates, and directory facilities to create a secure communication network.

Portal	A branded gateway to a variety of resources on the Internet. Examples include Yahoo!, MSN, Go, Excite, and many ISPs.
RealAudio	Commercial software program that plays audio on demand, without waiting for long file transfers.
Server	A machine that makes services available on a network to client programs.
Session	A specific, uninterrupted block of time that a user spends surfing the Net.
SET	Secure Electronic Transaction: a system for ensuring the security of financial transactions on the Internet. SET was supported initially by Mastercard, Visa, Microsoft, Netscape, and others.
SGML	Standardized General Markup Language: developed by the International Standards Organization (ISO) in 1986, SGML itself does not specify any particular formatting; rather, it specifies the rules for tagging elements. These tags can then be interpreted to format elements of a document in different ways.
Smart Card	A plastic card with an embedded microchip that can be loaded with data and used for telephone calls, stored cash payments, personal verification, storage of personal digital certificates, and other e-commerce or m-commerce applications.
SSL	Secure Sockets Layer: a program created by Netscape for secure message transmissions in a network. SSL uses the public-and-private key encryption system from RSA, an Internet security firm. SSL includes the use of a digital certificate.
Sticky	"Sticky" Web sites are those where the visitors stay for an extended period of time.
T-1	A high-speed (1.54 megabits/second) network connection.
T-3	An even higher-speed (45 megabits/second) Internet connection.
TCP	Transmission Control Protocol works with IP to ensure that packets travel safely on the Internet.
Telnet	A terminal emulation program for TCP/IP networks such as the Internet that allows users to enter commands that are executed as if they were entering these commands directly on the console of the computer to which they are "telneting."
Unique Users	The number of different individuals who visit a site within a specific time period.
UNIX	A computer operating system (the basic software running on a computer, underneath applications like word processors). UNIX is designed to be used by many people at once ("multiuser") and has TCP/IP built-in. Unix is the most prevalent operating system for Internet servers.
URL	Uniform Resource Locator: the global address of documents and other resources on the World Wide Web (and Internet generally).

Usenet	A worldwide bulletin board system consisting of over 14,000 forums (called newsgroups) that can be accessed through the Internet. These forums cover nearly every imaginable topic of interest.
Valid Hits	A further refinement of hits, valid hits are hits that deliver all information to a user. Excludes hits such as redirects, error messages, and computer-generated hits.
VAN	Value Added Network: a proprietary network over which EDI transactions and electronic funds transfer can take place.
Visits	A sequence of requests made by one user at one Web site. Usually, if there is a 30-minute or longer gap between requests, then a second visit is counted.
Vortal	A vertical portal, a portal directed at a particular industry.
VPN	Virtual Private Network: a way of setting up an Extranet or a wide-area Intranet, usually with the help of a telecommunications services provider.
VR (Virtual Reality)	Artificial, simulated, computer-based environments that appear and feel like the real environments that are being simulated.
VRML	Virtual Reality Modeling (or Markup) Language: a specification for displaying three-dimensional (3-D)objects on the World Wide Web. It is the 3-D equivalent of HTML.
WAP	Wireless Application Protocol: a secure specification that allows users to access information instantly via handheld wireless devices such as mobile phones, pagers, two-way radios, smartphones, and palmtop PDAs.
Web Portal	See Portal.
WML	Wireless Markup Language: a simplified version of HTML for creating content for WAP-enabled devices.
XML	eXtensible Markup Language: a pared-down version of SGML, designed especially for Web documents. If future browsers provide stronger support to XML, it may gradually replace HTML.

References and Bibliography

The following list provides references to the books, articles, and Web pages cited in the chapters. It also includes additional resources and serves as a comprehensive bibliography on online marketing and electronic commerce.

Abbott, Michele, Kuan-Pin Chiang, Yong-sik Hwang, Jerry Paquin, and Detlev Zwick (1999), "The Process of Online Store Loyalty Formation," in *Advances in Consumer Research*, 27.

Albers, S., and K. Peters (1997), "Die Wertschöpfungskette des Handels im Zeitalter des Electronic Commerce," *Marketing* 19.2 (69-80).

Albers, S., C. Paul and M. Runte (1999) "Virtuelle Communities als Mittel des Absatzes," O. Beisheim (ed.), *Distribution im Aufbruch*, Munchen: Vahlen, 955-66.

Amazon.de (1999), http://www.amazon.de/exec/obidos/subst/misc/author-review-guidelines, 9.51999.

Andelman, D.A. (1995), "Betting on the 'Net,'" *Sales and Marketing Management*, (June), 47-59.

Anders, G. (1999), "Finding the Needles," *Wall Street Journal*, November 22, R44.

Anderson, C. (1995), "The Internet: The accidental superhighway," *The Economist*, http://www.economist.com/commerce.htm.

Anderson, C. (1995), "The Internet: The Accidental Superhighway," *The Economist*, http//www.economist.com.

Anonymous (2000), "The World Can Be a Bidder," *The Economist* March 2, http://www.economist.com.

Ansari, A., and C. Mela (2000), "Targeting Electronic Content in Interactive Media," presented at *Second Marketing Science and the Internet Conference*, University of Southern California, Los Angeles.

Arbitron (2000), "Percentage of Ad Agencies Using the Following Types of Web Ads," http://www.emarketer.com/estats/050100 ads.html.

Arndt, Johan (1983), "The Political Economy Paradigm: Foundation for Theory Building in Marketing," *Journal of Marketing*, 47 (Fall), 44-54.

Aspen, R. (1998), "The Global Advance of Electronic Commerce: Reinventing Markets, Management, and National Security," A report of the Sixth Annual Aspen Institute Roundtable on Information Technology, Aspen, Colorado: Washington, DC: Aspen Institute and Society Program.

Auger, P. and J.M. Gallaugher (1997), "Factors Affecting the Adoption of an Internet-Based Sales Presence for Small Businesses," *The Information Society* (13), 55-74.

Bakos, Y.J. (1991), "A Strategic Analysis of Electronic Marketplaces," *MIS Quarterly* September, 295-310.

Balikowa, D.O. (1995), "Media Marketing: An Essential Part of a Free Press for Africa," *Media, Culture, and Society*, 17, 603-13.

Bandilla, W., and P. Hauptmanns (1999): "Internetbasierte Umfragen: Eine geeignete Datenerhebungstechnik fuer die empirische Forschung?" *Internet-Marketing*, W. Fritz (ed.), Stuttgart: Schaeffer-Poeschel, 197-216.

Bandopadhyay, S. (1999), "Web-Based Advertising: Panacea for All Advertising Woes?," R.R. Dholakia and S. Wilstrom (eds.), *Electronic Commerce: Behaviors of Suppliers, Producers, Intermediaries & Consumers*, Proceedings of COTIM((, RITIM: University of Rhode Island, Kingston.

Barabba, V., and Zaltman, Gerald (1991), *Hearing the Voice of the Market: Competitive Advantage through Creative Use of Market Information*, Boston: Harvard Business School Press.

Barol, Bill (1995), "What Is Cyberspace?" *Virtual City* 1 (1) Fall, 26-34.

Batinic, B.o.J. (1998), Umfrage-FAQ, dated January 9, 1998, http://www.psychol.uni-giessen.de/~Batinic/survey/frag_faq.htm.

Batinic, B.o.J. (1998), Umfragen-Metaliste, dated January 9, 1998, http://www.psychol.uni-giessen.de/~Batinic/survey/fra_andr.htm.

Batinic, M. (1997b), "How to Make an Internet Based Survey?" W. Bandilla, and F. Graulbaum, (ed), *SoftStat'97 - Advances in Statistical Software 6*, Stuttgart: Lucius and Lucius, 125-32.

Batinic, B. (ed.) (1997a), Internet für Psychologen. Göttingen: Hogrefe.

Batinic, B.B.M. (1997), "Fragebogenuntersuchungen im Internet," B. Batinic, (ed.), *Internet für Psychologen.* Göttingen: Hogrefe, 221-44.

Batnic, B. and M. Bosnjak (1997), "Fragebogenuntersuchungen im Internet," in: B. Batinic (ed.), *Internet fur Psychologen*, Goettingen: Hogrefe 1997, 221-44.

Benjamin, R., and R. Wigand (1995), "Electronic Markets and Virtual Value Chains on the Information Highway," *Sloan Management Review*, Winter, 62-72.

Berekoven, L. (1990), *Erfolgreiches Einzelhandelsmarketing*, Müchen.

Berekoven, L., W. Eckert, and P. Ellenrieder (1996) *Marktforschung*, 7th ed., Wiesbaden: Gabler.

Berry, L.L. and A. Parasuraman (1991), *Marketing Services: Competing through Quality.* New York: Free Press.

Berryman, H., and R. Layton-Rodin (1998), "Electronic Commerce: Three Emerging Strategies," *The McKinsey Quarterly*, 1.

Bezjian-Avery, A., B. Calder, and D. Iacobucci (1998), "New Media Interactive Advertising vs. Traditional Advertising," *Journal of Advertising Research*, July-August, 23-32.

Bless, H. J. and T. Matzen, (1995), "Optimierung von Verkaufsgesprächen und individuelle Produktpräsentation mittels PC," *Multi-Media und Marketing*, R. Hünerberg, and G. Heise, (eds.), Wiesbaden, 297-311.

Bloemer, J., and K. de Ruyter (1998), "On the Relationship between Store Image, Store Satisfaction and Loyalty," *European Journal of Marketing*, 32(5/6), 499-513.

Böhler, H. (1992) *Marktforschung*, 2. Aufl., Stuttgart: Kohlhammer.

Bohlin, S (2000), "Storaffärer driver andra våg av hem-pc," *Computer Sweden*, 8 (45).

"Borders Playing Internet Catch-Up" (1999), *The Providence Journal*, March 13, B1-2.

Bosley, A. (1994), "Internet Shopping and the Death of Retail," *The Internet Business Journal* 2 (October-November), 14.

Bradley, S.L. and R.L. Nolan, eds. (1998), *Sense & Respond: Creating Value in the Network Era*, Boston: Harvard Business School Press.

Brandtweiner, R. (1997) "World Wide Web Induced Disintermediation," N. Dholakia, E. Kruse, and D. Fortin (eds.), *COTIM '97 Conference Proceedings*, vol.2 Kingston, RI:RITIM, 61-66.

Brenner, W., and L. Kolbe (1997) "New Business Opportunities for Intermediaries on the Internet," *COTIM '97 Conference Proceedings*, 55-60.

Briggs, R., and N. Hollis (1997), "Advertising on the Web: Is There Response before Click-Through," *Journal of Advertising Research*, March-April, 33-45.

Bronold, R. (1999), "Mediengerechte Online-Forschung: DAs GfK Online-Forschungsprogramm," B. Batinic, A. Werner, L. Gräf, and W. Bandilla, (eds.) *Online Research*, Göttingen: Hogrefe, 36-42.

Brooker, K. (1998), "Online Investing: It's Not Just for Geeks Anymore," *Fortune* 138 (December 21), 89-98.

Brown, B. (1998), "Distance Education and Web-Based Training," paper present at the *Sooner Communication Conference*, Norman, OK, ERIC Document Reproduction.

Brown, S. (1995), *Postmodern Marketing*, New York: Routledge.

Bruhn, M. (1997), *Multimedia-Kommunikation*, München Beck.

Brynjolfsson, E., T.W. Malone, V. Gurbaxani, and A. Kambil (1994), "Does Information Technology Lead to Smaller Firms?", *Management Science* 40 (December), 1628-44.

Bryson, M.C. (1976), "The Literary Digest: Making of Statistical Myth, *The American Statistician* 30, 184-85.

Bucklin, R.E., an C. Sismeiro (2000), "How Sticky Is Your Web Site? Modeling Site Navigation Choices Using Clickstream Data," presented at *Second Marketing Science and the Internet Conference*, University of Southern California, Los Angeles.

Buettner, J.H. and A. Mann (1995), "Multimediale Kommunikations-und Vertriebspolitik mit VIA in: R. HHuenerbery and G. Heise (eds.), *Multimedia und Marketing*, Gabler-Verlag, 249-63.

Burke, R. A. (1997) "Do You See What I See? The Future of Virtual Shopping," *Journal of the Academy of Marketing Science* 25 (4) 352-60.

Burke, Raymond R. (1997), "Real Shopping in Virtual Store," Robert A. Peterson (ed.), *Electronic Marketing and the Consumer*, Beverly Hills, CA: Sage.

Business 2.0 (2000), "Top 15 Dot-Com Ad Spenders 1998-1999" March, 122,

Business Week (1999), quoted in *S.i. Systems-Online Advertising Statistics* http://www.sisystems.com/secrets/tipsi2.html.

"Cable TV Attracts High-Speed Speculation" (1997), November 10 Telephony, 7.

Cairncross, F. (1997), *The Death of Distance: How the Communication Revolution Will Change Our Lives*, Cambridge: Harvard University Business Press.

Campbell, C. (1994), "The desire for the new. Its nature and social location as presented in theories of fashion and modern consumerism," In: Silverston, R., Hirsch, E. (Eds.) *Consuming Technologies*. London: Routledge.

Cash, J.I. Jr. (1994), "A New Farmers' Market," *Information Week* December 26, 60. [commercial.scenarios.html].

Cavanaugh, C. (1999), *The Effectiveness of Interactive Distance Education Technologies in K-12 Learning: A Meta-Analysis*, Research report intended for practitioners and teachers, ERIC Document Reproduction Service No. ED 430 547.

Cavoukian, A. and D. Tapscott (1997), "Who Knows: Safeguarding Your Privacy in a Networked World," McGraw-Hill: New York.

Chen, G.M. (1998), "Intercultural Communication Via E-mail Debate The Edge," *The E-Journal of Intercultural Relations*, 1(4), http://kumo.sec.com /biz/theedge/chen.htm.

Chotourou, M.S., and J.L. Chandon (2000), "Impact of Motion, Picture and Size on Recall and Word-of-Mouth for Internet Banners," presented at *Second Marketing Science and the Internet Conference*, University of Southern California, Los Angeles.

Christensen, C.M., and R.S. Tedlow (2000), "Patterns of Disruption in Retailing," *Harvard Business Review* 78 (1) January-February, 42-45.

Clarke, R. (1999), "Electronic Commerce Definitions," Australian National University, http://www.anu.edu.au/people/Roger.Clarke/EC/ECDefns.html.

Coen, R.J. (2000). "Advertising Age," http://adage.com/dataplace/archives.

Cohn, M. (2000), "Internet U," *Spring House* 13(1), 46-59.

Colony, G.F. (1999), "My View: Killer Clicks," http://www.forrester.com/Marketing/.

Cortese, A., J. Verity, R. Mitchell and R. Brandt (1995), "Cyberspace: Crafting Software That Will Let You Build a Business Out There," Business Week (February 27), 78-86.

Crockett, R.O. (1999), "A Web That Looks Like the World," Business Week 3621, March 22, EB46.

Cronin, M.J. (1994), *Doing Business on the Internet: How the Electronic Highway Is Transforming American Companies*, New York: Van Nostrand Reinhold.

Cross, R. (1994), "Internet: The Missing Marketing Medium Found," *Direct Marketing* (October), 20-23.

Daft, Richard, and R. Lengel (1986), "Organizational Information Requirements, Media Richness and Structural Desing," *Management Science* 32(5), 554-71.

D'Aveni, R.A. (1994), *Hypercompetition: Managing the Dynamics of Strategic*

Davis, S., and B. Davidson (1991), *2020 Vision: Transforming Your Business Today to Tomorrow's Economy*, New York: Simon and Schuster.

Deck, S. (1998), "Car Buying on the Web," *Computer World* 32 (February 9), 40.

Decker, T., F. Vega, J. Shallit, and J. Wills (2000), "Debating Distance Learning," *Communications of the ACM* 43(2), 11-20.

Deighton, J. (1997), "Marketing in the Age of Addressability: Managing Conversations to Build Customer Equity," N. Dholakia, E. Kruse, and D. Fortin (eds.), *COTIM-97* Proceedings, Kingston, RI: RITIM, 169-70.

Dholakia, N. (1997), "The Webs and the Web-Nots: Access Issues in the Information Age,: *Telematics and Informatics*, May.

Dholakia, N. (1999), "Innovation at Warp Speed," RITIM Working Paper, Kingston, RI: Research Institute for Telecommunications and Information Marketing (RITIM), University of Rhode Island.

Dholakia, N., and R.R. Dholakia (1999), "Markets and Marketing in the Information Age," W. Fritz (ed.), *Internet-Marketing*, Stuttgart: Schaffer-Poeschel, 21-37.

Dholakia, N., R.R. Dholakia, M. Laub, and Y.S. Hwang (1999), "Electronic Commerce and the Transformation of Marketing," W. Fritz (ed.), *Internet-Marketing* Stuttgart: Schaffer-Poeschel, 55-77.

Dholakia, N., F.A. Fuat, and V. Alladi (1997), "Marketing in Postmodern Flavors," RITIM Working Paper, Kingston, RI: Research Institute for Telecommunications and Information Marketing (RITIM), University of Rhode Island.

Dholakia, R.R. (1995), "Connecting to the Net: Marketing Actions and Market Responses," paper presented at the *International Seminar of Impact of Information Technology*, CIET-SENAI, December 6, Rio de Janeiro.

Dholakia, R.R., and N. Dholakia (1994), "Deregulating Markets and Fast Changing Technology: Public Policy towards Telecommunications in a Turbulent Setting," *Telecommunication Policy* 18(1) 21-31.

Dholakia, R.R., and B. Pedersen (1994), "To Shop or Not to Shop the Interactive Way: Executive Summary," Research Report, Research Institute for Telecommunications and Information Marketing (RITIM), University of Rhode Island.

Diller, H. (1998), "Innovatives Beziehungsmarketing," *Absatzwirtschaft*, 90-98.

Dinsdale, A. (1995), "Introduction to Electronic Commerce: Issues, Concerns and the Future," http://www.netrex.com/business/ecommerce.html.

DomainStats.com (1999), http://www.domainstats.com.

Dreze, X., and F. Hussherr (1999), " Internet Advertising: Is Anybody Watching?" working paper, Marshall School of Business, University of Southern California, Los Angeles.

Dreze, X., and F. Zufryden (1998), "Is Internet Advertising Ready for Prime Time?" *Journal of Advertising Research*, May-June 7-18.

Durstewitz, M., (1997), "Erfordernisse und Grenzen des Einsatzes von Intranets in der Produktentwicklung und Qualitatssicherung," 39-50, D. Janetzko, B. Batinic, D. Schoder, M. Mattingley-Scott, and G. Strube, (eds.), CAW-97: Beitrage zum Workship "Cognition & Web." Freiburg: IIG-Berichte 1/97.

Economist (1999), "English and Electronic Commerce: The Default Language," *The Economist*, http://www.economist.com/PrinterFriendly.cfm?Story_ID=321735.

"EDI: Cornerstone of Electronic Commerce" (1995), *Candian Business* 68, May, 47f

Egermann, F. (1997), "The Compaq Optimized Distribution Model," N. Dholakia, E. Kruse, and D.R. Fortin (eds.), *COTIM-97* Proceedings, Kingston, RI: RITIM, 171-174.

"Electronic   Commerce   at   Bank   One"   (1995),   http://www.eft.
bankone.com:80/Main/EC/EC.htmld/index.html.

Elmasri, S., B. Navathe (1996), "*Fundamentals of Database Systems*, 2nd, Redwood City, CA: Benjamin/Cummings.

Esser E.H. (1998), *Computer-und Internetnutzung in privaten Haushalten*, Essen: Academic-Data Forschungsberichte 1/98.

Evans, P.B., and T.S. Wurster (1997), "Strategy and the New Economics of Information,: *Harvard Business Review* no5, September/October.

Fama, E.F. (1980), "Agency Problems and the Theory of the Firm," *Journal of Political Economy* 80 April), 288-307.

Fantapié, A., C. Hoffmann, S. (1996a), "Die optimale Online-Werbung für jede Branche-Was Nutzer von Unternehmensauftritten im Internet erwarten," München Vahlen.

Fantapié, A., C. Hoffmann, S. (1996b), *Werbung im Internet*, München: MGM Meida Gruppe.

Fattell, G. (1999), *The Development of Virtual Education: A Global Perspective*, London Commonwealth of Learning.

Fernandez, M. (1999), "Keynote Address of Manny Fernandez, Chairman of GartnerGroup," *Providence Business Expo*, March 17.

Field, D. (1998, June 15), "Delta's Marketing Chief Aims to Please Passengers," *USA Today*, 6B.

Firat, A.F., and N. Dholakia (1998), *Consuming People: From Political Economy to Theaters of Consumption*, London and New York: Routledge.

Fischer, C. (1987), "The Revolution in Rural Telephony: 1900-1920," *Journal of Social History* 21(1), 5-26.

Fittkau and Maass GbR (1999a), *W3B Uni-Ergebnisband*, Erhebung Oktober-November 1998, Hamburg: Fittkau and Mass.

Fittkau and Maass GbR (1999b), *WWW-Benutzer-Analyse*, W3B-Uni-Ergebnisband,

Fittkau, S. and H. Maaß, (1996), "Ergebnisse der W3B Internetumfrage 1996," http://www.w3b.de/W3B-1996/Ergebnisse/Zusammenfassung

Forskningsministeries (1999), "Danish firms' Use of IT 1998," *Marketing via homepage, Line of Business*, Section 4.3.11, (in Danish), http://www.fsk.dk/fsk/publ/1999/danskit/inde0007.htm#0001.

Förster, H.P., and M. Zwernemann, (1993), "Multimedia/Evolution der Sinne," Neuwied, Kriftel, Berlin

Fortin, D.R. (1998), "The Impact of Interactivity on Advertising Effectiveness in the New Media," Ph.D. dissertation, College of Business Administration, University of Rhode Island.

Fortin, D.R., and R.R. Dholakia (2000), "Examining the Effects of Interactivity on Social Presence and Involvement with an Online Advertisement," *Journal of Business Research*, forthcoming.

Friel, Daniel (1998), "Window on the Web," *Business Economics*, July, 66-67.

Fritz, W. (1995), *Marktorientierte Unternehmensführung und Unternehmenserfolg*, 2nd ed. Stuttgart: Schaffer-Poeschel.

Fritz, W. (1999e), *Internet-Marketing*. Perspektiven aus Deutschland und den USA, Stuttgart: Schaffer-Poeschel.

Fritz, W. (1999c): "Die Entwicklung des Internet-Marketing in der Versicherungs-wirtschaft im Jahresvergleich," W. Fritz (ed.), *Internet-Marketing*, Stuttgart: Schaeffer-Poeschel, 165-80.

Fritx, W. (1999d), "Das Internet als Herausforderung für das Handelsmarketing," O. Beisheim (ed.), *Distribution im Aufbruch*, Munchen: Vahlen, 993-1005.

Fritz, W. (1999a), "Electronic Commerce: What Is Different in Germany?" R.R. Dholakia and S. Wikstrom (eds.), *COTIM '99 Conference Proceedings*, vol.3, Kingston, RI.

Fritz, W. (1999b), "Electronic Commerce im Internet–eine Bedrohung für den traditionellen Konsumguterhandel?", W. Fritz (ed.), *Internet-Marketing*, Stuttgart: Schaffer-Poeschel, 107-45.

Fritz, W., and M. Kerner (1997a), "Online Marketing by WWW–Findings of a New Study," N Dholakia, E. Kruse, and D. Fortin (eds.), *COTIM '97 Conference Procedings*, Kingston, RI: RITIM, 39-42.

Fritz, W., and M. Kerner (1997b), *Online-Marketing im WWW in der Medien-branche*, research report, TU Braunschweig.

Fritz, W., and M. Kerner (1997c), *Online-Marketing im WWW im Finanz-dienstleistungssektor*, research report, TU Braunschweig.

Fritz, W., and M. Kerner (1997d), *Online-Marketing im WWW in der Versicherungs-wirtschaft*, research report, TU Braunschweig.

Fritz, W., and M. Kerner (1999), "Electronic Commerce: A Threat to Traditional Retailing?" R.R. Dholakia, and S. Wikstrom (eds.), *Cotim '99 Conference Proceedings*, Kingston, RI: RITIM (CD-ROM).

Fritz, W., M. Kerner, and S. Koennecke (1998), "Online-Marketing in der Computer-branche," *Jahrbuch des Absatz-und Verbrauchsforschung* 44(2) 151-62.

Fritz, W. and M. Thiess, (1986), "Das Informationsverhalten des Konsumenten und seine Konsequenzen für das Marketing," F. Unger (ed.), *Konsumentenpsychologie und Marketing*, Heidelberg, 141-76.

Garten, J.E. (2000), "World View," *Harvard Business Review*.

GfK Medienforschung (1998), Pressemappe zum GfK Online-Monitor. Nurnberg.

GfK Medienforschung AG (1999), *Online-Monitor*, 3, Welle, http://www.gfk.cube.net/.

Ghose, S., and W. Dou (1998), "Interactive Functions and Their Impacts on the Appeal of Internet Presence Sites," *Journal of Advertising Research*, April, 29-43.

Ghosh A. (1990), *Retail Management*, 2nd ed., Chicago: Dryden Press.

Ghosh, S., (1998), "Making Business Sense of the Internet," *Harvard Business Review*, March-April, 126-35.

Gibson, William (1984), *Neuromancer*, New York: Ace Books.

Gilder, G. (1995), "Telecosm: The Coming Software Shift," *Forbes ASAP*, August 28, 146-62.

Gilmore, R., and J.A. Czepiel (1987), "Loyalty as a Source of Differential Advantage in Telecommunications Marketing," paper presented at the *Telecommunications Marketing in the Information Era: Opportunities and Strategies*, Newport, RI.

Glomb, H.J. (1995), "Lean Marketing durch den Einsatz von interakitven Multi-Media-Systemen im Marketing-Mix," R. Hunerberg and G. Heise (eds.), *Multi-Media und Marketing*, Wiesbaden, 121-41.

Goble, C. Bechhofer, page and W. Solomon, et al. (1995), "Conceptual, Semantic and Information Models for Medicine," *Information Modeling and Knowledge Bases VI*, Amsterdam.

Godin, S. (1999), "'Permission Accomplished. Just Ask." *Business 2.0*. July, http://www.business2.com/content/magazine/marketing/1999/07/01/11833.

Goldberg, D. (1998), "Learning from a Distance," *Washington Post*, April, R04-R08.

Gottlieb, G. (1999), "Two States of Online Retail Revolution," *Netcommerce*, September, http://www.netcommercemag.com/september/4.html.

Gottlieb, G. (2000), "The Internet Retail Revolution," Netcommerce, December/January, http://www.netcommercemag.com/dec_jan/1.html.

Graf, L. (1997), "Pretest von WWW-Umfragen," D. Janetzko, B. Batinic, D. Schoder, M. Mattingley-Scott, and G. Strube (eds.), CAW-97: Beitrage zum Workship "Cognition & Web." Greiburg: IIG-Berichte 1/97, 51-62.

Graf, L. (1999), "Optimierung von WWW Umfragen: Das Online-Pretest-Studio," B. Batinic, A. Werner, L. Graf, and W. Bandilla, (eds.), Online Research. Gottingen: Hogrefe, 175-74.

Green, J. (1999), "Joyride for Car Dealers Nears Record Proportions," Brandweek, 40(25), S20-22.

Gregston, B. (1996), "The European Picture", Internet World, December, 52-55.

Griese, H., and P. Sieber (1999), "Electronic Commerce," Zurich: Werd Verlag.

Grover, M.B. (1999), "Lost in Cyberspace," Forbes 163 (March 8), 124-28.

Gudmundsdottir, S. (1996), "The teller, the tale, and the one being told: The narrative nature of the research interview," Curriculum Inquiry, 26(3), 293-306.

Guilford, D. (1999), "VW Woos its Young Drivers with Saturn-Style Festival," Advertising Age, 70(29), 12.

Gummesson, E. (1987), "The New Marketing: Developing Long-Term Interactive Relationships," Long Range Planning 20 (4), 10-20.

Gupta, S., and R. Chatterjee (1997), "Consumer and Corporate Adoption of the World Wide Web as a Commercial Medium," Robert A. Peterson (ed.), Electronic Marketing and the Consumer, Thousand Oaks, CA: Sage, 123-38.

Gurbaxani, V., and S. Whang (1991), "The Impact of Information Systems on Organizations and Markets," Communications of the ACM 34 (1), 59-73.

Gurley, J.W. (2000), "If i Won Wins, Do Portals Lose?" Fortune 141 (3), February 7, 190.

GVU (1998), GVU's 10th User Survey, http://www.gvu.gatech.edu/user_survey-1998_10html.

Hagel, J., and A.G. Armstrong (1997), Net Gain. Profit in Netz, Wiesaden: Gabler.

Hart, J., R. Reed, and F. Bar (1992), "The Building of the Internet: Implications for the Future of Broadband Networks," Telecommunications Policy, November, 666-89.

Hauptmanns, P. (1996), "Nonresponse: Who Responds and Who Does Not in an Enterprise Panel Survey?" Seppo Laaksonen, (ed.) International Perspectives on Nonreponse, Helsinki: Statistics Finland, 72-80.

Hecht, J., and P. Klass, (1999), "The Evolution of Qualitative and Quantitative Research Classes When Delivered via Distance Education," paper present at the Annual Meeting of the American Educational Research Association, Ontario, Canada, ERIC Document Reproduction Sercie No. ED 430 480.

Heeter, Carrie (1989), "Implications of New Interactive Technologies for Conceptualizing Communication," J. Salvaggio and J. Bryant (eds.), Media Use in the Information Age, Hillsdale, NJ: Erlbaum.

Hirschberger-Vogel, M. (1988), *Die Akzeptanz und die Effektivität von Standardsoftwaresystemen*, Berlin: Duncker and Humblot.

Hirschman, E. (1981), "Retail Research and Marketing," B.M. Enis and K.J. Roering (eds.), *Review of Marketing*, Chicago: American Marketing Association.

Hirschman, C.E. and M.B. Holbrook (1982), "Hedonic Consumption: Emerging Concepts, Methods and Propositions," *Journal of Marketing*, 46(Summer), 92-101.

Hodge-Hardin, S. (1997), "Interactive Television vs. a Traditional Classroom Setting: A Comparison of Student Math Achievement," paper present at *Mid-South Instructional Technology Conference Proceedings*, Murfreesboro, TN, ERIC Document Reproduction Service No. ED 430 521.

Hoffman, D.L. and T.P. Novak (1996a), "Marketing in Hypermedia Computer-Mediated Environments: Conceptual Foundations", *Journal of Marketing* July 50-68.

Hoffman, D.L., and T.P. Novak (1995c), "Marketing in Hypermedia Computer-Mediated Environments: Conceptual Foundations," July 11, http://www2000.ogsm.vanderbilt.edu/cmepaper.revision.july11.1995/cmepaper.html

Hoffman, D.L. and T.P. Novak (1995b), "Commercial Scenarios for the Web: Opportunities and Challenges", http://www2000.ogsm.vanderbilt.edu/nova k/jcmc,commercial.scenarios/jcmc.

Hoffman, D.L. and T.P. Novak (1995a), "The Challenge of Electronic Commerce," http://www2000.ogsm.vanderbilt.edu/intelligent.agent/index. html.

Hoffman, D.L. and T.P. Novak (1996), "Marketing in Hypermedia Computer-Mediated Environments: Conceptual Foundations," *Journal of Marketing* 60 (July), 50-69 [how_many_online/index.html].

Hoffman, D.L., and T.P. Novak (1997), "A New Marketing Paradigm for Electronic Commerce," *The Information Society* 13, 43-54.

Hoffman, D.L. W.D. Kalsbeek, and T.P. Novak, (1996), "Internet and Web Use in the United States: Baselines for Commercial Development," http:www2000.ogsm.vanderbilt.edu.

Hoflich, J. (1996), *Technisch vermittelte interpersonale Kommunikation*, Opladen: Westdeutscher Verlag.

"Hohe Zuwachsrate für Internet-Handler" (1999), *Frankfurter Allgemeine Zeitung*, 23, 20.

Höij, M (2000), "Västgöten som fick fart på Persson," *Computer Sweden*, Årgång 8 (45).

Holbrook, M.B. (1986), "Aims, Concepts, and Methods for the Presentation of Individual Differences in Esthetic Responses to Design Features," *Journal of Consumer Research*, 13(12), 337-47.

Holbrook, M.B, and E.C. Hirschman (1982), "The Experiential Aspects of Consumption," *Journal of Consumer Research*, 9(2), 132-40.

Holbrook, M., and R. Batra (1987), "Assessing the Role of Emotions as Mediators of Consumer Responses to Advertising," *Journal of Consumer Research* 14, December 404-20.

Hoque, Faisal (2000), *E-Enterprise: Business Models, Architecture, and Components*, Cambridge: Cambridge University Press.

Hunerberg, R., and G. Heise (1995), "Multi-Media und Marketing-Grundlagen und Anwendungen," R. Hunerberg, and G. Heise, (eds.), *Multi-Media und Marketing*, Wiesbaden: Gabler, 1-23.

Iconocast (2000), "Better Banner Variants" in discussion list iconcoclash@topica.com.

Intermedia Advertising Solutions (1999), "Top 10 Internet Advertisers in 1998," *S.i. Systems-Online Advertising Statistics*, http://www.sisystems.com/secrets /tipsi2.html.

James, D.L., R.M. Durand, and R.A. Dreves (1976), "The Use of a multi-attributes Attitudes Model in a Store Image Study," *Journa of Retailing* 52, 23-32.

Janal, D. (1995), "Book Review: Handbook Offers How-To Advice for Cyber Sales," *Network World*, May 1, 27.

Jarvenpaa, S.L., and P.A. Todd (1997a), Consumer Reactions to Electronic Shopping on the World Wide Web," *International Journal of Electronic Commerce* 1(2), 59-88.

Jarvenpaa, S.L. and P.A. Todd (1997b), "Is There a Future for Retailing on the Internet?" Robert A. Peterson (ed.), E*lectronic Marketing and the Consumer*, Thousand Oaks, CA: Sage, 139-54.

Jarzina, K.R. (1995), "Wirkungs- und Akzeptanzforschung zu interaktiven Multi-Media-Anwendungen im Marketing," R. Junerberg, and G. Geise, (eds.) *Multi-Media und Marketing*, Wiesbaden, 39-57

Jasco, P. (1998), "Shopbots: Shopping Robots for Electronic Commerce," *Online*, (July/August), 14-20.

Jaspersen, T. (1996), "Meßkriterien für die Online-Werbung: Ein Schritt in die richtige Richtung," *Absatzwirtschaft*, no. 11, 64-66

Jensen, M.C., and W.H. Meckling (1973), "Theory of the Firm: Managerial Behavior, Agency Costs and Ownership Structure," *Journal of Financial Economics* 3 October, 305-60.

Johansson, J., and J.E. Vahlne (1997), "The Internationalization Process of a Firm-A Model of Knowledge Development and Increasing Foreign Market Commitments," *Journal of International Business Studies*, (8)Spring/Summer, 23-32.

Jones, Russ (1994), "Digital's World-Wide Web Server: A Case Study," *Computer Networks and ISDN Systems* 27 November, 297-306.

Josse, H. (1998), "Zur Seriositat in der Online-Forschung," *Planung & Analyse*, 14-19.

Kalin, S. (1999), "The Worldlier, Wider Web," *CIO Web Business*, Section 2, March 1.

Kantor, A., and Michael Neubarth (1996), "Off the Charts: The Internet 1996," *Internet World*, December, 44-51.

Katz, J., and P. Aspden (1997),"Motivations for and Barriers to Internet Usage: Results of a National Public Opinion Survery," *Internet Research* 7 (3), 170-88.

Katz, M.L., and C. Shapiro (1985), "Network Externalities, Competition, and Compatibility," *American Economic Review* June, 424-40.

Katz, M.L. and C. Shapiro (1986), "Technology Adoption in the Presence of Network Externalities," *Journal of Political Economy* 94, 822-41.

Kienbaum Management Consultants GmbH (1999), *Electronic Commerce als Marketinginstrument noch nicht entdeckt*, htt;://www.kienbaum.de/norframes/de/aktuell/facts/ecstudie.htm.

Kim, Ch.K. (1999), "Improving Intercultural Communications Skills: A Challenge Facing Institutions of Higher Education in the 21st Century," In H. Hesse and Rebe, B. (ed.) *Vision und Verantwortund* {Vision and Responsibility], Hildesheim, Germand: 617-29.

Kirkpatrick, D. (1994), "A Look inside Allen's Think Tank: This Way to the I-Way," *Fortune* July 11, 78-80.

Klausing, H. (1998), "Quiz bei Quix. Was kommt nach dem Ende?" *Hannoversche Allgemeine Zeitung*, 238-23.

Klein, M. (1994), *Unfinished Business: The Railroad in American Life*, Hanover, NH: University Press of New England.

Klein, L. (1998), "Evaluating the Potential of Interactive Media through a New Lens: Search versus Experience Goods," *Journal of Business Research* 41, March, 195-203.

Kollmann, T., and Weiber R. (1996), "Die Akzeptanz technologischer Innovation-eine absatztheoretische Fundierung am Beispiel von Multimedia-Systemen," *Arbeitspapiere zur Marketingtheorie*, Universität Trier, Trier.

Kotler, P. and G. Armstrong (1996), *Principles of Marketing*, Prentice Hall

Kotler, P., and F. Bliemel (1995), *Marketing-Management*, (8. Aufl., Stuttgart: Schaffer-Poeschel.

Kover, A. (1998), "Why the Net Could Be Bad News for Bloomberg," *Fortune* 138 October 12, 220-22.

Krantz, J.H., J. Ballard, and J. Scher (1997), "Comparing the Results of Laboratory and World-Wide Web Samples on the Determinants of Female Attractiveness," *Behavioral Research methods, Investments, & Computers* 29, 264-69.

Krauss, M. (2000), "What to Do When the Electronic Exchange Comes?" *Marketing News*, April 24, 8.

Krishnamurthy, S. (2000), "A Critical Analysis of Permission Marketing," paper presented at Second *Marketing Science and the Internet Conference*, University of Southern California, Los Angeles.

Kroeber-Riel, W. (1979), "Activation Research: Psychobiological Approaches in Consumer Research," *Journal of Consumer Research* 5, March, 240-50.

Kuhlmann, E., M. Brünne, and B.H. Sowarka, (1992), *Interaktive Informationssysteme in der Marktkommunikation*, Heidelberg

Kurzweil, R. (1999), *The Age of Spiritual Machines: When Computers Exceed Human Intelligence*, New York: Viking.

Lechner, U., et al. (1998), *Die Bedeutung von Virtual Business Communities fur das Management von neuen Geschaftmedien,* www.businessmedia.net/ netacademy/publications.nsf/all_pk/1071, 9.5.1999.

Lee, B., and R. Lee (1995), "How and Why People Watch TV: Implications for the Future of Interactive Television," *Journal of Advertising Research,* November/December, 9-18,

Lee, H., and T.H. Clark (1996), "Impacts of the Electronic Marketplace on Transaction Cost and Market Structure," *International Journal of Electronic Commerce,* (Fall), 127-49.

Leibrock, L. (1997), "Privacy, Surveillance and Cookies," Robert A. Peterson (ed.), *Electronic Marketing and the Consumer,* Thousand Oaks, CA: Sage, 155-61.

Little, M.W., D.L. Cowles, and P. Kiecker (1997), "Examing Theory and Practice for Retail Electronic Markets: What Works and Why?" N. Dholakia, E. Kruse, and D. Fortin (eds.), *COTIM '97 Conference Proceedings,* vol. 2, Kingston, RI: RITIM 231-36.

Livinstone, S. (1994), " The meaning of domestic technologies. A personal construct analysis of familial gender relations," In: Silverstone, R., Hirsh, E. (Eds.) *Consuming Technologies,* London: Routledge.

Lohse, Gerald L., and Peter Spiller (1999), "Internet Retail Store Design: How the User Interface Influences Traffic and Sales," *Journal of Computer Mediated Communication* 5, December, 2.

Lyon, D. and E. Zureik (1996), "Surveillance, Privacy and The New Technology," In D. Lyon and E. Zureik (eds.), *Computers Surveillance and Priacyl,* Minneapolis, MN: University of Minnesota Press, 1-18.

Mainspring (2000), "Profits Depend on Customer Loyalty," April 4, http://www.nua.ie/surveys/?f=VS&rt_id=905355695&rel=true.

Malone, T.W., J. Yates, and R.I. Benjamin (1989), "The Logic of Electronic Markets," *Harvard Business Review,* May-June, 166-72.

"Managing Electronic Commerce" (1995), *Canadian Business* 68, May, 46-47.

Maneuvering, New York: Free Press.

MarketAdvisor (1999), "Interstitial/Banner Effectiveness Comparison," http//: emaker.com/estats/sell_ead2.html.

Martin, C.L. (1999), *Net Future,* New York: McGraw-Hill.

Martineau, P. (1958), "The Personality of the Retail Store," *Harvard Business Review* 36, January-February, 47-55.

Martinez, M.E. (1994), "Access to Information Technologies among School-Age Children: Implications for a Democratic Society," *Journal of the American Society for Information Science,* July.

Marx, G.T. (1999), What's in a name? Some reflections on the sociology of ananymity," *Information Society,* 15(2), 99-122.

Marx, Wendy (1996), "How to Make Web Ads More Effective," December 10, wysiwyg://7/http://www.netb2b.com/cgi-bin/netb2b/article.

May, Paul (2000,) *The Business of Ecommerce: From Corporate Strategy to Technology*, Cambridge: Cambridge University Press.

McGrath, P. (1999), "Knowing You All Too Well," *Newsweek*, (March 29), 48-50.

Mchugh, J. (2000), "Hall of Mirrors," *Forbes*, Feb. 7, 120-22.

McKenna, R. (1995), "Real-Time Marketing," *Harvard Business Review*, July-August, 87-95.

Meffert, H. (1992), *Marketingforschung und Kauferverhalten*, 2nd., Wiesbaden: Gabler.

Mehta, R. and E. Sivadas (1995), "Direct Marketing on the Internet: An Empirical Assessment of Consumer Attitudes," *Journal of Direct Marketing* 9 (4), 21-32.

Mesher, Gene (1996), "The Internet in Asia," *Internet World*, December, 56-57.

Mevenkamp, A. (1997), "Der Einsatz des WWW im Marketing," Abt. Marketing, Inst. f. Wirtschaftswissenschaften, Technische Universität Braunschweig, Braunschweig

MGM MediaGruppe München (1995), "Marktübersicht Online-Dienste," München

Midgette, M. (1999), "Are Your Costumers Being Fulfilled?" *NetCommerce*, July/August, http://www.netcommercemag.com/july/3.html, 6/20/2000.

Miller, S.E. (1996), *Civilizing Cyberspace: Policy, Power, and the Information Superhighway*, New York: ACM Books.

Mottl, J. (2000), "Learn at a Distance," *Information Week* 767, 75-78.

Mueller, M. (1993), "Universal Service in Telephone History: A Reconstruction," *Telecommunications Policy* 17 (5), 352-69.

Mulhern, F.J., (1997), "Retail Marketing: From Distribution to Integration", *International Journal of Research in Marketing*, 14, 103-24.

Mullaney, T.J. (1999), "Needed: The Human Touch," *Business Week*, December 13, 52-54.

Mundor, N., L. Kolbe, and W. Brenner, (1997), "Convergence of Media, Machines, and Messages," *Convergence*, 111-20.

Mundorf, N., D. Zwick, and N. Dholakia (1999), "Die Web-Praesenz fuehrender deutscher Industrieunternehmen," W. Fritz (ed.), *Internet Marketing*, Stuttgart: Schaefer-Poeschel, 81-107.

Narver, J.C., and S.F. Slater (1990), "The Effect of a Market Orientation on Business Profitability," *Journal of Marketing*, 54, 20-35.

National Academy of Sciences (1994), "Realizing the Information Future: The Internet and Beyond" http://xerexes.nas.edu:70/1/nap/online/rtif.

Nedstat (1997), "About the Nedstat Method," http://usa.nedstat.net/pro.html.

Negroponte, N. (1995), *Being Digital*, New York: Alfred P. Knopf.

Neuman, W.R., (1991), *The Future of the Mass Audience*, Cambridge, MA: Cambridge University Press.

Nielsen/NetRatings (1999), "Top 10: The Web's Stickiest Sites," *Infoworld*, December 6, 24, www.infoworld.com.

Nieschlag, R., E. Dichtl, and H. Horschgen (1997), *Marketing*, 18th ed., Berlin.

NUA Analysis 1999/2000, "Retial Sites Fail One Tenth of Shoppers," December 30, 1999, http://www.nua.ie/surveys/index.cgi.

NUA Analysis (2000), "Web Advertising Revenue 1996-2002," http://www. nua.ie/surveys/analysis/.

NUA Internet Surveys (1999): *How Many Online?*, http://www.nua.ie/surveys/.

OECD (1999), "OECD Communications Outlook 1999," *Paris: Organization for Economic Cooperation and Development*, http://www.oecd.org/dsti/sti/it/cm/prod/ com-out99.htm.

O'Flaherty, Dennis (1996), "Communications Breakdown: Will Multimedia Break the Net?" *Internet World*, October, 46-52.

Orme, P.M., D. Cordeiro, K. Cordeiro, J.K. Cohen, and N. Dholakia (1995), "Evolving Electronic Commerce: A Report from the Base Camp and the Digital Frontier," R.R. Dholakia and D. Fortin (eds.), *COTIM-95 Proceedings*, Kingston, RI: RITIM, 349-54.

Osman, M.Z. (1993), "A Conceptual Model of Retail Image Influences on Loyalty Patronage Behavior," *The International Review of Retail, Distribution and Consumer Research* 31, 149-66.

Pandya, A., and N. Dholakia (1992), "An Institutional Theory of Exchange in Marketing," *European Journal of Marketing* 26 (12), 19-41.

Patterson, S. (1999), "A History of the Adult Education Movement," doctoral dissertation, Nova Southeastern University, ERIC No: ED432696.

Paul, C., and M. Runte (1998), "Virtuelle Communities," S. Albers, M. Clement, and K. Peters (eds.) *Marketing mit Interaktiven Medien*, Frankfurt am Main, 151-64.

"People Design Technology," *Advertising Age*, from *S.i. Systems-Online Advertising Statistics*, http://www.sisystems.com/secrets/tipsi2.html.

Peppers, D., and M. Rogers (1993), *The One to One Future: Building Relationships One Customer at a Time*, New York: Doubleday.

Peppers, D., and M. Rogers (1997), *Enterprise One to One*, New York: Doubleday.

Peters, K., and N. Karck, (1998), "Messung der Werbewirkung,"S. Albers, M. Clement, and K. Peters, (eds.), *Marketing mit Interaktiven* Frankfurt, m., 237-52.

Peterson, R.A., S. Balasubramanian, and B.J. Bronnenberg (1997), "Exploring the Implications of the Internet for Consumer Marketing," *Journal of the Academy of Marketing Science* 25 (4), 329-46.

Petty R.E., J.T. Cacioppo, and D. Schumann (1983), "Central and Peripheral Routes to Advertising Effectiveness: The Moderating Role of Involvement," *Journal of Consumer Research10*, September, 135-46.

Picot, A., R. Reichwald, and R.T. Wigand (1998), *Die grenzenlose Unternehumng*, 3rd ed., Wiesbaden: Gabler.

Piller, F., and D. Schoder (1999), "Mass Customization und Electronic Commerce," Zeitschrift für Betriebswirtschaft 69 (10), 1111-36.

Polanyi, K. (1944), *The Great Transformation*, New York: Farrar and Rinehart.

Preissner, A. (1999): "Warten auf online.de," *Manager magazin*, no. 3, 188-95.

Quelch, J.A., and L. Klein (1996), "The Internet and International Marketing," *Sloan Management Review 38, Spring, 60-75.*

Rafaeli, S. (1988), "Interactivity: From New Media to Communication," R. Hawkins et al. (eds.), *Advancing Communication Science: Merging Mass and Interpersonal Processes*, Newbury Park, CA: Sage, 110-34.

Rafaeli, S. (1990), "Interacting with Media: Para-Social Interaction and Real Interaction," B. Ruben and L. Lievrouw (eds.), *Mediation, Information and Communication*, New Brunswick, NJ: Transaction, 125-81.

Rask, Morten (1999), "Strategies of International Marketing on the Web used by Danish Companies," Paper presented at the Conference on telecommunication and information markets, Providence, Rhode Island, USA.

Rayport, J.E., and J.J. Sviokla, (1994), "Managing in the Marketspace", *Harvard Business Review 72 (6)*, November-December, 141-50.

Reidenberg, J.R. (1995), "Information Flows and The Global *Infobahn*: Toward New U.S. Policies," In W.J. Drake (ed.), *The Information Infrastructure,* New York: The Twentieth Century Fund Press, 251-68.

Reips, U.-D. (1995), Das Web-Labor fur Experimentelle Psychologie, http://www.uni-tuebingen.de/uni/sii/Ulf/Lab/Web/ExpPsyLabD.html [since April 1998 also http://www.genpsyserv.unizh.ch].

Reips, U.-D. (1997), "Das psychologische Experimentiere im Internet," B. Batinic (ed.), *Internet für Psychologen*, Gottingen: Hogrefe, 245-65.

Reips, U.-D. (1999), "Theorie und Techniken des Web-Experimentierens," B. Batinic, A. Werner, L. Graf, and W. Bandilla, (eds.) *Online Research*, Gottingen: Hogrefe, 27-91.

Rengelshausen, O. (1997), "Werbung im Internet und in kommerziellen Online Diensten," G. Silberer, (ed.), *Interaktive Webung* Stuttgart: Schaffer-Poeschel, 101-45.

Rheingold, H. (1993), *The Virtual Community: Homesteading on the Electronic Frontier*, Reading, MA: Addison-Wesley.

Rheingold, H. (1994), *Virtuelle Gemeinschaft. Soziale Beziehungen im Zeitalter des Computers*, Bonn: Addison-Wesley.

"The Right Connections" (1995), *Canadian Business* 68, May, 43-44.

Roche, E.M., and M.J. Blaine, (1997), "Research Note: The MIPS Gap," *Information Technology in Developing Countries* 7 (3), July, 15-16.

Rogler, M. (1998), "Bei der Jugend Piepts," *Werben & Verkaufen*, no.9, 100-02.

Roland Berger and Partners (1999) *Erfolgsfaktoren im E-Commerce*, Frankfurt am Main: Roland Berger and Partners.

Ross, S. (1973), "The Economic Theory of Agency: The Principal's Problem," *American Economic Review* May, 134-39.

Roth, D. (2000), "Meet eBay's Worst Nightmare," *Fortune* 142 (1), July 26, 199-206.

Rust, R.T., and R.W. Oliver (1994), "The Death of Advertising," *Journal of Advertising* 23 (4) 71-78.

Sahlins, M.D. (1972), *Stone Age Economics*, Chicago: Aldine-Atherton.

Sarkar, M.B., B. Butler, and C. Steinfield (1995), "Intermediaries and Cybermediaries: A Continuing Role for Mediating Players in the Electronic Marketplace," R.R. Dholakia and D. Fortin (eds.), *COTIM-95 Proceedings*, Kingston, RI: RITIM, 82-92.

Schlender, B. (1996), "Sun's Java: The Threat to Microsoft Is Real", *Fortune* 134 (9), November 11, 165-70.

Schmidt, I. (1998), "Auf dem Weg zum E-Commerce," *Technischer Vertrieb*, no. 1, 26-29.

Schmidt, W.C. (1997), "World-Wide Web Survey Research: Benefits, Potential Problems, and Solutions," *Behavioral Research Methods, Instruments, & Computers*, 29, 274-79.

Schnell, R. (1993), Homogenitat sozialer Kategoren als Voraussetzung fur "Reprasentativitat" und Gewichtungsverfahren. Zeitschrift fur Soziologie, 22, Heft 1:16-32.

Schnell, R. (1997), *Nonresponse in Bevolkerungsumfragen. Ausmaß, Entwickluyng und Ursachen*. Opladen: Leske and Budrich.

Schnell R., Pl Hill, and E. Esster (1993), *Methoden der empirischen Sozialforschung*, Munchen and Wien: Oldenbourg aufl. 4.

Schuster, F. (1997), "Programming Online-Questionnaires with HavaScript and Java," W. Bandilla, and F. Faulbaum (eds.), *SoftState '97-Advances in Statistical Software*, vol. 6, Stuttgart: Lucius and Lucius, 159-66.

Schutz, P. (1998), "Aktuelles Stichwort. Community Building," *Absatzwirtschaft*, no. 9, 31.

Schutzer, D. (1995), "Get Ready for Electronic Commerce," *ABA Banking Journal*, June 47-48.

Schwankert, S. (1996), "The Giant Infant: China and the Internet," *Internet World Online*, http://www.iw.com/current, accessed November 8.

Seeger, H. (1998), "Kommerz mit Kommunikation?" *Global Online*, no. 4-5, 34-38.

Sen, Saurava (1995), "The Internet: Wiring into the World," *India Today*, September 15, 128-29.

Seybold, P. (1999a), "Lighting the Fire to Acquire," *Business 2.0*, April, http://www.buisnes2.com/content/magazine/marketing/1999/04/01/11517.

Seybold, P. (1999a), "Kighting the Fire to Acquire," *Business 2.0*, April 2, http://www.business2.com/content/magazine/marketing/1999/04/01/11517.

Shapiro, C., and H.R. Varian (1998), "Versioning: The Smart Way to Sell Information," *Harvard Business Review* 76, November-December, 106-14.

Shiffrin, R.M. (1976), "Capacity Limitations in Information Processing, Attention and Memory," *Handbook of Learning and Cognitve Processes, vol.4: Attention and Memory*, Estes (ed.), Hillsdale, NJ, 177-236.

Short, J., E. Williams, and B. Christie (1976), *The Social Psychology of Telecommunications*, London, John Wiley and Sons.

Sivadas, E., J.J. Kellaris, and R. Grewal (1995), "One-to-One Marketing: The Internet as a Segmentation Tool," R.R. Dholakia and D. Fortin (eds.), *COTIM-95 Proceedings*, Kingston, RI: RITIM, 250-57.

Solomon, M.R. (1996), *Consumer Behavior*, 4th ed., Upper Saddle River, NJ: Prentice Hall.

SRI International (1996), "Exploring the World Wide Web Population's Other Half," http://future.sri.com/vals/vals-survey.results.html.

Stauss, B. (1998), "Internet-Kunden_Kommunikation. Globale Kundenkritik in World Wide Web und Newsgroups," *Marktforschung and Management*, 139-44.

Steiger, P. (1995), "Die Akzeptanzprufung bei Multimdedia-Anwendungen," G. Silberer, (Hrsg.), *Marketing mit Multi-Media*, Stuttgart: Schaffer-Poeschel, 269-308.

Stoll, C. (1996), *Die Wuste Internet*, Auflt. 4, Frankfurt am Main: Fischer.

"Streitgesprach E-Commerce. Das Ende der Gewinne?" (1998), *Absatzwirtschaft*, no. 10, 48-54.

Sun, S. and G.A. Barnett (1994), "The International Telephone Network and Democratization," *Journal of the American Society for Information Science*, July.

Sundelin, I (1999), "PC-boomen över för denna gång," *Dagens Nyheter*, 21st October.

Surprenant, C.F., and M.R. Solomon (1987), "Predictability and Personalization in the Service Encounter," *Journal of Marketing*, 51, April, 86-96.

Tanzer, A. (1997), "Computers before Cars," *Forbes*, October 6, 45.

Tapscott, D. (1995), *The Digital Economy*, New York: McGraw-Hill.

Taylor, S., and S. Thompson (1982), "Stalking the Elusive Vividness Effect," *Psychological Review* 89 (2), 155-81.

Taylor, W.C. (1996), "Who's Writing the Book on Web Buiness?... (amazon.com)," *Fast Company*, no. 5, October/November, 132-33.

Tedesehi, B. (2000), "Easier-to-Use Sites Would Help E-Tailers Close More Sales," *New York Times*, June 12, C14.

Tomic, V. (1998), "Global Update: Internet Spreads Its Reach," *Telephony*, March 16, 32-36.

Treacy, M., and F. Wiersema (1995), *The Discipline of Market Leaders: Choose Your Customers, Narrow Your Focus, Dominate Your Market*, Reading, MA: Addison-Wesley.

Tse, S., D. Sutton, P. Tsang, and C. Stuart (1995), "The World Wide Web: Changing the Way We Work, Learn and Play," R.R. Dholakia and D. Fortin (eds.), *COTIM-95 Proceedings*, Kingston, RI: RITIM, 165171.

Turkle, S. (1995), *Life on the Screen: Identity in the Age of the Internet*, New York: Simon and Schuster.

Turoff, M., and S.R. Hiltz (1998), "Computer-Mediated Communications and Development Countries," *Telematics and Informatics* 5 (4), 357-76.

Tuten, T.L., (1997), Getting a Foot in the Electronic Door: Understanding Why People Read or Delete Electronic Mail. ZUMA-Arbeitsbericht 97.08.

Urban, G.L., and E. von Hippel (1998), "Lead User Analysis for the Development of New Industrial Products," *Management Science*, 569-82.

Van Eimeren, B., E. Oehmichen, and C, Schroter (1997), "ARD_Online-Studie," *Onlinenutzung in Deutschland. Media Perspektiven*, 548-57.

Van Eimeren, B., E. Oehmichen, and C, Schroter (1998), "ARD_Online-Studie," *Onlinenutzung in Deutschland. Media Perspektiven*, 423-35.

Van Heck, E. (2000), "The Cutting Edge in Auctions," *Harvard Business Review*, March-April, 18-19.

Vaughn-N., J. Steven (1996), "The NC Follies," *Internet World*, December, 72-73.

Venkat, R., and F.H. Sobey (1999), "Internet Advertising: Role of Involvement and Ad Characteristics," R.R. Dholakia and S. Wikstrom (eds.), *Electronic Commerce: Behaviors of Suppliers, Producers, Intermediaries & Consumers*, Proceedings of COTIM99, RITIM: University of Rhode Island, Kingston.

Venkatesh, A., R.R. Dholakia, and N. Dholakia (1996), "New Visions of Information Technology and Postmodernism: Implications for Advertising and Marketing Communications," W. Brenner and L. Kolbe (eds.), *The Information Superhighway and Private Households*, Heidelberg, Germany: Physica-Verlag, 319-38.

Verity, J.W. and R.D. Hof (1994), "The Internet: How It Will Change the Way You Do Business," *Business Week*, November 14, 80-88. [website/mefo/s1d011.htm].

Vlahos, L. (1995), "Hanging Ten on the Internet: Booksellers Brave Cyberspace," *American Bookseller*, September, 23-27.

Walther, J.B. (1996), "Computer-Mediated Communication: Impersonal, Interpersonal and Hyperpersonal Interaction," *Communication Research* 23, February, 3-42.

Wheelock, J. (1994), "Personal computers, gender and an institutional model of the household." *Consuming Technologies: Media information domestic spaces*, (eds.) Silverston, R. and E. Hirsch, 97112.

Wells, G., and R. Petty (1981), "The Effects of Overt Head Movement on Persuasion: Compatibility and Incompatibility of Responses," *Basic and Applied Social Psychology* 1, 219-30.

Werner, A. (1997), "The Problem of Self-Selection-Some Solutions," W. Bandilla and F. Faulbaum (eds.), *SoftStat '97-Advances in Statistical Software*, vol. 6, Stuttgart: Lucius and Lucius, 167-74.

Weston, R. (1995), "Five Ways to Do Business on the Internet," *Inc. Technology*, no. 3, 75-77.

White, S. (1999), "The Effectiveness of Web-Based Instruction: A Case Study," paper present at the *Joint Meeting of the Central States Communication Association and the Southern States Communication Association*, St. Louis, MO (ERIC Document Reproduction Service no. 430 261.

Wigand, R.T., and R.I. Benjamin (1996), "Electronic Commerce: Effects on Electronic Markets". *Journal of Computer Mediated Communication*, 1 (3), http://www.usc. edu/dept/annenberg/vol.1/issue3/wigand.html.

Wilk, R. (1995), "Learning to be Local in Belize," In D. Miller (ed.), *Worlds Apart: Modernity through the prism of the local*, London: Routledge, 110-33.

Wilk, E. (1999a), "The Personal Touch: Handling Customer Service Online," *Netcommerce*, December.

Wilk, E. (1999b), "The Personal Touch Handling Customer Service Online," *Netcommerce*, December, http://www.netcommercemag.com/dec_jan/ 7.html.

Williams, F., R. Rice, and E.M. Rogers (1988), *Research Methods and the New Media*, New York Free Press.

Williamson, O.E. (1975), *Markets and Hierarchies*, New York: Free Press.

Winger, B. (1998), Zum Stand der privaten Nutzung von Online-Diensten. Wissenschaftlicher Bericht FZKA 6152 des Forschungszentrums Karlsruhe, Technik und Umwelt.

Yahoo! (1997), "WWW Server Log Analysis Tools," http://www.yahoo.com/ Computers_and_Internet/Software/Internet/World_Wide_Web/Servers/Log_Analysi s_Tools.

Yakhlef A., (2000), "The Internet as an Opportunity to Rethink The Role of Intermediary," *Consumption, Markets ad Culture*, 4(1), 39-55.

Zaichkowsky, J. (994), "The Personal Involvement Inventory: Reduction, Revision, and Application to Advertising," *Journal of Advertising* 23 (4), 59-10.

Zajonc, R., and H. Markus (1982), "Affective and Cognitive Factors in Preferences," *Journal of Consumer Research* 9, September, 123-31.

Zellweger, P. (1997), "WebBased Sales: Defining the Cognitive Buyer," *Electronic Markets* 7 (3), 10-16.

Zeitalter des Electronic Commerce, *Marketing*, Vol. 19, No. 2, 69-80.

Zerdick, A., et al. (1999), *Die Internet-Oekonomie*, Berlin and Heidelberg: Springer.

Zgodzinski, D. (1996), "Third-World Internet," *Internet World Online*, http://www.iw.com/current.

Zimmermann, H. (1995), "The Electronic Mall Bodensee: A Virtual Marketplace for Private and Commercial Customers," R.R. Dholakia and D. Fortin (eds.), *COTIM-95 Proceedings*, Kingston, RI: RITIM, 11-17.

Zimmermann, H. (1998), *Regionale elektronische Marktplatze: Infrastrukturen nicht nur fur den elektronischen Hande*, http://www.businessmedia.net/ netacademy/publications.nsf/ass_pk/1033, 9.5.1999.

Index

Contributors

MICHELE ABBOTT is an independent Marketing Consultant based in Minneapolis. She holds an MBA from the University of Minnesota.

WOLFGANG BANDILLA received his Ph.D. from the University of Mannheim in 1986. He is a Senior Project Director at ZUMA, Center for Surveys, Methods and Analyses, in Mannheim. His primary research interests include methodology and methods of empirical research and data collection, especially computer-assisted data collection.

STEPHAN BENNEMANN is Research Associate in the Department of Business Administration and Marketing at the Technical University of Braunschweig in Germany. His research focuses on the evolution of e-commerce in Germany.

CAMILLA CARLELL is a Doctoral Candidate in the School of Business at Stockholm University in Sweden. Her research focuses on long-term observational and interview-based study of Internet-based shopping behavior of families in Stockholm.

KUAN-PIN CHIANG is a Doctoral Candidate in the Marketing and E-Commerce Areas in the College of Business Administration at the University of Rhode Island. His research focuses on electronic retailing, pioneering advantages in Internet-based markets, and consumer behavior in e-commerce settings.

NIKHILESH DHOLAKIA is Professor of Marketing and E-Commerce in the College of Business Administration at the University of Rhode Island. He holds a B. Tech. degree from Indian Institute of Technology, and MBA from Indian Institute of Management, and a Ph.D. in Marketing from the Kellogg School of Northwestern University. His research focuses on Information Age strategies in the global economy and on global consumer culture.

RUBY ROY DHOLAKIA is Professor and Director, Research Institute for Telecommunications and Information Marketing (RITIM) in the College of Business Administration at the University of Rhode Island. She obtained her BS and MBA from the Haas School of Business at the University of California at Berkeley. She holds a Ph.D. in Marketing from the Kellogg School at Northwestern University. Her research deals with information technology adoption by households and with consumer behavior in electronic marketplaces.

DAVID R. FORTIN is a Senior Lecturer in the Department of Management, University of Canterbury, New Zealand. He earned his Ph.D. in Marketing from the University of Rhode Island, writing a dissertation that received acclaim from the Marketing Science Institute (M6SI). With multiple publications in e-commerce and interactive advertising, Dr. Fortin's work has received awards and international recognition. He is the director of Web-L@b, an online experimental consumer research project at the University of Canterbury.

WOLFGANG FRITZ is a Professor of Marketing and Head of the Department of Business Administration and Marketing at the Technical University of Braunschweig, Germany. He is also an Honorary Professor of International Marketing at the University of Vienna, Austria. Dr. Wolfgang Fritz has published 10 books and around 200 articles in the fields of marketing and general management in leading German and international journals. Among his honors are the Karin-Islinger Award of the University of Mannheim, Germany, and the national Scientific Award of the German Marketing Association.

MARIA FROSTLING-HENNINGSSON is a Doctoral Candidate in the School of Business at Stockholm University in Sweden. She is also on the research staff of Telia, the telecommunications company that leads in wireline, wireless, and broadband services in Scandinavia.

PETER HAUPTMANNS is a sociologist working at the Emscher-Lippe Association for Communication and Data Technology in Germany. He specializes in Internet-based methods of market and consumer research.

MARTIN KERNER is working on his Ph.D. Dissertation in the Area of Marketing at the Technical University of Braunschweig in Germany. He has worked with Professor Fritz in pioneering studies of e-commerce evolution in many sectors of the German economy.

CHAI KIM is Professor and Director of the Institute for International Business in the College of Business Administration at the University of Rhode Island. He has pioneered a method of cross-national learning using Internet-based debates.

MARTIN LAUB is a Senior Consultant at Andersen Consulting in Frankfurt, Germany. His work has ranged from implementation of Enterprise Resource Planning systems to various projects on e-commerce. He was a Fullbright Fellow in the United States and earned his MBA at the University of Rhode Island.

TOBIAS LÜHRIG is a Consultant with McKinsey and Co in Berlin, Germany. In addition to earning his Engineering degree from the Technical University of Braunschweig in Germany, he also obtained an MBA and an MS in Mechanical Engineering from the University of Rhode Island.

ANDREAS MEVENKAMP is Information Manager for Corporate Purchasing at Continental AG, Germany. Earlier he was IT Project Manager Central at Boehringer Mannheim GmbH. He has participated in various projects in multimedia and new media at Technical University of Braunschweig, Manchester University, IBM, Siemens Nixdorf Informationsysteme AG, and Continental AG.

NORBERT MUNDORF is Professor of Communication Studies and a Faculty Associate with the Research Institute for Telecommunications and Information Marketing (RITIM) at the University of Rhode Island.

JERRY PAQUIN is a consultant with Information Technology Academies (ITA), a Providence, Rhode Island based venture to promote computer and network education, supported by Cisco Systems and other companies. She earned her MBA from the University of Rhode Island.

MYUNG-HO PARK is the Dean of the College of Business Administration at Keimyung University in South Korea. He has been a Visiting Professor at the University of Rhode Island. Dr. Park earned his Ph.D. at the University of Alabama and specializes in the study of retailing, including the emerging methods of Internet-based retailing.

MORTEN RASK is an Assistant Professor in International Business, Marketing, and E-business ad Department of Business Studies, Aalborg University, Denmark. He holds a Ph.D. in International Business and his current research is on m-commerce, e-business portals and e-marketplaces and e-books. He also has practical work experience from Silicon Valley, using the Web to conduct market and competitor analysis.

JESKO SCHRÖDER is Research Associate in the Department of Business Administration and Marketing at the Technical University of Braunschweig. He has also worked at Volkswagen AG in Germany.

SOLVEIG WIKSTRÖM is Professor of Marketing in the School of Business, Stockholm University, Sweden. She is the author of award-winning books in the field of marketing and electronic business. At Stockholm University, she directs a research program on interactive marketing and consumer behavior.

DETLEV ZWICK is a Doctoral Candidate in Marketing at the College of Business Administration at the University of Rhode Island. He is currently working on an in-depth study of "investors as consumers" in the fast-growing electronic stock markets of the United States and Europe. He has published several papers on consumer culture and e-business.